SOCIAL POLICY REVIEW 1990–91

Edited by

Nick Manning

Reader in Social Policy, University of Kent

LONGMAN

In collaboration with the
Social Policy Association

SOCIAL POLICY REVIEW 1990–91

Published by Longman Group UK Limited, Longman Industry and
Public Service Management Publishing Division,
Westgate House, The High, Harlow, Essex CM20 1YR.

First published 1991

British Library Cataloguing in Publication Data
Social policy review – [No. 3] –
   1.   Great Britain. Social policies
   361.6′1′0941

0–582–08788–0

Printed in Great Britain by
Antony Rowe Ltd, Chippenham, Wiltshire

Contents

Contributors

John Baldock Lecturer in Social Policy, University of Kent.

Martin Baldwin-Edwards Department of Social Policy, University of Manchester.

Eric Blyth Senior Lecturer in Social Work, Huddersfield Polytechnic.

Michael Cahill Senior Lecturer in Social Policy, Brighton Polytechnic.

Angela Dale Reader, Social Statistics Research Unit, City University.

John Ditch Senior Research Fellow, Social Policy Research Unit, University of York.

Adalbert Evers Senior Research Fellow, European Centre for Social Welfare Policy and Research.

John Ferris Lecturer in Social Policy, University of Nottingham.

Ian Gough Senior Lecturer in Comparative Social Policy, University of Manchester.

Melanie Henwood Fellow in Health Policy Analysis, King's Fund Institute.

Michael Joffe Lecturer, Academic Department of Public Health, St. Mary's Hospital Medical School.

Kirk Mann Lecturer in Social Policy, University of Leeds.

Catherine Marsh Joint Lecturer in Sociology, and Econometrics and Social Statistics, University of Manchester.

Jo Roll   Senior Research Officer, Family
                                     Policies Study Centre.

Søren Villadsen   Associate Professor of Economics
                                     and Planning, University of
                                     Roskilde.

Gerald Wistow   Senior Lecturer in Health and
                                     Social Care Management, Nuffield
                                     Institute.

1 Introduction

Nick Manning

Looking back over 1990, the most dramatic domestic event has been the resignation of Margaret Thatcher as Prime Minister. For much of the last decade the British social policy community has been coming to terms first with the rhetoric of Thatcherism, and subsequently in more recent years with the real impact that this policy direction has at last been having on social policy. As with the Bush succession to Reagan, initial impressions have been that Major is prepared to countenance a less abrasive approach to social problems and issues. Sensing this, the electorate has registered a more even judgement about its likely choice in the next election, which will loom increasingly large over the social policy debates of the coming year, and which will therefore form a major focus for next year's edition.

However, it is too early for this edition to cover such developments. Consequently, the opportunity has been taken to reflect at slightly greater depth on social policy concerns which have been emerging over the last few years, and which have not lent themselves easily to the annual cycle of review which normally forms a major part of the contents. Chapters have been commissioned in three distinct areas. First is the growing problem of environmental sustainability and the question of the way in which social policy might respond in general, together with some examples of specific concern. Second is a continuation of last year's focus on the international context, but with a more specific examination of European developments, both in particular countries and at the level of the EC in general, which as Thatcher's departure suggests will increasingly affect domestic social policies. Third is a group of chapters which examine the relationship between work and welfare, particularly the consequences for welfare and social policy of the dramatic changes we have seen in the labour market over the last ten years.

The greening of social policy

We begin with a discussion of the greening of social policy. Even two years ago this notion seemed absurdly on the fringe of our perennial preoccupation with the dismantling of the welfare state. Now however, signalled yet again by Margaret Thatcher in a speech late in 1988, global warming, pollution, and other concerns about the quality of the environment that we all take for granted, have emerged as lively political issues. The first two pieces by Michael Cahill and John Ferris are both focused on the substantive nature of the politics of green issues, and thus the impact that these must inevitably have on social policy, and the responses that might come from the social policy community. Clearly, this impact can operate at two levels. First is the possibility of a new position or paradigm in the pantheon of social ideologies with which we locate policy arguments. Second is the articulation of new social needs to which existing policy instruments are being asked to respond. Cahill identifies the range of green concerns from light to dark green. While the former can for example accommodate many current patterns of development through the use of such principles as the 'polluter pays', the latter envisages a complete revolution in social and economic life in favour of small self-sustaining communities. Cahill concludes that greater personal and ethical responsibility is a major implication for social policy, if economic development is to become 'sustainable'.

Ferris describes a more complex interweaving of arguments. Three positions, technocentrism, deep ecology, and social ecology, are identified. The first two roughly correspond to Cahill's light and dark greens. The third, however, is a 'red/green synthesis' favoured by Ferris as the best prospect for establishing links between ecology and social policy. Here he notes that green policies prefer autonomous work to wage labour, a basic income, community based services, and are in general suspicious of the traditional Keynesian welfare legacy. He sees much overlap with the participatory and decentralised approach of welfare pluralism, mixed as for Cahill with more self-reliance.

These general surveys of green social policies are matched by two pieces which examine in detail the kind of specific issue which for most of us are the origins of our consciousness of the fragility of our environment. Mike Joffe presents a wide ranging account of food as a social policy issue. The history of food production, distribution and consumption demonstrates that it has been a key factor in the steady rise of the health status of western populations over recent centuries. It is not surprising that in this century food dropped out from the agenda of political concerns, and was left to the market. However there is growing concern about potential links between our general diets and coronary heart disease, cancer, and obesity, as well as more specific dangers associated in recent years with certain foods. This was felt to be in part a result of food production changing from an agricultural to an industrial activity, with associated technological innovations such as mechanically recovered meat. Similarly, the creation of designed-processed food uses common ingredients such as fats, sugars, starch, and texturisers, but these are highly packaged to meet marketing rather than nutritional criteria. More recent scares about salmonella, listeria, and bovine spongiform encephalopathy have added specific weight to these general concerns. Joffe is critical of the cultural and consumer explanations of these patterns of food consumption, preferring to blame economic interests and ministerial divisions than to 'blame the victims'.

Technological threats to the environment are also to be found in medicine. Eric Blyth reviews the Human Fertilisation and Embryology Act, 1990, due to be implemented in 1991. This is an attempt to regulate the rapidly growing field of assisted reproduction. Despite the understandable desire from the estimated 15 per cent of potential parents who are childless to undergo procedures such as in vitro fertilisation and gamete transfer, average failure rates are 90 per cent. In addition, elevated rates of fetal abnormality, spontaneous abortion, ectopic pregnancy, perinatal mortality and disability, and maternal illness can result. Regulation is clearly justified. But the assumptions embedded in the Act, Blyth argues, give great legitimacy to medical views and hence legitimate a number of assumptions about 'normal' family structures and parenting practices held by doctors which are not strictly medical concerns. What is and what is not natural in this area is a matter of dispute, and highlights the difficulty in green views which claim to privilege nature over human culture.

The European Community and social policy

Greens also appeal to the idea of community as much as nature. But community has a long history in the service of a variety of social planners, and has been enjoying something of an official revival in recent times in many European countries. This in itself might be enough to sensitise a critical nose to an ironic turn in its career. Not surprisingly therefore divergent views as to its current use can be found in the next two papers on the turn to community in the UK and Europe, respectively. Wistow and Henwood take the view that the white paper 'Caring for People' (1989) is a major step forward in thinking about community care. It acknowledges the needs of carers as a central issue. It is need rather than service oriented. It recognises that there are serious organisational divisions in previous policy. The main problem in their view is that proper implementation is unlikely as a result of resource limits, traditional lack of policy and practice coordination, and contradictory needs of carers and the cared for. However they conclude that the right argument has been won in principle, and the way is now presumably open for specific lobbying to take place to press for full implementation.

The view from Europe, however, suggest Baldock and Evers, is far less sanguine. Indeed they argue that in endorsing the above line put forward by Henwood and Wistow, the British Labour party is pressing for the implementation of a policy that is contrary to almost every principle of welfare espoused by Labour since the war. They arrive at this conclusion via a study of similar policies planned or implemented in Sweden, the Netherlands, and Germany as well as the UK. They suggest that in all these countries there is a steady retreat by the state from accepted welfare commitments, towards selective and minimalist provision incompatible with previous conceptions of the social rights attached to citizenship. Their evidence is taken from policies being developed towards the predicted sharp rise in the numbers of the frail elderly in these countries. These include a package of three policies which together herald the arrival of the 'enabling' state: the 'marketisation' of social care services; support of voluntary and private agencies; and payment of informal carers. This they suggest amounts to the deliberate limiting of citizens' social rights under the guise of extending other rights.

Whether or not comparative analysis will always lead to such a dramatic reversal of analytic conclusions, it clearly lends a much greater depth to our understanding of social policy changes in any individual country. The other chapters in this middle section help to do that. Three of these refer to the European Community. John Ditch sets out a very useful guide to the origins and growth of social policy at the European Community level. Social policy was thought of as having a clearly subordinate status to economic policy in the early years of the EC, and although several articles of the Treaty of Rome referred to social policy issues, they were only meant to facilitate the smooth operation of the labour market. Although the social action programme of 1974 raised the profile of social issues in the EC, it was not until the appointment of Jacques Delors as President in 1984 that a noticeable turn towards social policy occurred. The Single European Act of 1987, financial reforms, qualified majority voting, the 1989 Social Charter, and finally the 1992 single market have all followed (as indeed has the resignation of Margaret Thatcher). Ditch introduces all this clearly, and on the way explains such Euro-terms as harmonisation, subsidiarity, and social dumping.

However, there is a lingering feeling that all this may amount to very little in concrete terms. Have our social policies really been much affected by the EC? Gough and Baldwin-Edwards set out to answer just this question by posing the counterfactual of Britain *not* having joined the EC. Their conclusion is that there has been substantial effect in principle in the areas of promoting sex equality, and in the reduction of discrimination against EC nationals in areas such as employment, public housing, higher education, and income support. There has also been greater funding of vocational training. The main area of no change is health care. Nevertheless they observe that in practice the core activities of our main social policies have been little affected. In a concluding explanation they attempt to demonstrate the incompatibility between the corporatist social policy regimes of the founder EC members, and the liberal/social democratic regime mixture typical in Britain. EC social policy regimes have been traditionally employment-based and, in the courts, rights-based. This contrast to Britain, they conclude, may not be resolvable without British constitutional reform.

It is sometimes difficult to grasp the concrete consequences of the general nature of EC developments while looking across the whole range of social policy. The final two chapters in this section thus address specific and related areas in European social policy. Jo Roll's study of lone parents in the EC was undertaken on behalf of the EC's programme on equal opportunities for women. Lone parents are a rapidly expanding group right across the EC, consequent upon a number of changes in family structure, with Denmark and Britain having the highest number at 19 per cent of all families. These families experience below average incomes, but their sources of income vary widely across the EC. The mix of main sources (employment, maintenance payments, and social security) is determined by varying policies towards guaranteeing maintenance, and social security; employment is used by lone parents in response to the remaining income gap. Clearly this is an example where the EC's interest in employment opportunities for women might make a more uniform policy possible. For example although Denmark and the UK have the highest rates, their policies are sharply contrasting. Denmark has universal child benefit with a lone parent supplement, advance maintenance payments, generous employment leave for childcare, and one of the highest levels of childcare services in the EC. As Roll concludes such generous support of all families is a most effective policy for lone parents.

In the latter case, as Søren Villadsen shows, Danish support for children is particularly dependent on the Scandinavian welfare model which is fighting a rearguard action against heavy criticism from which it is unlikely to emerge unscathed. He links this in part to EC membership, and expects that the eventual membership of

Sweden and Norway will herald similar policy reconstruction. A
feature of the reconstruction of the Danish welfare state is that
it has been done in the guise of a progressive decentralisation
heralded as bringing social policy closer to citizens through the
local commune. There are now in effect 275 welfare states
in Denmark with a diminishing emphasis on equality between
them, or on citizenship rights. This closely mirrors the earlier
observation of Baldock and Evers about the incompatibility of
pluralist policies and basic citizenship rights. More recently in
Denmark, poor economic performance, growing unemployment
and poverty, and declining public expectations about the hopes
for poor people (now at the bottom of the Eurobarometer table
alongside England and Ireland) mean that political rhetoric stressing
personal responsibility, strengthening the family, and supporting
social networks is increasingly seen as the alternative to social
democratic traditions of basic service provision and welfare guarantees. Villadsen concludes that central government has all but
abandoned labour market policies, and that the Danish welfare
state is in such deep trouble that the future heralds fundamental
changes of social citizenship and political culture.

The labour market and social policy

The seriousness of the Danish situation is expressed here in terms
of labour market policies as social policies. This viewpoint has not
perhaps been clear enough in British social policy debates, although
it was of course a fundamental prerequisite of the Beveridge plan.
The final section therefore contains three chapters which make this
their focus. Angela Dale sets out the historical and changing situation
of women in the British labour market. This clear introduction to
the general structure and dynamics of the labour market is an
essential prerequisite to policy considerations and explanations.
The main pattern has been a period of expansion during the
'long boom' followed by contraction, underlying which has been a
growing segmentation and ultimately polarisation. Married women
were actively recruited from the 1960s onwards to meet labour
shortages, but in contrast to France, for example, part-time work
was deemed essential so that traditional child care activities would
not be undermined. Much of the labour market is segregated by
sex, and hence little affected by legislation designed to ensure equal
opportunities and pay. Indeed deregulation in the 1980s appears to
have resulted in an increasingly polarised labour market according
to data from the ESRC's initiative on social change and economic
life. However from the 1990s a period of skilled labour shortage
will return which may result in a 'trickle down' of opportunity to all

workers, and in addition provide government and employers with an incentive for better support of child care.

Of course such a 'trickle down' may well fail to appear. The question then would be a more fundamental one of the principles upon which work is distributed, and the extent to which this is in any sense just. Catherine Marsh examines this question, arguing first of all that work is a positive welfare good, both financially and psychologically. She then considers the principles upon which this good should be distributed, and rejects both utility and desert in favour of a right to work. Finally she proceeds to explore the policy implications of such a right both in principle and in historical practice, including a surprisingly wide range of examples from the USSR, Sweden and the USA. Given the origin of much EC social policy in a concern to secure effective employment of the European labour force, some of these examples make instructive reading; but the general political tide would not now appear to be flowing in this direction.

The final chapter by Kirk Mann returns to a traditional treatment of work and social policy in Titmuss's conception of the social division of welfare as structured through employment. He, too, is interested in the growing divisions that have appeared in the labour market in recent decades. This development necessitates an extension of the Titmuss model, he argues, to take account of the way workers struggle to secure advantages from employers with uneven success. Some groups manage successfully to extract benefits from employers that others do not; similarly some employers are better at resisting these demands than others. The nature of recent industrial developments ('post-fordism') with a growing imperative for a flexible and rapid response to markets has exacerbated these divisions and created an employers' strategy of separating core and peripheral workers. However using evidence from an original survey of 38 enterprises in a range of industries in Leeds, Mann suggests that it is the relative organisational effectiveness of workers that is the crucial variable determining work-based social divisions. With this addition to the Titmuss model, Mann concludes that it remains a powerful explanation of patterns of work and social policy which has not achieved the recognition it deserves.

A final comment is appropriate about the life and times of the *Social Policy Review*. This issue continues to build upon the new developments initiated last year in terms of its structure and contents. It is once again produced in collaboration with the Social Policy Association, which has provided editorial advice and financial help. From next year a major new era for the *Social Policy Review* will begin when the Social Policy Association takes over as publisher. This will strengthen its connection to the social policy community both through the availability of space for conference papers, and through greater accessibility for individual readers. The 1990s promises to be a decade of further marked changes in social policy. As the dust settles on the conservative assault on traditional policy assumptions, there remain substantial and growing changes in economic, social and political structures which pose a challenge to both the practice and analysis of social policy.

2 The greening of social policy?

Michael Cahill

The late 1980s witnessed a remarkable shift in British politics when Mrs Thatcher, in a speech to the Royal Society in the autumn of 1988, signalled her government's intention to put environmental concerns at the top of its agenda. Although many would argue that the ensuing policy, embodied in the white paper *This Common Inheritance*, has not matched her rhetoric Mrs Thatcher's volte-face on this issue gave 'green politics' an importance which in this country it had never previously enjoyed (Department of the Environment, 1990). The other major parties have vied with the Conservatives in their claims to be the 'greenest', publishing substantial environmental policy papers, while in June 1989 the Green Party was granted serious attention for the first time when it gained 15 per cent of the vote in the Euro-Elections (Labour Party, 1990; Liberal Democrats, 1990). The market place has likewise been changing with green products arriving on the shelves in response to the identification of 'green consumers' by market analysts. This chapter outlines the background to the changed consciousness on ecological issues paying particular attention to the critique of western society made by the Green Parties and suggests that this critique challenges social policy to broaden its vision and to reorder its priorities.

The background to the publication of the white paper in September 1990 lay, in part, with the increasing public disquiet over the quality of life in this country. In the 1980s public squalor had returned to the streets of London. The quality of the nation's drinking water had become a matter of some concern. Most British beaches failed to pass the European Community's standards for cleanliness. Quite apart from the headline-hitting case of Camelford where tons of poison were dumped into the reservoir there is a long term concern about the amount of nitrates leaching into the underground water supplies. The quality of our food has become a major consideration as the press reported cases of 'mad cow disease', the contamination of milk by dioxins, the problem of

salmonella in eggs. This is in addition to the long-running fears
over the environmental consequences of the production of energy
by nuclear power stations.

The intellectual arguments for the government's white paper can
be traced to the Pearce Report, *Blueprint for a Green Economy*,
published in the summer of 1989. Pearce argues that economic
development now has to mean more than an increase in economic
growth; it must also include a measure of the quality of life:
the health of the population, the standard of education and
social well-being. Pearce also made an important contribution
by introducing the concept of 'sustainability' into the schema of
market economics. In the Pearce Report there is a recognition that
'future generations should be compensated for reductions in the
endowments of resources brought about by the actions of present
generations' (Pearce, 1989, p3). This must include 'environmental'
wealth – soil, forest, wildlife, water – just as much as monetary
capital. What Pearce does not acknowledge is the fact that with
increasing population levels in the world there is a question as to
whether one would want to bequeath to future generations the
existing standard of living or some diminished version. In order
to achieve the former economic production would have to greatly
increase with consequent environmental pollution. Greens would
argue that existing living standards in the West are unsustainable
at present because they can only be enjoyed by a minority of the
world's population. Clearly if the entire population of the world
were all to live at the level of western nations ecological catastrophe
would be imminent. Pearce advocates a form of environmental
accounting in which the forests, lakes and natural resources of
a country would be measured each year along with the GDP
and other conventional economic measures – a process that has
been undertaken in Norway and France (Pearce, 1989, pp95–104).
Pearce recommends using prices to ensure that the costs of resource
depletion are built into market transactions: a carbon tax is a prime
example. This is one illustration of 'the polluter pays principle' in
which a standard for acceptable environmental behaviour is set and
the costs of achieving this are met by the producer and, in addition,
by setting pollution charges on the products which eventuate.

The origins of the concept of sustainability can be traced back to
the Club of Rome Report *Limits to Growth*, published in 1972, a
document which foreshadowed many of the ecological concerns
of our time. This report concluded that if present growth trends in
world population, industrialised food production etc continued then
the probable result would be a 'a sudden and uncontrollable decline
in both population and industrial capacity' (Meadows *et al*, 1974,
p23). A sustainable economy and society had to be created which
was built on the recognition that there were limits to the economic

growth which the planet could endure. If Pearce has naturalised sustainability, making it part of the British debate, then perhaps it has been at the expense of the wider global concern which suffused the Club of Rome Report and Brundtland. For the Brundtland Report, as befits a United Nations document, points to the dramatic changes which have to be made if the population of the poor world is to eat at the same level as the rich world (Brundtland, 1987). For Brundtland sustainability was defined in general terms: 'meeting the needs of the present without compromising the ability of future generations to meet their own needs' (Brundtland, 1987, p43). Brundtland put centre-stage the needs of the world's poor linking the debates on development and ecology. The damage that is being done to the planet is mainly caused by the quarter of the world's population who live in the developed countries. Per capita they consume far more than the three quarters who live in the developing countries. They consume fifteen times as much paper, twelve times as much energy, and ten times as much steel (Robertson, 1989, p2).

The response to the global picture presented by these reports reveals two kinds of green thinking. On the one hand, the 'dark green' sees the way of life of industrial societies as leading to environmental catastrophe and as a result believes we have to withdraw from much of the organisation of industrial society and move towards a nil-growth society with much smaller populations and a far lower standard of living. In contrast, the 'light green' view, which is the majority perspective of those interested in these issues, is premised on the belief that it is possible to retain our industrial way of life providing we 'clean up our act' and remove the polluting consequences of industrial processes. This is a bipartisan political perspective which unites both front benches in the House of Commons. It finds its most popular expression in the green consumerism which has persuaded many people to change their washing-up liquid, fit a catalytic convertor and use unleaded petrol and is now embodied in the government's white paper *This Common Inheritance* with its checklist of 'action for all' specifying what each individual can do to protect the environment.

The challenge of the Green Parties

If Chris Patten is correct and the white paper sets the environmental agenda for the 1990s then the debate in this country will continue to be conducted in the language of light green politics. Nonetheless there is a more far-reaching challenge presented by 'dark' Greens with considerable implications for social policy. To understand this one needs to remember that although the beginning of Green politics in its present form can be dated back to the 'limits to growth' thesis of the early 1970s the leading Green Party in Western Europe, Die Grünen, came out of a coalition of social movements, chiefly the feminists and peace groups (Bramwell, 1989; Hulsberg, 1988, Parkin, 1989). This meant that the founding members were already disenchanted with the western way of life. Because of its size and its representation in the national and state parliaments Die Grünen has explored many of the tensions and critical issues in Green politics to a greater extent than the other smaller parties in Western Europe.

Fundamentalists in Germany and elsewhere believe that the ecological crisis is an outcome of industrialism which has for centuries raped Nature and treated the natural environment as subordinate to the concerns of human beings. They want to see 'industrial disarmament' with a return to much lower levels of consumption and production and an end to the many economic and social processes whereby we damage the planet. The best known spokesman for this tendency is Rudolf Bahro, although he resigned from Die Grünen in 1985 because he thought the party was compromising the Green cause with too much of an adjustment to electoral considerations. Believing that the key to survival for the human race and the planet lies in the abandonment of the industrial way of life, he advocates small communities, comprised of at most three thousand people who would be economically self-sufficient, insofar as that was possible, using the surrounding land to earn a living and perhaps trading with other communities in their area. They would be in touch with other communities and contribute that which was necessary to the infrastructure of the country – transport and information needs, for instance. For Bahro production in industrial societies has become an end in itself –

> The result is that today we consume around ten times as much energy for a worker to be able to sit in front of the TV in the evenings with his bottle of beer as was needed in the 18th century for Schiller to create his life's work.
>
> (Bahro, 1986, p4)

People must learn to live off the land and build communities which are outside of the industrial system.

What makes Bahro a fundamentalist is that he believes that our basic attitudes, which are oriented towards possessions and 'having', must change and as these derive from the capitalist mode of production which emerged in the last two hundred years then this too must be ended. This fundamentalist Green vision is one which tries to move the way of life of western societies towards that of countries in the poor world – to the extent that it is a culture based on a local economy. Bahro is best understood as part of the prophetic tradition in the Green movement – his utopian thinking, which earned him a term of imprisonment in East Germany for his first book *The Alternative*, motivates people to act and is not concerned with the details of social policy, beyond the fact that it would be intrinsically local and decentralised. Of course this vision is of limited general appeal to populations in Western Europe as it would mean the reduction of standards of living and personal consumption. The small communities idea bears some resemblance to the call for a return to such a way of life which was made by Alasdair Macintyre in *After Virtue* as an alternative to the moral chaos of western societies.

> What matters at this stage is the construction of local forms of community within which civility and the intellectual and moral life can be sustained through the new dark ages which are already upon us.
>
> (Macintyre, 1985, p263)

However Bahro's message appeals to a significant minority of the population for it shows how a society might be envisaged in which a different standard of values to those of western materialism prevailed. The votes cast for Green Parties in the 1980s, although obviously not all cast by fundamentalists, do indicate, nonetheless that post-materialists as defined by Inglehart – those concerned with the quality of life and motivated by other than economic ambitions – exist in some numbers (Inglehart, 1977); although it does seem difficult for Green Parties in Western Europe to move beyond around 10 per cent of the vote (Eckersley, 1989).

Bahro displays a concern for spiritual (not necessarily religious) values which is shared by most Greens. It marks Green politics off from the conventional parties. The British Green Party in their 1983 election manifesto had a section on 'The Spirit' which criticised the contemporary preoccupation with 'having', rather than being, arguing that the ecological crisis was at root a spiritual crisis for men and women who have become alienated from their own nature as well as Nature.

The theme of 'one world' is increasingly being taken seriously in mainstream politics as countries are forced into co-operation on environmental issues. Many dark Greens in their analysis start from the theme of 'one world' and reach some uncomfortable conclusions about our western way of life, pointing out that it is based around consumerism and the profligate use of non-renewable resources. They argue that the kind of society which would enable the present world population to survive at some tolerable standard, which is emphatically not what is enjoyed by millions of people in the Third World today, would have to have very low levels

of energy use, localised forms of agriculture and production for
use rather than exchange. It would entail: 'a marked reduction in
commercial production and consumption and a marked increase
in domestic and neighbourhood production' (Trainer, 1985, p247).
This is for most economies a long way into the future, yet there
are small-scale local examples of economic decentralisation which
Greens believe point the way forward. (See Robertson, 1989;
Dauncey, 1988.) One of these is the 'Local Employment and
Trade System' or LETS which originated in Canada in 1983.
This is a community-controlled barter system where members
agree to do work, provide a service for another member and
will then receive payment in 'Green dollars' which are invisible,
simply credit recorded on the system's computer. They have to
be used within the local economy as they have no meaning in
the wider economy and this is said to encourage local self-reliance
(Dauncey, 1988, Ch4).

Green Party policies

The policies of the Green Parties across Europe are usually a
mixture of the fundamentalist and the realist or, to put it another
way, the dark green and the light green. The Green Party in the
United Kingdom is perhaps typical of many western European
Green parties in that its social policies are much more idealistic,
fundamentalist and vague than its environmental policies, which
only seem to be a few years ahead of the government. For example
at the 1987 General Election the Green Party called for taxes on
pollution. It is in the sphere of social policy that the idealism of the
Green position emerges most clearly.

The policies of the Green Party on work and social security
demonstrate this. Greens do not bemoan the disappearance of
full employment in western economies, for they are disenchanted
with the 'work ethic'. The emphasis on work in our society is
for them seen as an emphasis on paid work which relegates the
domestic work, most often performed by women, to an inferior
level because it is unpaid. Yet it is in the home that children are
reared, that people relax and find their sense of identity, and that
the sick and disabled are cared for. Ultimately Greens want to see a
society in which most work is performed at home – paid or unpaid.
In this they are working with a trend which has now got underway
towards more homeworking or 'telecommuting' (Kinsman, 1987).
The advantages of this vision of the home are a strengthening of
communal life and the conservation of energy which will not be
required for journeys to work. Greens want to reorder economic
priorities so that caring work is given a value by society, which

means at present that it should be paid. Hence the Basic Income scheme is one policy which all Green Parties subscribe to, although it is not a policy which is peculiar to them, having supporters across the political spectrum. (For a good review of schemes see Walter, 1989.) Irvine and Ponton in their recent book *A Green Manifesto* advocate replacing all welfare benefits with the Basic Income which would be available to all including children, who would be paid at a lower rate (Irvine and Ponton, 1988). It would be financed from taxation but they do not state how much the tax level would need to be in order to sustain it. Clearly problems occur if the tax rate is so high as to constitute a disincentive. In line with the population policies of the Green Party the Basic Income would not be paid to third and subsequent children, who presumably would be ineligible for any benefits until they achieved adulthood. It is not clear from Green Party literature how the classic problem for social security policy of those who do not want to work will be dealt with – it is open to the obvious criticism that it will subsidise these people without providing them with an incentive to work, although they might be said to be doing caring work in their homes and families. In this area Green Party policy is open to the obvious objection that men and women are not motivated by altruism in the organisation of their daily life and their dealings with the state.

Limits and lifestyles

The response of social scientists to the Club of Rome report *Limits to Growth* published in 1972 was minimal; yet was this so surprising when one considers that at that time the ecological crisis was something that was going to occur when, at some unspecified date, resources would become scarce? E.J. Mishan had already identified many of the costs of economic growth challenging the view that it improves social well being. Although he made references to the ecological consequences of growth economies, his primary concern was to delineate the extent to which this economic growth – measured in terms of sales of motorcars, television sets, greatly increased air travel and the advent of mass tourism – had exacerbated problems of alienation, loneliness and congestion (Mishan, 1967). Fred Hirsch was one of the few who did make a response and in *The Social Limits to Growth*, published in 1977, he identified the ceaseless encouragement to consumption in western societies as the root of the ecological problem; because capitalism encourages individuals to operate in self-maximising ways, they try to achieve 'positional goods' which will enable them to overtake their neighbours. These can be either private goods – like consumer durables – or public goods – like higher education. In industrialised societies policy difficulties could emerge because of the 'tyranny of small decisions'. He concluded that this process needed to be contained by adherence to a strict social morality (Hirsch, 1977, p117).

As critics pointed out it was difficult to see how a consensus on individual and social morality could be created – which agency would ensure that it would come about? (Ellis and Kumar, 1983, p168). The answer from Greens in the 1990s would be 'in all our interests' for we all depend upon Nature to provide the wherewithal to live our lives. If global warming and ozone depletion start to seriously interfere with the operation of industrial society then one can envisage the material conditions for a revival of a consensus on morality. In the meantime, it may not be too fanciful to suggest that the growing Green consciousness in western societies is preparing the way for this. Some of the proponents of the 'limits to growth' thesis believe that the elevation of consumerism to the status of an ideology in western industrial societies has eroded morality. The traditional restraints upon the pursuit of self-interest disappeared with the decline in religious belief or shared collective values. Much of the moral imperative for Greens derives from their heightened sense of the future and the environment which will be available to people in future generations. Our consumption of non-renewable resources must be restrained so that they can be conserved for use by future generations (Daly, 1987).

The Greens urge us to cut back on our personal consumption of goods for they argue that this leads to resource depletion and the immiseration of the third world, which supplies raw materials and cash crops for first world consumption and production. Many of the activities which are accepted as part of leisure – foreign holidays and travel for pleasure – would be discouraged as they waste valuable non-renewable resources and erode other cultures. Greens argue that advertising and the mass media need to be curtailed in order to cut back on consumption. Running through the Green message is a preoccupation with the way in which we live our lives, that we have to live more simply and need to find our satisfactions outside of consumer products.

The Green alternative to consumer capitalism is a conserver economy: an economy dedicated to recycling, make do and mend and products which would have a long life. Within the country, people would live in small communities which would not necessitate them travelling very long distances. So in effect what many Greens are saying is that we need to think globally and *live* locally. As a result motor cars would not be required for the great majority of the population who would prefer to walk or cycle or use public transport. The satisfactions which would be gained from this life would lie in the fact that one produced 'own work' in a local community where one would be known and valued (see Robertson, 1989). There would be an enormous emphasis on the production of food – by each household insofar as this was possible – and food consumed would be of that grown in the region. There is a presumption that the conserver economy would have to be self-sufficient in food production and a number of estimates suggest that this food policy would mean that Britain could not sustain a population much above 30 million (Dobson, 1990, p94). Population control as envisaged by some Greens would be a combination of 'carrot and stick' policies: bonuses paid for periods of non-pregnancy, tax benefits for small families, higher pensions for those who have had small families along with bonuses paid to those who are sterilised and an end to infertility research (Irvine and Ponton, 1988, p23).

Personal responsibility

The Green critique of industrial society is a sustained assault on the assumptions which underlie much contemporary thinking about the self and society. They argue that the acquisition of material goods has become an end in itself and for many people a substitute for satisfying human relationships; the damage to the planet that is being caused by human beings is because they are out of harmony with themselves as well as nature. They point to the work of Richard Easterlin who, summarising the work of a number of cross-national surveys, has shown that for different countries with different income levels the reported differences in 'happiness' are small (Easterlin, 1974). They would cite the restricted or minimal self of which Christopher Lasch writes, the defensive ego-centred individual who regards each encounter with others as an opportunity to maximise his own advantage, as an individual constructed by the hedonistic calculus of consumer society (Lasch, 1980).

The development of consumer capitalism has been partly responsible for the weakening of individual morality and the Greens emphasise that their society would require an ethic of personal responsibility. It can be argued that this should be revived in the subject of Social Policy and Administration which, after all, came out of the confluence of different traditions which all had in common an ethic of personal responsibility: the reformist social philosophy of New Liberalism, the ethical socialism of the early Labour Party and the citizenship ideas of the Charity Organisation Society. It is arguable that ethical socialism was the dominant current and this was about the linkage between social reform and 'individual' reform: its evolutionary perspective deemed that individuals would need to change their behaviour as well as governments introducing legislation to tackle social problems. Social Policy and Administration should attend to the phenomenon of consumerism but with a critical focus: we need to consume in order to live but do we need to consume above a certain level? Does an individual 'need' more than four times the national average earnings? An ethical social policy informed by ecological considerations would need to embrace the issue of personal responsibility and ally this to structural change.

In many ways it would come into conflict with modernity: a Green ethic may not tolerate some of the personal freedoms available in contemporary society. The small communities of a Green society would not be able to afford the expense of some of these freedoms. If people lived in smaller communities then presumably they would not be able to shake off their past so easily. It would not be possible for individuals to create new identities by moving house to another part of the country and changing their work and circle of friends. There would be fewer 'mobile individuals'. Yes, this is a restriction of personal 'freedom' but it would be the cost of these small communities staying together. These options are part of modernity but it is a modernity which with certain forms of technological industrialism has begun to erode the basis for human life on our planet.

Towards a Green Social Policy

The extent to which one thinks it necessary to construct a Green Social Policy depends on the extent to which one believes that the ecological crisis can be solved by industrialism itself with a series of 'technical fixes' which can reduce global warming, ozone depletion and the other problems which the planet faces. The authors discussed above do not accept that they can and do not think our present way of life in the west should continue anyway, based as it is upon exploitation of third world people and the earth's resources.

A Green Social Policy programme can be envisaged along three dimensions: the personal, the community and the national level. At the level of the individual it is important that personal responsibility be stressed; it is axiomatic in so much discussion of the environmental crisis that individuals need to take responsibility for their contribution to the problem. It has been the particular contribution of Green thinking to stress the individual responsibility which should accompany an ecological politics. Nonetheless this entails a range of options from Green consumer purchases through the food that one eats, where one banks right through to the simplification of life urged by the Lifestyle Movement with its motto 'Live simply so that others may simply live'. As we have seen it is at the local level that Greens would want to see the creation of an infra-structure which would facilitate ecological decisions by individuals. It is a truth universally accepted by Greens that power has to be devolved to the locality with an enormous strengthening of powers and revenues of local government. Yet as has been pointed out this lies at variance with the plans of many Greens for environmental controls which presume a strong central government. (See Dobson, 1990, p128.) The controls that would be needed on advertising and the market in order to encourage ecological lifestyles suggest a continuing need for such a strong centre. The future will inevitably see considerable resistance to Green strategies which threaten consumer capitalism. The battle between the two ideologies may well be fought in the realm of consciousness; at the same time it is clear that the Greens advocate organisations of citizens in order to provide and produce services for themselves. Both the local and central state will have to shed services. Greens seem to envisage a return to the voluntarism which characterised much welfare provision before World War One, exemplified in the friendly societies, co-operative movement and the myriad of working-class self-help organisations. There is an emphasis on individuals coming together to provide services rather than relying on the state-employed professionals who are seen to 'disable' their clients (Irvine and Ponton, 1988 p83).

Implications for Social Policy and administration

The subject of Social Policy and Administration was born out of a dissatisfaction with, and documentation of, the damage wrought to individuals by industrialism. Now, at the end of the twentieth century, it is possible to see the damage that industrialism has inflicted on nature. Social Policy is presented with a multi-faceted challenge by Green ideology. The first is to take seriously once more the linkage between a social philosophy imbued with Green principles and the world of Social Policy. Green thought in this country can be viewed as a continuation of the Romantic critique of industrialism which embraced Ruskin, Morris and Tawney. In Social Policy from Tawney, through Titmuss to Townsend there has been a strong vein of moral critique but the Greens are not afraid of moral prescription. Perhaps now the ethical basis which underlies some arguments for Social Policy needs to be enunciated more clearly?

The second challenge is to widen the scope of Social Policy studies by reinterpreting traditional concerns with inequality and unfairness. This can take a variety of forms and space only permits a sketch of how this might be attempted. (See Cahill and Squires, forthcoming).

Because the Green perspective starts from the concern with pollution, damage to the ecosphere and the waste of energy it does not mean that the concern with inequality and unfairness will be made redundant, merely that it will be reinterpreted and made more relevant to a society which is beginning to realise the implications of the limits to growth. One of the most obvious of these issues is transport and specifically the role of the motorcar. A generation ago there was no public discussion on the desirability of motorcars – it seemed that there was a consensus in the society that they were desirable for all. E. J. Mishan was a notable exception when he wrote that 'the invention of the automobile is one of the great disasters to have befallen the human race' (Mishan, 1967, p173). Cars were part of the personal freedom which increasing affluence had brought to all.

The environmental consequences of this unthinking elevation of one mode of transport are plain to see today: large parts of cities destroyed in order to make way for motorcars, the very high levels of pollution found in many urban areas, the increasing congestion of traffic. All this is now part of public and policy debate such as the work of Stephen Plowden and Mayer Hillman who have produced such a range of informed, policy-relevant work on transport with a bias to the disadvantaged road users i.e. pedestrians. (See, for example, Plowden, 1985; Hillman, 1979.) Yet the socioeconomic consequences of the car as king of the road are largely undocumented: although the reality is there on the outer area council estates where car ownership is low and the bus service, since deregulation, is poor and expensive, the isolation of groups like the disabled, the elderly and those who live in the countryside and do not have a car. These are real and felt inequalities which are part of a wider system of inequality but still nonetheless require attention in their own right. Community care, patch, decentralisation, inner city policy – it is hard to think of a debate in social policy in the last decade which has not had a substantial connection with transport and it is equally hard to think of many studies which have acknowledged it. The reasons for this are to be found in the consensual understanding that private car ownership is one of the bases of our society, in much the same way as private home ownership. To look across the Channel is to see the peculiarity of this viewpoint where public transport is given much higher status and regard. A Green Social Policy challenges us to re-examine this acceptance of the motorcar as the preferred form of transport, not because it relies on a non-renewable energy source which contributes to global warming, not because it is responsible for thousands of deaths and accidents each year but rather because of the real and felt inequalities it creates and reinforces. It really is a vehicle of inequality.

A Green Social Policy would concern itself with the creation of sustainable communities, based around the forms of renewable energy which most people have available to them: walking and cycling. At present walking reflects the unequal distribution of resources and power in our society: the National Consumer Council in its report *What's Wrong with Walking?* pointed out that:

> Walking as a means of transport is of central importance to women rather than men, to those on low incomes rather than to those on high incomes, and to the very young and very old rather to those of working age
>
> (National Consumer Council, 1987, p3).

Transport policies in Britain have been devised on the basis of enhancing mobility. The costs of this mobility-for-some-but-not-for-others need to be counted more accurately, not just the deaths and accidents but the dislocation and uprooting of communities caused by the construction of roads. A Green Social Policy would promote access as a key concept and enhance the travel options of those without private cars.

How one gets to this point is of course a matter of political strategy and debate. Indeed, restrictions on car use and discouragement of car ownership look as though they will be one of the tests for western democratic societies as they grapple with the need for measures to prevent or postpone ecological crisis, for would not such a policy be a major vote loser? Transport is but one part of urban policy and the mobility created by the motor car has encouraged the urbanisation of the countryside as more and more people leave the cities in search of a place to live which is quiet and peaceful. This has taken its most acute form in the South East of England with scores of commuter villages being created. Do we wish this development to continue or do we wish to create sustainable cities which would be environments where the economically advantaged would want to live?

Post-materialism?

It is one of the ironies of history that just as the 1980s ended with the people of Eastern Europe removing their state-socialist regimes and voting for governments committed to market solutions, so in Western Europe there was increasing support for environmental pressure groups and Green Parties which challenged the elevation of market criteria as dangerous to the planet. It is now some time since Inglehart identified 'post-materialists'. But if the growth of green consciousness entails the spread of these post-materialist values then the greening of social policy may not be far away. All this is a long way on from the perspective of the government's white paper, *This Common Inheritance*, with its bid to set the environmental agenda for the 1990s, but then we must remember that the Green Parties claim to be constructing a politics for the next century.

References

Bahro, R (1986) *Building the Green Movement*. Heretic Books.

Bramwell, A (1989) *Ecology in the 20th Century: a history*. Yale University Press.

Brundtland Report (1987) *Our Common Future*. Oxford University Press.

Cahill, M and Squires, P (forthcoming) *Welfare for a New World*. Basil Blackwell.

Daly, H E (1987) 'The economic growth debate: what some economists have learned but many have not.' *Journal of Environmental Economics and Management*, Vol 14, pp323–336.

Dauncey, G (1988) *After the Crash: the emergence of the rainbow economy*. Green Print.

Department of the Environment (1990) *This Common Inheritance*. Cm 1200, HMSO.

Dobson, A (1990) *Green Political Thought*. Unwin Hyman.

Easterlin, R (1974) 'Does economic growth improve the human lot? Some empirical evidence' in David, P A and Reder, M (eds), *Nations and Households in Economic Growth*. Academic Press.

Eckersley, R (1989) 'Green politics and the new class'. *Political Studies*, Vol 37, No 2, pp205–23.

Ellis, A and Kumar, K (eds) (1983) *Dilemmas of Liberal Democracies*. Tavistock.

Hillman, M and Whalley, A (1979) *Walking is Transport*. Policy Studies Institute.

Hirsch, F (1977) *Social Limits to Growth*. Routledge, Kegan Paul.

Hülsberg, W (1988) *The German Greens*. Verso.

Inglehart, R (1977) *The Silent Social Revolution*. Princeton University Press.

Irvine, S and Ponton, A (1988) *A Green Manifesto*. Optima.

Kinsman, F (1987) *The Telecommuters*. John Wiley.

Labour Party (1990) *An Earthly Chance*. London.

Lasch, C (1980) *The Culture of Narcissism*. Abacus.

Liberal Democrats (1990) *What Price Our Planet?* Hebden Royd.

Macintyre, A (1985) *After Virtue*. 2nd. ed., Duckworth.

Meadows, D *et al* (1974) *The Limits to Growth.* Pan.
Mishan, E J (1967) *The Costs of Economic Growth.* Staples Press.
National Consumer Council (1987) *What's Wrong with Walking?* HMSO.
Parkin, S (1989) *Green Parties: an international guide.* Heretic Books.
Pearce, D (1989) *Blueprint for a Green Economy.* Earthscan.
Plowden, S (1985) *Transport Reform.* Policy Studies Institute.
Porritt, J (1984) *Seeing Green.* Blackwell.
Robertson, J (1989) *Future Wealth.* Cassell.
Trainer, F E (1986) *Abandon Affluence!* Zed Books.
Walter, T (1989) *Basic Income.* Marion Boyars.

3 Green politics and the future of welfare

John Ferris

All that is solid melts into air, all that is holy is profaned. (Communist Manifesto 1848)

Men fight and lose the battle, and the thing they fought for comes about in spite of their defeat, and when it comes turns out not what they meant, other men have to fight for what they meant under another name

(William Morris 1889).

The concept of 'post-industrial society' lacks precision, but it provides a convenient metaphor that will be used in this essay because it captures the prevailing sense of transition that characterises social policy now. Green politics emerged on the public policy agenda during the past decade but as yet have had little impact on social policy. This essay is aimed at establishing links between ecological concern and social policy. It reflects the view that the concept of sustainability, popularised by the Brundtland Report (United Nations 1987), does have important implications for models of welfare.

Science and technology harnessed to capitalist industrialism have been Janus-faced, the forces unleashed by the industrial revolution have been creative and destructive. Human power and mastery over the natural world have been extended beyond anything envisaged in pre-industrial societies. At the same time forces have been unleashed and are now embodied in organisations that can destroy human communities, erode deeply held beliefs and shape the destinies of individuals and nations alike. The systems we have created have both the power to create and the power to destroy. The euphoria of the 1960s and optimistic projections of infinite technological and economic growth have now been superseded by a darker and more troubled view of the future. Contemporary consciousness of ecological threats to human survival is historically unprecedented. Moreover there is now ample scientific justification for unease.

This is the global and historic context in which the familiar parameters of social policy which have shaped the modern welfare state are now shifting. Old problems like poverty and disease have not been solved, they have assumed global dimensions and demand new approaches and solutions. New problems, related specifically to ecological destruction and the advance of technology, are pressing for attention, for example urbanisation in the third world, contaminated food and water, famine. It therefore seems evident that the social policy agenda for the next decade and beyond will have to expand if these problems are to be tackled. These are matters scarcely envisaged by the architects of the welfare state. The social policies associated with twentieth-century social democracy and liberalism were a civilised response to the 'great transformation' (Polayni, 1944). However new problems call for new values and solutions and these must include social policy.

Since 1945 social policy in every developed nation has been explicitly related to the objective of increasing the rate of economic growth. The basic assumption has been that growth would increase both social and private welfare. For socialists it would provide the basis for expanded collective provision (Crosland, 1955). For liberals it would enhance welfare by allowing wealth to 'trickle down' (Friedman and Friedman 1980). Social spending has also, within these broad assumptions, been viewed as an independent contributor to growth (O'Connor, 1973; George and Wilding, 1984, Ch. 4). The 'Faustian' dreams of virtually infinite growth and progress have been challenged by critical economists (Daly and Cobb, 1989; Hirsch, 1977; Ekins, 1986; Gorz, 1989). Central to the critical arguments is the idea that we live in a world where we are obliged to acknowledge that we face biophysical and social constraints. Central to the Green critique of industrialism is the idea of limits, of life within ecological and cultural boundaries. The challenge to industrial prometheanism has, if taken seriously, profound implications for social policy which we have scarcely begun to address. The very idea of limits is an anathema to social scientists and political elites schooled in the doctrines of Enlightenment – whether liberal or socialist.

A starting point for reassessment then is the finance for welfare. If the critique of economic growth is seen as persuasive then it follows that we can no longer expect to pay for welfare from the increments of growth in the ways that have been possible for most of the post-war era. Ever-expanding public spending budgets are not sustainable. Nor on the other hand should it be assumed that wealth will 'trickle down'. Market welfare creates rich and poor, and morally unacceptable degrees of inequality. This is not to argue that further economic growth is not possible but simply to assert that it would impose increasingly unacceptable social and ecological costs. The concept of sustainability advanced by the Brundtland Report is an acknowledgement of this political reality – even though its formulation of the problem and proposed remedies are ambiguous and contestable.

Post-enlightenment liberalism and socialism which shape the parameters of contemporary thinking about social policy were both premised on the conquest of nature. It is becoming very difficult to evade awareness of the costs of this 'victory'. Rather than liberation from the historic bonds of scarcity we have to recognise at least the possibility of the destruction of the planet. Such considerations form the core of the ecological critique of industrialism. Ecological movements worldwide have drawn attention to the problems and placed the idea of limits on the policy agenda. It is no longer a question of saving 'socialism' or 'capitalism' but humanity itself on a threatened planet.

Although ecological movements have frequently invoked utopian ideas and sometimes advocated romantic pre-industrial views it seems more appropriate to see ecological protest as a very modern response to the negative and manifestly destructive aspects of modernity rather than as a negation of modernity per se. The Green critique of enlightenment has often been historically uninformed and one-sided, but as Adorno and Horkheimer forcefully argued in the 1940s, modernity was never an unmixed blessing:

> The fallen nature of modern man cannot be separated from social progress. On the one hand the growth of economic productivity furnishes the conditions for a world of greater justice; on the other hand it allows the technical apparatus and the social groups which administer it a disproportionate superiority to the rest of the population.
>
> (Adorno and Horkheimer, 1944, pxiv)

In the developed nations ecological movements have had a middle class character and have often been rather conservative in seeking to defend what is worth defending and opposing the blind destructive forces unleashed by late capitalism eg nuclear power and weapons (Hulsberg, 1987; Papadakis, 1983). Two main objectives seem to have emerged from over a decade of green politics and ecological thought.

- The articulation of a common interest in human survival and with this an attempt to found universal ethics that would support the common interests by sustainable development.
- To affirm unequivocally our human responsibility for other species and the eco-sphere which sustains them. This responsiility has been conferred upon us by evolution (as the dominant species). We are the only species with the power to destroy everything that exists.

Given these objectives ecological movements are implicitly faced with the 'task not of conservation of the past but the redemption of the hopes of the past' (Adorno and Horkheimer, 1944, pxv). On this interpretation Green politics represent a modernist critique of enlightenment, not a rejection of enlightenment.

These objectives transcend social policy, of course, but it is becoming evident that ecological ethics so conceived do have substantive relevance for social and economic policy. Social policy, especially in Britain, has traditionally been concerned with distributive justice. Only in recent years has there been much concern with production and reproduction. In the new context of ecological concern the old questions of classical economics of 'what' is produced and 'how' can no longer be safely left to orthodox economists. Economic reason has become one of the principle targets of the ecological critique (Daly and Cobb, 1989; Gorz, 1989; Henderson, 1981). Feminists have usefully re-read Titmuss (Rose, 1981). Perhaps it is now appropriate to re-read him in the light of ecological preoccupations. Titmuss in *The Gift Relationship* (1970) and elsewhere stressed the ethical construction of community and the importance of not repressing gift relationships by allowing the market to coerce people into situations where they have less freedom to exercise moral choice. This argument could plausibly be extended to behaviour which damages the environment eg the extravagant private use of the motor car in congested towns and cities. The concept of 'sustainability' provides the necessary cue (UN, 1987; Peace *et al*, 1989; Redclift, 1987). Ecological awareness makes it possible to recognise the multiple interdependencies in society and between human societies and nature. The concept of sustainability foregrounds questions about basic needs and issues of equity. Distributive justice must figure prominently in debates about sustainable development. Green policies without a coherent social dimension are self-defeating. This point has not apparently been accepted by many fundamentalist Greens (Devall and Sessions, 1985; Devall, 1990).

More positively, a social policy agenda that seriously addresses the quality of life might perhaps have more appeal than it has in the past. There are compelling reasons for establishing links between ecology and social policy. The main obstacles to such links being made are; firstly the ring-fencing of environmental concerns by Governments (and it must be said by environmental pressure groups) which leads to overly technocratic responses prevailing. Secondly, the explicitly misanthropic values being advocated by the increasingly influential 'Deep Ecologists'. Liberals hope that a series of technical/regulatory fixes will solve environmental problems without corresponding changes in other policy areas. The 'Deep Ecologists' in their rejection of anthropocentrism are rejecting implicitly any attempt to reconcile the 'rights of man' with the 'rights of nature' and give priority to the latter (Dobson, 1990, Ch2).

Environmentalism, deep ecology and social ecology

It has now become conventional in ecological writing to make a sharp distinction between environmentalism and radical ecology. This distinction has been popularised by Jonathan Porritt in his references to 'deep' and 'shallow' Greens. (Porritt and Winter, 1989). The point of the distinction was to create the intellectual/ philosophical basis for a sharp break with liberal and socialist ideology, perceived as being inextricably bound up with industrialism. As a slogan it has no doubt been useful but it is too simple and evades the complexities of defining Green values and policy agendas. It is necessary to make a threefold distinction if we are interested in making links between ecology and social policy. A useful typology has been provided by O'Riordan (1981, Ch1).

Following O'Riordan's typology it is necessary to distinguish between 'technocentrism' and 'ecocentrism' and then to recognise that a fundamental schism is now opening up within ecocentrism. Jonathan Porritt and others within the British Green Party have understandably sought to minimise and gloss over the important ethical and political divisions that exist within the Green movement (Porritt and Winter, 1989; Parkin, 1989). These distinctions are however important if the objective of sustainable development is to be taken seriously.

Technocentrism

Environmental reformism as described by O'Riordan is characterised by the belief that present and foreseeable environmental problems can be managed by technocratic means. There would be no need to fundamentally change institutional frameworks or sacrifice accepted economic growth objectives from this perspective. The measures associated with environmental reformism are well established and familiar, eg pricing techniques via taxes that would force polluters to meet the external costs of pollution and compensate victims, legal regulation, scientific and technological innovation to reduce pollution and increase productivity, as well as to find substitutes for depleted resources. From this perspective there would be no need to link ecology with social policy. Nor would there by any need to reduce reliance on the market as the main determinant of policy. Virtually all the environmental policies adopted by British governments to date have been 'technocentric' in O'Riordan's terms. The 'environment' in this perspective remains the domain of scientists and technical specialists.

Deep ecology

Within the 'ecocentric' approach described by O'Riordan it is apparent that in Britain and the USA that the 'Deep Ecology' tendency has become more influential during the 1980s. Along with a general adherence to rather vague variants of anarchism, deep ecologists insist upon the primacy of biocentric ethics and reject all forms of humanism as anthropocentric. There are four main elements in deep ecology.

1 The primacy of nature as the context of human activity.
2 Ecological, evolutionary and physical laws should dictate human morality. (As we are part of nature natural 'laws' can be discovered intuitively 'by thinking like a mountain'; Sessions and Devall, 1985.)
3 Other species and life forms have intrinsic worth or value. Human beings are only one among many species and should not therefore be privileged.
4 Human population should substantially decrease in order to allow non-human life to flourish.

The explicitly anti-humanistic positions of the 'Deep Ecologists' (Naess, 1988) have been widely criticised as deeply malthusian and even eco-fascist. Two particular areas have been subject to controversy. The first is the idea of species equality – the notion that a rat's life is as valuable as a human life. The second is that 'developing nations' should be left to solve their own problems without aid from the West. Migration of human populations to wilderness territories or from poor to rich nations is also opposed from the stand point of population control and conservation. It is difficult to reconcile any form of social policy with the radical biocentrism of the deep ecologists, other than negatively.

Social ecology

The most polemical critic of deep ecology has been Murray Bookchin (1982). Bookchin's conception of social ecology is essentially a reformulation of classical anarchism. It is explicitly humanist and emphasises equality, decentralist strategies, participation and soft-technology. While many Greens are sympathetic with Bookchin's anarchism it is also widely acknowledged that while he is strong on social criticism he is also weak on action proposals. Bookchin's anti-statism and opposition to any kind of

electoral politics leaves few options open to those who have
no taste for sectarian politics and marginal 'life-style' solutions.

The term 'social ecology' could be legitimately extended to
those who are committed to a red/green synthesis (Frankel, 1986;
Ryle, 1987; Redclift, 1987). From this left perspective all forms of
biocentrism are rejected as untenable and unethical. Evolution itself
for better or worse has created human consciousness and with this
supremacy over other species. Our power to destroy life on earth
means that the planetary eco-system and all other species are de
facto dependent upon human decision. Nature itself has conferred
responsibility upon the human race. This is a given not a normative
argument. Nevertheless from an informed ecological standpoint
socialism has been insufficiently materialist in ignoring biophysical
constraints on social and economic development. It would appear
that some form of red/green social ecological perspective offers
the best prospect of establishing links between ecology and social
policy. Not least because such a perspective would see a positive
role for state and international organisations in providing an ethical
regulatory framework as well as the need for decentralised citizens
initiatives favoured by anarchists like Bookchin.

Instrumental vs ecological rationality

In practice the distinction between environmentalism and radical
ecology may not be as sharp as many Green fundamentalists
would like. Even so environmentalism as generally understood
does not provide adequate ground for linking ecology to social
policy. In public policy terms it is a distinct and separate area.
Moreover, because environmentalism is premised on the idea
of finding technical solutions to specific problems it remains
on the level of responding to symptoms. It does not address
the wider realm of ethics and cultural values which have been
identified as an important element in the contemporary ecological
crisis. The controversies surrounding Deep Ecology highlight these
wider concerns and the desire to address causes. Environmentalism
operates at the level of instrumental rationality and is the specialised
domain of technical and political elites, precisely the groups who
have been so slow to respond to increasing evidence of ecological
malaise.

Green politics have emerged because of popular pressure
from grassroots campaigns and public reactions to disasters like
Chernobyl and Bhopal. It is in this context that attempts at
developing new values and ethics must be seen. Typically governmental and industrial elites have sought to restrict the environmental
agenda in ways consistent with free market economics and the
priorities of capitalist development. As Andre Gorz warned over

a decade ago, capitalism will seek profits in clean-up campaigns even as they pollute (Gorz, 1980). Environmentalism does not challenge this.

A new kind of rationality is required which would include both instrumental and practical reason. John Drysek (1987) argues that practical reason is Aristotelian and that, while concerned with pragmatic solutions to problems, it also involves the collective cultivation of virtuous behaviour. Instrumental reason is essentially technical and involves the manipulation of people and things. Ecological rationality would therefore include science and ethics as well as aesthetics. It is concerned with the objects of action as well as technical means. The point that needs to be stressed here is that social ecology would have to address how we live together in human communities as well as our interactions with nature and therefore would have to take on board substantive social policy issues. This is precisely what environmental reformism and biocentric Deep Ecology fail to do.

Paradigm thinking and the new pluralism – some implications for social policy

As the Green movement has gained in influence there have been numerous attempts to articulate distinctive ecological values. Fritjof Capra (1983) is representative and has probably been the most influential writer in this genre.

> What we need is a new 'paradigm' – a new vision of reality; a fundamental change in our thoughts, perceptions, and values. The beginnings of this change, of the shift from the mechanistic to the holistic conception of reality, are already visible in all fields and are likely to dominate the present decade
>
> (Capra F 1983, pxviii).

Capra, like other authors in this genre, is aiming at a non-academic readership. It is social movement literature not social science. This means it is about the articulation of belief and an attempt to offer ideological identity to movement activists. Like any ideology Green 'new paradigm' thinking aspires to hegemony. Capra asserts that the 'new paradigm' will come to displace the old positivist paradigms. The Kuhnian framework is explicit. Whatever the validity of such an approach it is evident that substantive social policy is at best implicit and marginal to the main objectives of ideologists like Capra. The main elements in the 'new paradigm' which has certainly attracted widespread support can be briefly summarised.

Holism

Cartesian approaches to philosophy and science are rejected as overly reductive in favour of holism. (Capra favours a mix of Taoist religion and systems theory.) There are many variants on this mix but an Eastern religion and Western 'holistic science' have become the norm. The aim is to find methodological frameworks for unifying discrete phenomena and the complex inter-relationships between events, things, and processes.

Globalism

It is held that the nation state is becoming obsolete because of transnational patterns of interdependency. There are no purely national solutions to environmental, energy and resource problems. This argument is developed with particular force in relation to North-South relations. Globalism implies a new world order where the rich nations cease living parasitically off the poor nations who have over the past century been providing natural resources and cheap labour to the affluent 'North'.

Limits

Economic growth of the pattern we have seen for the past century is now widely perceived as facing biophysical limits. Population, pollution, and resource constraints were the parameters adopted in the Club of Rome study 'Limits to Growth' (Meadows, *et al*, 1973). Following this report arguments for zero-growth became common. The neo-malthusian assumptions underlying such approaches are now controversial and the more flexible concept of sustainable development has become the new orthodoxy (Pearce, *et al*, 1989).

Decentralisation

This has both economic and political dimensions and is linked to the value placed on self-reliance. Ricardo's economic law of comparative advantage is reversed. Self-reliance implies reducing economic dependency, especially in the sphere of basic needs. With regard to wants and luxuries we need to establish more balanced trading relations. Politically the aim is to enhance community by empowering local/regional populations. Sometimes this is linked with the idea of bioregionalism – natural geographic areas which can be relatively self-sufficient in resource terms. The ecological metaphor of species diversity is extended to human society. Diversity has intrinsic value and is likely to be safeguarded by federalist political structures and enhanced local autonomy.

Co-operation and mutual aid

Zero-sum games, it is held, can be replaced in political and economic life by win-win games arising from co-operative bargaining strategies and adherence to mutual aid norms. This implies local collectivism with common interests being identified by consensual decision making processes working via confederalist structures.

Self-reliance

This has been widely advocated as an intrinsic value for individuals, households, and communities. It includes the idea of self-determination and 'new paradigm' writers argue that it can be distinguished from neo-conservative ideas of self-help, which reflect methodological individualist assumptions, because self-reliance is grounded in cultural norms of reciprocity and mutuality. Interdependence is acknowledged but the objective is to reduce destructive competition and dependence upon ecologically damaging products and modes of life.

Sexual equality

The feminist critique of patriarchy has been generally accepted by 'new paradigm' writers. Industrial society, it is held, is pervaded by patriarchal values. 'Masculine' values of competition, egoism, detached rationality are promoted while 'feminine' values like empathy, intuition, altruism are systematically devalued. Attitudes towards nature, it is held, have been shaped by patriarchal values. The quest to dominate nature is mirrored in human societies by male domination of women.

Non-violence

Gandhian non-violence has been freely drawn upon in the elaboration of the 'new paradigm'. Non-violent action and resistance have been widely used in campaigns against ecological destruction and the oppositional movements against nuclear weapons and power. Non-violent philosophy has also been drawn upon in campaigns against sexism and racism.

Social policy in an ecological society

Green politics are multi-issue as the elaboration of 'new paradigm' values clearly indicates. The political problem for Greens is not that their agenda is too narrow but potential overload. Given this it is not surprising that social policy has received little attention. One of the few British writers who has attempted to tease out the implications of 'new paradigm' thinking for social policy is James Robertson (1985). In his scenarios for the future of post-industrial society his declared preference is for what he calls the S.H.E. option (Sane, Humane, Ecological). This scenario is not so much a prediction as an exercise in value clarification and the delineation of a possible future. Robertson takes the position that it is neither desirable or feasible to reconstruct the full-employment Keynesian Welfare State. Centralised social services are therefore included in his critique of industrial institutions.

The S.H.E. future assumes a comprehensive redefinition of work and along with this the eventual separation of work and income. Robertson argues for more job-sharing, part-time jobs, career sabbaticals, sexual equality in paid and unpaid work. He lays particular stress on the importance of informal sector activity. Overall the main thrust of Robertson's S.H.E. scenario is to elevate autonomous work over wage labour. Underpinning this strategy is his advocacy of the idea of a guaranteed minimum income. Basic income proposals are linked to the idea of citizen rights to an income irrespective of their work contributions. They also imply steeply progressive taxation of income and wealth. Implicitly at least Basic Income proposals are aimed at setting the range of income inequality (Jordan, 1989).

Robertson is anti-state and pro-community. His preference is for communal self-reliance and a greatly extended informal sector. The logic of this approach is pushed into spheres like education, health and housing with proposals for de-professionalisation. Small schools run by parents, alternative and preventative medicine, self-build housing and local community action are seen as the alternative route to a new pattern of welfare in community (Robertson, 1985). Virtually all the substantive proposals put forward are informed by the de-institutionalist ideas of Ivan Illich and judiciously interwoven with the post-industrial sociology of Gershuny *et al* (Frankel, 1987, p.38). While it is certainly possible to view Robertson's S.H.E. scenario as hopelessly utopian, woefully incomplete and schematic this is to miss the point which is that Robertson, like other 'new paradigm' authors, is concerned with value clarification and pointing a direction for future policies.

While the positive prescriptive elements in Robertson are certainly open to criticism it is nevertheless the case that the critical content of his arguments have close affinity with left-libertarian critiques of the welfare state and state socialism (Frankel, 1987, pp65–66). First there was widespread disbelief in the welfare state as an adequate response to problems of poverty and inequality. As Frankel shows, this scepticism is based on ample documentation and cogent argument. Research on racial and gender inequality has dispelled myths about the establishment of social rights of citizenship and the false claims of welfare universalism. Ultimately the welfare state could not be persuasively defended because it was an answer to the problems of 'full-employment' societies. Second, corporatist modes of organisation and policy implementation typically excluded the interests of minorities and marginalised social groups. Over the past decade there have been demands for more participatory structures and provision for excluded minorities. In the absence of political and constitutional change the market has in some respects been a more effective response to the new particularism than the cumbersome structures of the corporatist welfare state and its false universalism.

Robertson and other Green writers have therefore exposed a real problem in attempting to articulate a new range of universal values and to include within these space for individual interests and needs. What is important in this literature is that there is an attempt to draw up a new agenda and indicate new directions for social and economic policy. Unfortunately much of this Green writing is fundamentalist and leaves little space for political debate or choice. The apolitical stance adopted and pervasive anti-statism conveniently ignore the contradictory role of the modern state where as well as seeking to promote the accumulation of capital it also offers degrees of protection to the workers. The logic of accumulation creates the need for legitimation and protective public policy (Gough, 1981; Offe, 1984). This argument is even stronger if the analysis is extended to the natural environment. Policy change emerges from opposition to specific policies and practices that are seen not to be effective or are ethically unacceptable. While abstract ideological models and utopian blueprints obviously influence policy change, social conflicts and incremental adaptation have historically been more important. The novelty of 'Thatcherism' is precisely that it is an ideological blueprint.

A sharper and more realistic frame for green policy has been indicated by the 'realo's' in the West German Green movement. (Weisenthal, 1989) This view of Green politics is reflected in Claus Offe's observation:

> I am deeply convinced that all future political designs will be mixed and to some degree 'electic' designs. Political development in this sense would take the form of a more multi-faceted and pluralistic combination of different forms of economic, technological and political rationality
> (Offe, 1984, p292–299).

The centralising and authoritarian cast of neo-conservatism has its origins in extreme idealism. Behind every absolutist ideal there is a big stick. There is no reason to believe that Green fundamentalism would not be equally authoritarian. Dogmatic adherence to abstract principle is not the way to solve ecological problems. While the decentralising thrust of Green ideology is attractive it is difficult to identify practical alternatives to the protective and regulative functions of the state (and of course supra-national equivalents like the EEC and the UN). However attractive communitarian solutions and values might be, the fact is that communities are attenuated and fragmented in the advanced industrial societies and therefore do not offer a real alternative to state agencies and institutions. This is of course as true for environmental policies as it is for social policy in areas like education, health care, and other social services. They are simply too important to be left to the unregulated vagaries of the market, informal sector and voluntary initiative.

Post-industrial society and ecological realism

Green politics have emerged as a response to the problems created by industrialism and the relentless drive for economic expansion. They are now part of the post-industrial political landscape along with such phenomena as global media networks and flexible specialisation. While the established left-right language is far from meaningless it has become misleading. The old language no longer represents the complex political landscape now taking shape. The old industrialised working class is fragmenting with economic restructuring. Nation states which provide the framework for social policies are increasingly interdependent, especially as their populations have become more mobile across national boundaries. Party politics based on aspirations of ideological hegemony within nation states appear anachronistic in this emerging post-industrial world.

Political parties still attempt to devise policy agendas around core values while political culture itself is like a supermarket. It is now possible to choose political identities and policy agendas like a high street consumer out shopping. The brand names are familiar, 'enterprise culture', 'feminism', 'anti-racism', 'Green' etc., etc. Despite the political dominance conferred by electoral power on neo-conservatism in Britain it is clear that there is a high degree of pluralism in social structure and political values. This has implications for social policy. Recent debates about equality illustrate the problem. Particularistic concerns like gender, race and nation receive more attention than universalistic themes like class and citizenship. Recent texts like *Social Policy – a Critical Introduction* (Williams, 1989) and the journal *Critical Social Policy* exemplify the new pluralism even while seeking to defend social policy universalism. Likewise, poverty research is obliged to analyse a range of specific groups and categories of need rather than 'the poor'. While there are certainly strong arguments for universal basic needs provision it is also the case that it is difficult to envisage all-embracing welfare measures that can address all needs and interests. The problem of what particular infrastructure of universalism and socially acceptable selectivism is needed, identified by Titmuss in the 1960s is no nearer solution (Titmuss, 1987, p154).

Welfare pluralism is frequently seen as some kind of Trojan horse for market welfare and anti-welfare statism. Such an interpretation fails to acknowledge the de facto complexity and pluralism of 'post-industrial' society (Beresford and Croft, 1986). A pioneering attempt at outlining some of the elements of a feasible decentralised welfare system with the capacity to address particularistic needs was put forward by Hadley and Hatch in *Social Welfare and the Failure of the State* (1981). Their ideas show affinity with the 'new paradigm' ideas of writers like James Robertson but are more realistic in terms of what needs to be done to create more participatory structures of social service provision. Welfare pluralism can be seen as offering a coherent perspective to those who are interested in the development of green social policies.

The four main features of the decentralised system proposed by Hadley and Hatch were:

1 Pluralistic service provision
2 Maximum possible decentralisation
3 Contractual service delivery organisations
4 Participatory democracy.

They were harshly criticised by many on the left in the early 1980s for adopting anti-welfare positions. In essence these criticisms focused on the charge that they were simply legitimating new right 'rolling back the state' policies. While they were certainly, and in many respects rightly, critical of centralism they were not seeking to replace state welfare with market welfare. The main thrust of the book was directed towards a stronger and more coherent role for voluntary and informal welfare and the creation of viable communities and participatory structures. Moreover, unlike Robertson, they did give some consideration to financing such a system. The idea of welfare pluralism can be radicalised and linked with basic income proposals. Such ideas if linked with Claus Offe's 'mixed eclecticism', where he advocates a multi-faceted and pluralistic combination of different forms of economic, technological and political rationality, is entirely consistent with the Green value of diversity. It also acknowledges the need for wide-ranging social experiment to find more suitable energy-efficient ways of living. Socialist conceptions of the 'public sphere' have been too ready to equate 'public' with 'state organisation'. Welfare pluralism might

offer the best prospect of both re-valuing the public sphere
and providing the means for strengthening 'civil society' (Keane,
1988).

After a decade of cuts and defensive welfare politics the outlines
of a more pluralistic and decentralised welfare system can be
discerned. While the welfare state in Britain has certainly been
'rolled back' this has had unforeseen consequences. There are new
alliances between welfare professionals and service users emerging,
eg the strength of support for Health Service professionals in their
defence of the NHS. Local authorities under pressure from central
government have developed new relationships with community
groups and the voluntary sector – impelled by common interests
in the protection of valued services. Housing policy has provided
novel examples of such alliances. Public tenants are organised on
historically unprecedented levels, faced as they are by the opting-
out provisions of the Housing Act 1988 (Ginsburg, 1989). While
there has of necessity perhaps been a great deal of attention paid
to privatisation and the new managerialism, relatively little attention
has been given to researching new forms of decentralised welfare
and patterns of co-operation between professionals and service
users. The increasingly important grant economy that underpins
the so-called 'voluntary sector' has been seriously neglected. The
Government's handling of community care illustrates the knowledge
gap. Policies with respect to homelessness have revealed a similar
ignorance of the 'grant economy' and the ways in which it interlocks
with social security. Piecemeal tinkering and crude attempts at
social engineering have been manifestly unsuccessful. In the fields
of housing and social security it is evident that successive Ministers
did not understand the system that they created (Ferris and Whynes,
1990).

Three themes seem to have emerged from the changes that have
occurred over the past decade. Taken together they can be seen as
essential elements in a Green approach to social policy that is not
overly biocentric or subordinate to environmental reformism.

1. Democracy and citizenship

The coercive aspects of the Welfare State have been thoroughly
documented. The new-right solution has shown itself to be authoritarian and anti-democratic. The enabling and redistributive role
of welfare has been under relentless pressure in Britain and
America. Economic coercion can only be resisted by an extension
of democratic rights of citizenship. New forms of functional representation could potentially enlarge the scope of social rights.
Citizens not clients is the appropriate language for social policy
in a sustainable ecological society (Frankel, 1987).

2. Self-reliance

Green conceptions of self-reliance should be sharply distinguished from neo-conservative ideas of self-help. If we understand by self-reliance the capacity to resist political and economic domination, this distinguishes it from the methodological individualist assumptions of the new right. Self-reliance from an ecological standpoint has to be seen in the context of multiple interdependencies and human communities. It certainly implies a responsibility to give as well as take. Normatively Green politics are premised on mutual aid, co-operation, and self-determination. Centralism in social policy is inconsistent with such values (Ekins, 1986).

3. Political and social pluralism

Dogmatic and sterile debates over the issue of state versus market have contributed very little to clarify the important questions raised by the threats of ecological collapse. Both capitalism and socialism have contributed to the present crisis. Neither is uniquely fitted to offer solutions. Given key preconditions, markets can be the most efficient means of meeting need at the lowest cost but the advantages of markets have been exaggerated out of all proportion. The preconditions for efficient markets are stringent, first that they are genuinely competitive and second that they are bounded by the moral context of community. Only viable communities can define limits. Unregulated markets erode both conditions. We need the efficiency provided by markets and the ethics that arise from the community and which are embodied in public policy. The concept of sustainable development is premised on social justice and efficiency. In Britain especially the public sphere has been subject to sustained denigration. The voluntary and informal sectors have been equated with community but in a dishonest way because of the tendency not to acknowledge the flows of taxpayers' money that sustain these sectors. Green thinking about social policy will therefore need to address the links between sectors in the context of post-industrial pluralism. Basic income proposals might be linked to an explicit 'grant economy' in forms that are designed to strengthen civil society (Keene, 1988; Offe, 1984).

Conclusion

It is evident from current debates in ecological movements and Green parties that green politics are neither a single issue or ideologically unified. There are many shades of green. The experience of the West German Greens has been salutory because they achieved a degree of electoral success and political influence.

The German Greens like other Green parties have the characteristics of a social movement and an electoral party seeking power. The tension between these attributes has forced internal disputes to the surface of public debate in Germany. The major cleavage has been between the fundamentalists and realists. There are common values shared by both sides but the fundamentalists want to maintain a social movement identity while the realists take values as given and are more concerned with means and political influence. Social movement activists are concerned with extending movement values. Realists argue that values will never be unitary and that it will be necessary to attract the electoral support of voters who do not necessarily accept the whole Green package.

Political realism means seeking to reconcile conflicting values and strategies. Of necessity it has to use the language of rational choice; strategic bargaining, priorities, trade-offs. Green realists like Helmut Weisenthal (1989) have argued persuasively for Greens to acquire greater learning capacity and organisational sophistication. While this will certainly mean drawing the line around basic values like democracy, equality, and the protection of nature, at present the Greens are so far from holding real power that esoteric debates about 'life-style' and philosophical ecology are politically irrelevant. The realist strategy leaves open the possibility of value change and argues the case for creating the space for social experiments to test new proposals. To fundamentalists this is reformist tinkering. Fundamentalism, being more concerned with 'identity', responds to post-industrial relativism with absolutism. These problems of course face all modern political parties and social movements, as Socialist parties have painfully learned over the past decade. The Greens are not unique.

What is potentially more damaging to the prospects of Green politics and policies are the disputes between misanthropic Deep Ecology and humanistic social ecology. The arguments between Greens in this debate are not about means but ultimate aims. The substance of the humanist critique of Deep Ecology is its harsh malthusianism where its advocates are prepared to accept Garret Hardin's 'Life Boat' ethics and demographic triage (letting human populations starve to reduce world population) (Hardin, 1968). The hidden social policy agenda in these approaches are increasingly restrictive immigration controls and demographically led 'family policies'.

Environmentalism also has implications for social policy that are given token lip-service and not made explicit in policy debates and proposals. 'Making the polluter pay' has become a fashionable slogan, (Pearce *et al*, 1989). Any such measures, however, whether directed at consumers or producers have serious distributional consequences. While this may be acknowledged by economists they also tend to leave these out of their analysis. Measures aimed at protecting wilderness and natural habitats will have consequences that will effect the livelihoods of human beings in terms of employment, health and social services, education, housing. Rural planning will of necessity have to address social and environmental concerns. Energy and transport policies concerned with sustainability will likewise have to interlock with urban policies. While Greens have been right to emphasise ecological priorities they also need to appreciate the complexities of linking these priorities with other policy areas and in pluralistic political and social systems.

Green parties and ecology movements have now been able to put the issues of the environment and biophysical constraints on the public policy agenda. To achieve this it probably was necessary to adopt fundamentalist positions and from these attempt to generate, debate and elaborate new values. Finding effective solutions will require a different strategy that builds on previous historical experience and divergent value perspectives.

Such a strategy, however it develops, if it does, would have two distinctive features. It would have to start from the position that is explicitly humanist and seeks to preserve a viable future for humanity. 'Prometheanism' would have to be replaced by a philosophy of prudence. Every technological and economic development should be in principle reversible. We cannot afford the mistakes of the past century. The future is not predictable so all decisions should be governed by caution (Jonas, 1984). It will be necessary to experiment to find viable ways of life compatible with sustainability and this will imply adopting pragmatic tactics to achieve ecological aims. There is no single logic or rationality that might lead to a sustainable future. Social policy could play a useful if modest role in securing such a future along with other disciplines.

References

Adorno, T and Horkheimer, M (1973) *The Dialectic of Enlightenment.* Allen Lane.

Beresford, P and Croft, S (1986) *Whose Welfare?* Lewis Cohen Centre.

Bookchin, M (1982) *The Ecology of Freedom.* Cheshire Books.

Capra, F (1983) *The Turning Point.* Flamingo.

Crosland, C A R (1956) *The Future of Socialism.* Cape.

Daly, H E and Cobb, J B (1990) *For the Common Good.* Green Print.

Devall, B and Sessions, G (1985) *Deep Ecology.* Gibbs Smith.

Devall, B (1990) *Simple in Means, Rich in Ends.* Green Print.

Dobson, A (1990) *Green Political Thought.* Unwin-Hyman.

Drysek, J (1987) *Rational Ecology.* Blackwell.

Ekins, P (ed) (1986) *The Living Economy*. Routledge, Kegan Paul.

Ferris, J S and Whynes, D (1989) *Homeless Young People in Nottingham*. Nottingham CPRU.

Frankel, B (1986) *The Post-Industrial Utopians*. Oxford Polity.

Freidman, M and Freidman, R (1980) *Free to Choose*. Secker & Warburg.

George, V and Wilding, P (1984) *The Impact of Social Policy*. Routledge, Kegan Paul.

Gorz, A (1980) *Ecology as Politics*. South End Press.

Gorz, A (1989) *The Critique of Economic Reason*. Verso.

Gough, I (1981) *The Political Economy of Welfare*. Macmillan.

Ginsburg, N (1989) 'The Housing Act 1988 and Its Policy Context'. *Critical Social Policy*, Issue 25, pp56–81.

Hadley, R and Hatch S (1981) *Social Welfare & The State*. Allen & Unwin.

Hardin, G (1968) 'The Tragedy of the Commons'. *Science*, Vol. 162, pp1243–1248.

Henderson, H (1978) *Creating Alternative Futures*. Berkeley University.

Hirsch, F (1976) *Social Limits to Growth*. Harvard University.

Hulsberg, W (1988) *The German Greens*. Verso.

Jonas, M (1984) *The Imperative of Responsibility*. Chicago University.

Jordan, B (1987) *Redefining Welfare*. Blackwell.

Keane, J (1988) *Democracy & Civil Society*. Verso.

Meadows, D *et al* (1974) *Limits to Growth*. Pan.

Naess, A (1988) *Ecology, Community & Lifestyle*. Cambridge University.

O'Connor, J (1973) *The Fiscal Crisis of the State*. St Martins Press.

Offe, C (1984) *Contradictions of the Welfare State*. Hutchinson.

O'Riordan, T (1981) *Environmentalism*. Pion.

Papadakis, E (1984) *The Green Movement in West Germany*. Croom Helm.

Parkin, S (1989) *Green Parties*. Heretic Books.

Pearce, D *et al* (1989) *Blueprint for a Green Society*. Earthscan.

Polayni, K (1944) *The Great Transformation*. Gollancz.

Porritt, J (1984) *Seeing Green*. Blackwell.

Porritt, J and Winner, D (1988) *The Coming of the Greens*. Fontana.

Redclift, M (1987) *Sustainable Development*. Methuen.

Robertson, J (1985) *Future Work*. Temple Smith.

Rose, H (1981) 'Rereading Titmuss: The Sexual Division of Welfare' *Journal of Social Policy* 10:4, pp477–502.

Ryle, M (1987) *Ecology & Socialism*. Radius.

Titmuss, R (1970) *The Gift Relationship*. Allen & Unwin.

Titmuss, R (1987) *The Philosophy of Welfare*. Allen-Unwin.

Weisenthal, H (1984) 'Grun Rational', *Kommune*, No 4.

Falkenberg, G and Kersting H (eds) (1985) *Eingriffe Im Diesseits*. Klartext.

Williams, F (1989) *Social Policy*. Polity.

World Commission on Environment & Development (UN) (1987) *Our Common Future*. Oxford University Press. (*The Brundtland Report*.)

4 Food as a social policy issue

Michael Joffe

Introduction

Ten years ago, there was little public interest in food, and little public challenge to the individualistic view that the consumer has free choice and should therefore take the blame for any health problems. At that time too, widespread concern over environmental issues was only just beginning. A great deal of progress has been made, especially in 'green' issues, and it has now become part of ordinary commonsense that many problems require tackling on a large scale, even by supra-national agreements. Gains have not been confined to ecological matters, however. Concern over food quality has become headline news, and, crucially, attempts from various quarters to shift blame to consumers and homemakers have been resisted. The food chain has become visible, as a system of production involving agriculture, processing and distribution, as well as regulation and monitoring.

   The purpose of this chapter is to present a description of the food sector in all its aspects, in a way that is relevant to policy making. It starts with a global perspective on the modern history of the food supply, aiming to highlight the major processes which have brought about the present pattern of production, distribution and consumption. The consequences for public health are then described, starting with the substantial improvements which have occurred historically in Britain and in other developed countries, and the subsequent temporary submerging of food as a public concern. Current nutritional and health problems are then described, in the context of changing patterns of production, distribution and consumption, and drawing out the implications for policy making institutions. Emphasis is placed on the inter-relation between economic, technological, health-related, ecological and social dimensions of the food sector. Food safety is then considered, drawing on two case studies which have received a great deal of public attention,

Salmonella in eggs, and bovine spongiform encephalopathy (BSE
– 'mad cow disease').

Food in modern world history

A few generations ago, throughout the world, the threat of
under-nutrition or starvation hung over many people, especially
the poor. Food production was only just adequate in most areas,
even though most people worked in agriculture. A series of bad
harvests could tip the balance; the start of the French Revolution of
1789 was immediately preceded by a grain shortage (Doyle, 1980,
pp158–167).

In the regions where capitalist development has been successful,
this is no longer the case, despite massive population growth and
simultaneous decline in the proportion of the population working
in agriculture. The process began in eighteenth-century England,
where new crops, drainage and other simple improvements in
technique led to increased productivity (Mathias, 1983, pp53–70).
This 'agricultural revolution' preceded the industrial revolution and,
despite its fundamental economic importance, is far less famous
than the rise of factories and railways. Indeed, the agricultural
revolution made industry economically possible, by achieving
sufficient productivity to allow industrial workers to be fed even
though they produced no food. However, the threat of under-
nutrition was reflected in high mortality rates, especially from
infectious disease (McKeown, 1979, p59). This was compounded
by the effects of enclosures in the countryside and appalling working
conditions in the mushrooming industrial towns.

The growth of British industry was such that additional sources
of food were required: agricultural imports, paid for by exports
of industrial goods. In the mid-nineteenth century, a 'cheap
food' policy was adopted, allowing industrialists to keep wage
costs low. This victory for the proponents of Free Trade led to
a progressive decline in British agriculture: prices were undercut
by cheap imports, particularly from the newly planted lands
of North America, which were being opened up by railroads
and made accessible by steel-hulled trans-Atlantic steamships
(Ashworth, 1960, pp53–70). Thus the British food supply became
commercialised a hundred years ago, at a time when the rest
of western Europe was still dominated by peasant agriculture.
Adulteration of food was commonplace, for example dilution of
flour with chalk. The inadequacy of the nutritional level was exposed
in the early twentieth century, during the Boer War, by the high
proportion of army recruits who had to be rejected owing to poor

physique (Report of the Interdepartmental Committee on Physical Deterioration, 1904).

During the twentieth century, the availability of food increased to the point where under-nutrition became rare. This was due partly to imports from additional sources overseas, such as New Zealand, Australia and Argentina, and partly to a government-led renewal in British agriculture, especially the system of subsidies introduced after the Second World War. The farming interest, represented by the National Farmers' Union (NFU), has become very powerful. Productivity has continued to grow, along with ever-increasing inputs of chemicals and machinery, to the extent that surpluses have developed. This process has been fuelled by the price support system of the Common Agricultural Policy (CAP), after Britain became part of the European Economic Community. However, problems remain: adverse health effects related to nutrition, and adulteration and other problems with food quality, compounded by the results of technological change. These will be discussed below.

In post-war Britain, only a few per cent of the workforce have been employed in agriculture. However, there has been growth in the food processing industry and in other food-related employment, so that about one in six workers are in some part of the food industry, turning agricultural produce into processed food, which requires less domestic preparation. Many of these jobs are low-paid, and the majority of workers are women. Thus, as an increasing number of women has joined the paid labour force, many of them helping to produce food for consumption in others' homes, housework (including food preparation) has become ever more mechanised (Tilly and Scott, 1987, pp214–225).

The cheap food policy, and the associated destruction of peasant agriculture, is unique to Britain. North America and the other 'new' lands never had a peasantry, and commercial food production developed along with the economy as a whole. The western European food economy has developed in quite a different way, although with the same underlying dynamic of increasing agricultural productivity together with industrial development. Thus although continental Europe has experienced devastating political upheavals since 1789, its food system has been less disrupted than in apparently peaceful Britain. The links of production and consumption have not been so affected by commercial pressures, and culinary traditions have stood a better chance of surviving intact. However, the differences are becoming less marked, and high-input agriculture, the CAP and changing food processing technology are leading in the same direction as in Britain.

The history of food in Eastern Europe and Russia has been quite different, and has played a crucial part in the political history of the Soviet Union. In the Tsarist Empire, the level of poverty and under-nutrition was far worse than in western Europe. Inhabitants of the nascent industrial and administrative towns could be fed, because the feudal system made possible extraction of an agricultural 'surplus' while serfs were frequently on the brink of starvation. This rural/urban relationship was compounded by a geographical dimension, that the bread-bowl was in the south, chiefly the Ukraine, whereas the large towns were in the far less fertile north. The end of serfdom led to a key problem: how to feed the towns?

The early Soviet Union faced this problem, and in the context of the Civil War the answer was forced requisition – 'war communism'. During the 1920s, the re-introduction of the market (New Economic Policy) was initially successful, but in the absence of a rapid increase in productivity, the procurements crisis inevitably followed. The intra-Party struggles of the late 1920s were primarily concerned with striking a balance between industrial investment and the problem of agricultural productivity and the procurement of food. The chosen policy was forced 'collectivisation', which was followed by the death of many millions of peasants. This was the substantive issue which led to the emergence of Stalinism and an ever-narrowing power base for the regime, culminating in the Purges of the later 1930s. Soviet agriculture never prospered, despite a series of policy measures and capital injections since the death of Stalin, and food shortages remain a major weakness of the Soviet economy (George and Manning, 1980).

The prosperity of developed capitalist regions has been mirrored by poverty in many parts of Asia, Africa and Latin America. They are often grouped together as the Third World or the South, although in many ways their diversity is more evident than their homogeneity. Their common feature has been their place in the world economy, and the massive inequality of technological and organisational capacity which has allowed their subjugation by the developed world: from sugar and slavery in the Caribbean and the plunder of Bengal, through the colonial phase, to the present position of dependence on a few commodities and their world prices, and debt. It is impossible to do justice here to the complexity of the histories of these very different regions, and in any case there is no shortage of books on the subject (George, 1989).

Food is a more obvious feature of the history of the South than of the North, mainly because actual famine occurs regularly and severe under-nutrition is endemic, and also because the South is largely agricultural. However, the economic position of these regions is better thought of as a problem of income generation, severe enough to affect the basic necessities of life, than as a food-related problem. The poverty of areas such as Bengal dates from the destruction of native industries, especially textiles, due to price-undercutting by imports from industrial Lancashire together with colonial laws. Reliance on cash crops for export, often at the expense of subsistence, is a symptom of the lack of an alternative commodity to export. Much Southern agriculture is devoted not to food production but to drugs for the west (tea, coffee, tobacco, heroin, cocaine), as well as to sugar and exotic fruits. The international economic position is considerably worsened by agricultural subsidies and price support within the developed world, such as the CAP, which hamper access to these rich markets. There are also detailed policy questions, such as the continuing encouragement of sugar beet production in the EEC and the USA, despite the dependence of many Southern countries on sugar export (Franklin, 1988, pp83–87).

The geographical definition of 'the South' should not be allowed to obscure the very great socio-economic inequalities within such societies, typically greater than in the developed world. Rapid population growth combined with landlessness or agrarian poverty have enhanced the lure of the cities, swelling peri-urban slums. The United Nations projects that by the year 2025, the world population will have grown from 4.9 billion (in 1985) to 8.2 billion, and of this 3.3 billion growth, 3.1 billion will be in less developed countries, 2.7 billion of that being in urban areas, largely in shanty towns (Dogan and Kasarda, 1988). For residents of such places, poverty and social marginalisation are combined with the inherent problems of urban food supplies, such as deterioration during the long time from field to kitchen, which is exacerbated in a hot climate.

In principle, technological advance is a means of escape from perpetual agricultural backwardness. However, the Green Revolution of the 1970s had only patchy benefits, and the considerable drawbacks of increasing rural social inequalities, and dependence on new crop varieties which require continuing input of expensive and ecologically damaging chemicals, locking the producer into a one-sided relationship with multi-national corporations. More generally, ecological disaster threatens many areas as a result of deforestation, monoculture, over-use of pesticides and other chemicals, and other measures which were implemented with the promise of bringing development. This background suggests that the imminent bio-technological revolution may prove to be a mixed blessing.

A final twist is the 'demonstration effect', the impact on the poor of being exposed to a vision of the affluent life-style. The world food economy is now dominated by massive multi-national corporations. *Coca-cola* and *MacDonalds* have global reach, and artificial infant feeds are advertised using images of plump, healthy babies. Such articles are not only major items of expenditure for those on a low income; like tobacco they also add directly to the existing health problems of the South.

Food, public health and public policy

In England and Wales, death rates have been falling rapidly since the latter part of the nineteenth century (McKeown, 1979, pp29–71). Detailed analysis of the time-course of this process in relation to the dates of introduction of various specific medical interventions has demonstrated that the latter made only a small and relatively recent contribution, the greatest improvement having happened earlier. It is well known that the great engineering achievements of clean water and effective sewerage made an important contribution, notably to the decline of cholera and typhoid. However, only 21 per cent of the total fall in mortality since the mid-nineteenth century is attributable to the near-elimination of lethal water- and food-borne infectious diseases. The principal cause of this unprecedented improvement in health is the improvement in nutrition consequent on the increased *per capita* availability of food. In addition, infant mortality, which made a major contribution to overall mortality, only fell rapidly after 1900, when clean milk became reliably available. Other contributory factors have included contraceptive practices and an improvement in standards of hygiene.

Similar developments have occurred in other parts of western Europe, and in similar societies in North America and elsewhere. Large-scale infant mortality, fatal infectious disease and starvation have all but disappeared, and the pattern of ill-health has become dominated by cancers and by disorders of the circulatory system, especially coronary heart disease (CHD). These principally affect people in later life, so that the vast majority of babies born into such societies can reasonably expect to live for several decades.

The contrast with the South, especially its more impoverished regions, could not be starker. The preponderance of infant mortality and infectious diseases is directly connected with the scarcity of food and also of clean water and fuel, as well as other less important factors. However, this does not mean that the afflictions of the developed world are accurately called 'diseases of affluence', as coronary heart disease and most cancers are more frequent among the less prosperous within those societies. More important, from the viewpoint of the South, is that such diseases could well be added to the burden of under-nutrition, if 'developed' patterns of food and tobacco consumption take hold in the less developed areas of the world.

As western prosperity has increased during this century, food has disappeared from the agenda of political or public affairs for several decades. Although it could be argued that this was simply because the problem of under-nutrition had been solved, or the perception that this was so, there are other reasons. During the twentieth century, the policy agenda has become dominated by two types of concern: economic issues, including concrete struggles over wages and working conditions as well as the more abstract world of government economic and welfare policy; and those areas which were specifically seen as spheres of legitimate political debate, ones in which the public sector was a major owner and/or controller, such as education, housing, energy and transport. Food has been left to the market, albeit one profoundly distorted by state support, and for some decades it was tacitly assumed that such sectors of the economy could be left to themselves. If there were problems (other than 'purely economic' questions of subsidies, monopoly power, prices and wages), their source must be sought in the decisions of individuals. The consumer is sovereign, it was argued, and must be held accountable for any apparent defects in the system.

One of the interesting aspects of the recent resurgence in public concern over the food supply is that this view is necessarily challenged, whether explicitly or not (Politics of Health Group, 1979). There is a parallel here with other issues, for example the campaign against tobacco. More generally, the environmental movement is as concerned with the activities of the private sector as of the state, and 'green' radicalism does not make the assumption that nationalised industry is necessarily better than capitalism. In a political environment which places greater emphasis on the efficiency and the inevitability of the market, the focus has shifted: neither to destroy capitalism, nor to nationalise its controlling heights, but to ensure safe, beneficial and sustainable activity throughout the economy. The state is important, but less as an active participant than as a regulator, which includes fiscal policy (eg the CAP; tax incentives for lead-free petrol; a proposed 'carbon tax') and production targets (eg quotas for fisheries and for dairy farming) as well as setting standards and monitoring compliance; controls on information are also relevant (eg tobacco advertising).

The 'state' in this sense is increasingly international: in Europe, the European Commission is (or soon will be) sovereign in most of these areas. Inevitably, powerful commercial interests are well organised to lobby in such policy-making bodies. The other components of democratic society are less effectively represented: those concerned to put the consumer view, and/or to guarantee food safety; trades unions with members working in various parts of the food chain; those concerned with the impact of poverty and inequality on nutrition and health; and those who take an ecological perspective, or even just the long term view.

Nutritional problems in Britain

Although outright under-nutrition is now uncommon, there are three major inter-related nutritional concerns: (a) the nutritional quality of a large section of the food supply; (b) the range of food effectively available to particular sections of the population, especially those on low incomes; (c) the implications of the prevailing pattern of food consumption for health and the environment.

We have already seen that food production has been transformed from a predominantly agricultural and domestic activity to a largely industrial process. Agriculture itself has become more like industry, and has increasingly become linked to industrial inputs, especially chemicals. The food processing industry has developed new techniques, under the stimulus of competition.

At their most extreme, these can be characterised as the ruthless application of technology to economic ends. The product, although still apparently recognisable as a food in some traditional sense, is manufactured from components rather than prepared from ingredients. For example, there is a large number of synthetic products, sweet or savoury, with similar lists of ingredients: sugars, fats, starch, milk protein, refined flour, homogenates, texturizers, flavourings and preservatives. Their variety results from the in-genuity of the designer rather than being an inherent property of the food. Although such articles contain sufficient calories and the major nutrients, their content of vitamins, minerals and fibre may be inadequate. Also, the production process leads to a wide separation of quality and appearance, removing the consumer's ability to judge.

Another example of technological innovation is mechanically recovered meat (MRM), a process which removes all soft tissue from bone, resulting in a sludge bearing little resemblance to what is usually thought of as meat (muscle). Together with other parts of the carcass such as spleen and eyeballs, MRM is a component of many meat products, such as sausages, pies and pates. Nothing is wasted.

The food industry as a whole faces the structural problem that the quantity of food demanded does not grow, especially in a modern society with a stable and increasingly sedentary population, making it difficult to expand turnover as other industries do. This accentuates the tendency for relatively few large companies to dominate many sections of the industry, as these market leaders can grow by taking over the smaller concerns. Another response has been to 'add value' to products, thereby selling more than the original ingredients, as long as customers are willing to buy the result. Thus, crisps are an expensive form of potatoes together with fat, salt and flavouring. At the upper end of the market, the same economic logic can give rise to improved variety and (sometimes) quality of food, for example by allowing the import of more exotic fruits, the sale of gourmet items and 'health' foods, and fulfilling the demand for organically grown produce at premium prices.

The domination by large companies has been most pronounced in particular sectors, notably the manufacture of frozen food, meat products, bread and flour, tinned food, breakfast cereals and margarine, and more recently in retailing. Such concentration has been slower to develop in the case of fresh foodstuffs, such as fruit and vegetables. This has resulted in higher levels of availability and advertising in the former group compared with the latter.

However, the distinctions among producers have become less important with the rising dominance of the retail sector, dominated by the supermarket chains. They are now responsible for the large majority of food sales (eg eight companies accounted for 90 per cent of food sales in London in 1985, 59 per cent being due to just two companies (Lewis, 1985)). Even the large producers have had to adjust to this reality, and the concomitant trend towards supermarkets' 'own brand' produce. The requirements of the retail sector have become predominant, especially durability of food so that it survives the long distribution chain in saleable condition, and also its attractiveness.

Distinctions within the retail sector are now a major determinant of patterns of consumption, and therefore of price and of the availability of different sorts of food. The recent trend towards very large 'superstores', located away from high street shopping areas, has led to further segmentation in an already stratified market. People with access to cars are able to benefit from the low prices and greater choice provided in larger stores. People on low incomes tend to be restricted to small shops which typically are more expensive and have a smaller range of goods, especially of fresh foods. The policies of the major retail chains reinforce the market conditions underlying this tendency (Lewis, 1985).

Thus although poverty is basically a question of income genera-tion, a less severe version of the problem of under-nutrition in the South, it is accentuated by certain aspects of modern food manufacture and by the pattern of retailing. Deficiencies in vitamins and minerals and low intakes of fibre are commonplace. The most seriously affected groups are low income families, the elderly, people with disabilities, and the increasing number of homeless people (Cole-Hamilton and Lang, 1986). Women tend to bear the brunt, by giving their families priority over their own needs. Pregnant women have additional nutritional needs, which may be beyond the available income, and this may contribute to higher rates of low birthweight and of perinatal and infant mortality among those of lower social class. Children from low-income households may be at risk of under-nutrition, failure to thrive, vitamin and mineral deficiencies and poor dental health, as well as poor nutrition generally. Additional problems are faced by people from ethnic minorities who prefer to maintain traditional eating patterns, as the necessary foods may be expensive and difficult to obtain locally (Cole-Hamilton and Lang, 1986).

People from low-income households sometimes have to miss meals for economic reasons, as food is a relatively flexible item of expenditure. They also tend to eat more fatty and sugary food, which provide inexpensive calories, and less fruit, vegetables and high fibre foods compared with those from high-income households. The extent to which these things happen is very sensitive to changes in the level of benefit, and to other factors such as the decline in the nutritional quality of school meals following abolition of statutory standards. Value for money is the prime consideration, and it appears that people with low incomes shop more efficiently in terms of nutrients per pound (Cole-Hamilton and Lang, 1986).

Health, the environment, and consumer demand

Current scientific evidence strongly suggests that patterns of food intake affect the risk of serious diseases. Although the evidence is not conclusive, it is probable that coronary heart disease is associated with the consumption of fats, especially saturated fat which is especially abundant in food of animal origin. A government committee, set up owing to concern at the internationally high rates of CHD in Britain, recommended in 1984 that fat consumption should be markedly reduced (Committee on Medical Aspects of Food Quality, 1984). There are other reasons for encouraging a decline in fat intake, and more generally for the consumption of sugars and salt to decrease and that of fibre to increase. These include possible links with certain cancers, and gastro-intestinal disorders more generally (National Advisory Committee on Nutrition Education, 1983). Indeed, it is possible to identify a disease pattern related to the low fibre, high fat/sugars/salt diet which has developed particularly in countries with a highly commercialised and industrial food production system.

Another consequence of this consumption pattern is a high prevalence of obesity, which predisposes to diseases such as osteo-arthritis of the lower limbs. Many products of the food industry are calorie dense, for example confectionery, and have been criticised as containing 'empty calories', in the sense that they are relatively poor in nutrients other than fats and sugars. A further consequence is the existence of a highly lucrative slimming industry.

The policy of the European Commission has accentuated some features of this unhealthy food supply in countries such as Britain, even though the latter has complex roots, and is more similar to the commercialised system in the United States than in much of the rest of Europe. This is because the Common Agricultural Policy has largely supported the overproduction of relatively unhealthy foods such as butter and sugar (beet). The role of EC policy has particular importance for the future, as there is a danger that the relatively healthy diet of southern Europe will be displaced by the unhealthy consumption patterns of northern Europe, rather than the other way around.

Thus, both the operation of the market and the policy process have been even-handed or 'blind' in relation to health criteria. It is interesting that recent discussions on the need to move towards free trade in agriculture, in order to fulfil requirements under GATT negotiations, have been innocent of concern over public health implications.

This points to a gap in formal policy making institutions. There are at least two possible interpretations, both of which may be partly true: first, that criteria of social responsibility take a subordinate role to those of economic policy, which in turn are largely shaped by commercial vested interests. Second, that there is fragmentation, so that (in Britain) the Ministry of Agriculture, Fisheries and Foods represents the food production industry, but health aspects fall within the brief of the Department of Health; or in the European context, that different Directorates General are responsible. The solution implied by the second is in terms of inter-departmental committees to ensure coordination. In practice, the best hope is that those with an independent voice, for example voluntary organisations, will voice their concern in the hope of bringing effective pressure to bear politically.

The term 'criteria of social responsibility' includes the ecological dimension, which is at last being taken seriously in public policy formulation. It would be mistaken to assume that the present abundance of food will continue indefinitely, even apart from the question of world population growth. Climatic change could pose a threat to the continuing productivity of agriculture. Long run deterioration in soil quality, to which chemical inputs together with monoculture may contribute, needs to be taken seriously. There are competing models of change here: to move towards an overall reduction in chemical usage (low input agriculture), or to promote 'pure and natural' organically grown produce for those who want it, and who can pay the price. The latter course implies segmentation of the market, while ignoring the larger perspective.

The type of agriculture is also important: it has long been recognised that vegetable production is a great deal more efficient than meat production, except where the latter takes place on marginal land which is otherwise useless. There are further implications, on a global scale: the connection between the destruction of tropical rain forests and the expansion of beef production has been well publicised. As mentioned above, there are also health-related grounds for recommending a radical decrease in the quantity of meat consumed, implying a decline in its production. Thus in this instance, health and environmental criteria point in the same direction, but in opposition to the interests of the meat production/distribution chain (including the employment implications), and to the high cultural value given to meat as a food.

Such cultural considerations must be given due weight, but not over-emphasized as is sometimes the case (Blaxter, 1990). Experience shows that food consumption patterns can change rapidly. The developments in the food production industry described previously have brought about large changes, for example the trend towards food which is quick to prepare. Continental and ethnic influences have enriched and diversified the diet, both through specialised restaurants and cookery books. Changes are made on the grounds of health, for example the fall in egg consumption following the *Salmonella* affair (see below), and more general alterations in response to nutritional guidelines.

The likely future shifts in consumption patterns need to be taken into account by policy makers. For example, if scientific evidence were increasingly to support – or a television programme were to publicise – the hypothesis that consumption of fatty fish protects against coronary heart disease, this would increase the demand for fish, raising questions concerning both the long-term adequacy of fish stocks and pollution of the seas.

Food safety and agriculture

Unease has been growing for more than a decade over the use of chemicals both in agriculture and as food additives. However, the major shift in public awareness of the importance of food safety in the past few years has focused mainly on infectious agents such as *Salmonella*, *Listeria* and Bovine Spongiform Encephalopathy (BSE – 'mad cow disease').

The incidence of infection with a particular strain of *Salmonella* known as *enteritidis* phage type 4 had been rising for some years before the story broke into the public arena. As a result of their routine monitoring activity, scientists at the Communicable Diseases Surveillance Centre (CDSC) documented the increase as it occurred (*Lancet*, 1988). No effective action was taken and the number of cases continued to grow. Public health professionals became increasingly aware of the rise, but Environmental Health Officers and public health doctors are organised on a local basis (local authorities and district health authorities, respectively), and could only continue to deal with outbreaks on a local basis, even though the source of these recurring outbreaks was outside their localities.

However, the matter did not rest there. The media played an important role in bringing the situation to public attention, and were provided with information not only by CDSC but also by those who understood the sources of contamination within the poultry industry: Professor Richard Lacey and the London Food Commission provided evidence concerning the contamination of animal feeds, and highlighted the inactivity of the Ministry. Attempts to place the responsibility on declining standards of hygiene in domestic kitchens and in catering establishments were unsuccessful. Thus a breakthrough in public understanding occurred: the spotlight was focused 'upstream' on the poultry industry, and the victims of the disease escaped the blame on this occasion.

Political pressure culminated in an admission by the Minister then in charge that the problem lay at the production end. Thus action was taken, both over regulation and in addressing the economic interests of the producers by offering up to 19 million pounds in compensation. (The principle that the polluter should pay was not adhered to in this instance.) The government and the Ministry of Agriculture had to abandon their favoured approach of advising the consumer rather than direct intervention. Since this was done, the rapid rise in the number of cases has tapered off, although there has been no decline.

However, because it was necessary to make the issue public in such a way that it became a 'scare story', some of this publicity was counter-productive. If perceived to apply at an individual level, together with other concurrent news stories concerning the safety of food and water, it encouraged the view that 'nothing is safe', which has the corollary that no specific effective action can or should be taken. The episode also raised the question of the rationality of different strategies of action. For any particular member of the public, the risk of contracting serious disease due to *Salmonella* is very small. It would therefore be irrational to devote substantial personal effort to effecting major behavioural change. In contrast, at the population level the risk is certain: the number of annual cases exceeds ten thousand. Action at this level is therefore rational.

Salmonella enteritidis is only one of four diseases attributable to contaminated animal feed which have occurred during the 1980s. Cattle have been subject to outbreaks of botulism, apparently as a result of being fed on hen-house waste, and cattle feed laced with lead caused deaths among cattle and financial loss by farmers. In those cases the animals were severely affected but the human danger was slight. The fourth disease is BSE. All indicate the consequences of treating animal welfare as a ruthless exercise in the combination of economics and nutritional science. In each case, in addition to any implications for human health, farmers have suffered financially as a result of their trust in their suppliers of animal feedstuffs.

BSE is a new disease of cattle which was first recognised in November 1986, though the first cases probably occurred in April 1985 (Southwood *et al*, 1989). Over 20,000 cases have now been recorded, with devastating consequences for the affected farmers and the British beef industry more generally, and considerable cost to the taxpayer.

It has a long incubation period: current estimates are that 2.5 to 8 years may elapse between exposure to the causative agent and developing signs of the disease. Once established the illness progresses to an inevitably fatal outcome within two weeks to six months. The central nervous system is affected, with abnormal gait and posture, and behavioural abnormalities. It is very similar to scrapie, a disease of sheep which has been widely prevalent in Britain for at least two centuries, but was previously unknown in cattle.

The best evidence of the cause of BSE comes from epidemiological studies conducted by MAFF's Central Veterinary Laboratory (Southwood *et al*, 1989). A computer simulation model points to the period 1981–82 as the start of the epidemic, exposure having been mainly as calves. At least until now, BSE is mainly an English disease, especially affecting herds in southern and eastern England. In most affected herds, it is usual for only a few animals to be affected. The feature which has been found to be common to all cases is the use of commercial concentrates as feeds, specifically meat and bone meal. The uneven geographical spread may reflect the tendency for meat and bone meal to be distributed within quite a small radius. It is unclear why some sources of meat and bone meal are apparently sources of infection, whereas others are not.

Apart from the economic disaster which BSE has brought to many farmers, the main concern has been whether the disease may spread to humans. The most reassuring evidence that it will not do so is the apparent non-transmissibility of scrapie from affected sheep. There are two human diseases which are similar, and which have been transmitted by an infectious agent: Kuru, and Creutzfeld-Jacob Disease (CJD).

Kuru used to be a widely prevalent disease in New Guinea, which was maintained in the population by the ceremonial handling and consumption of affected human brains. The evidence suggests the absence of human-to-human transmission, and an incubation period having an upper limit of more than 30 years, although children were affected as well as adults, suggesting that the lower limit of the incubation period was a fairly small number of years (Gajdusek, 1977; Alpers, 1987). Cases of CJD have been reported which resulted from corneal transplants, from electrode implantation or surgical instruments, or from hormone preparations derived from cadaveric human brains (Rappaport, 1987). The suggestion that naturally occurring CJD results from the ingestion of scrapie-infected material from sheep has never been substantiated, and a case has been reported in a life-long vegetarian (Southwood *et al*, 1989).

Thus the unexpected spread of the scrapie agent to cattle, and the possibility that it may spread to humans, indicate the complexity and unpredictability of biological systems, and the folly of treating them as if they followed mechanistic laws. However, although it seems self-evident retrospectively that feeding sheep material to cattle was obviously wrong, it is not easy to specify criteria which could be applied in such cases before the event. Many current practices in agriculture and food production are unnatural, and some of these are positively beneficial (for example, pasteurisation of milk), just as nature is sometimes harmful – as in the case of the toxin causing botulism, one of the most potent poisons known.

Another way of putting the same view is to consider what would have been the likely response, if in 1980 the argument had been advanced that feeding sheep remains to cattle should be discontinued, on the grounds of a health risk to the cattle if not also to humans. The reply would have been, that there was no evidence that the scrapie agent could cross those species barriers, and it would have been unanswerable at that time. This raises an uncomfortable question for policy makers: given the unpredictability of biological (and more generally, ecological) systems, what resources should be devoted to policy-orientated research which attempts to predict future problems, how should this be organised so that it is independent of vested interests, and crucially, what weight should be given to the findings in the development of economic and social policy?

Conclusion

The great decline in gross under-nutrition in the developed areas of the world has shown the potential gain which can result from economic development. However, there are no grounds for complacency. Some food-related problems are symptoms of a more general economic situation, of the inequitable distribution of income generating opportunities. This is particularly so in the less developed countries, but also affects some of the inhabitants of the developed parts of the world. More specific to food is the requirement to protect the achieved gains from ecological disturbances such as the effects of soil deterioration, over-fishing and global warming. Second, in addition to the question of quantity, it is increasingly necessary to consider qualitative aspects, safety as well as nutritional quality, and to relate these to technological developments.

Food is not only important and interesting in its own right. It also provides an interesting example for social policy analysis, because its production and distribution are located almost wholly within the private sector. In this context, public policy is not confined to the activities of national and supra-national governmental bodies, but includes also measures to influence industrial and commercial practices, requiring an analysis of the latter in all their aspects.

Thus, in the case of food, we have looked at supply, equity of distribution, technology, quality, and ecological implications within the whole sector, considered against the background of the historical processes which brought these about. Further elements which could be considered include wage levels and opportunities for employment, ethnic aspects, the gender division of labour, the degradation of language by publicists with vested commercial interests, and health and safety at work.

An analysis of this kind, extended to other sectors, when taken together could be described as a description of the material basis of civil society. Such sectors include housing, energy and transport, health and social care, the weapons industry and defence, and information (the latter example indicates that a 'sector' can be defined not only as an area of economic activity, but equally as a key *social* area).

A sector is a good focus for analysis because it is large enough to be concerned with more than sectional concerns, but at the same time its concreteness has immediate relevance for actors in the real world, such as companies, trades unions and ministries. The focus is therefore accessible to these interest groups, and also to other institutions and individuals such as relevant voluntary organisations and academics, as in the case study of the *Salmonella* outbreak described above, showing the operation of public policy as a democratic process.

References

Alpers, M P (1987) 'Transmissible slow virus encephalopathies (kuru)'. In Weatherall, D J, Ledingham, J G, Warrell, D A (eds) *Oxford Textbook of Medicine*, Vol 1. Oxford University Press.

Ashworth, T S (1960) *An Economic History of England 1870–1939*. Methuen.

Blaxter, M (1990) *Health and Lifestyles*. Routledge.

Cole-Hamilton, I and Lang, T (1986) *Tightening Belts: a report on the impact of poverty on food*. London Food Commission.

Committee on Medical Aspects of Food Quality (1984) *Diet and Cardiovascular Disease*. Department of Health and Social Security, London, HMSO.

Dogan, M and Kasarda, J D (1988) 'Introduction'. In Dogan, M and Kasarda, J D (eds) *The Metropolis Era*, Vol 1. Newbury Park, Sage.

Doyle, W (1980) *Origins of the French Revolution*. Oxford University Press.

Franklin, M (1988) *Rich Man's Farming: the crisis in agriculture*. Routledge.

Gajdusek, D C (1977) 'Unconventional viruses and the origin and disappearance of Kuru'. *Science*, Vol 197, pp943–60.

George, V (1989) *Wealth, Poverty and Starvation*. Harvester.

George, V and Manning, N (1980) *Socialism, Social Welfare and the Soviet Union*. Routledge and Kegan Paul.

Lancet Editorial (anonymous) (1988) 'Salmonella enteritidis phage type 4: chicken and egg'. *Lancet*, Vol ii, pp720–22.

Lewis, J (1985) *Food Retailing in London*. London Food Commission.

McKeown, T (1973) *The Role of Medicine*. Blackwell.

Mathias, P (1983) *The First Industrial Nation: An Economic History of Britain 1700–1914*, 2nd edition. Methuen.

National Advisory Committee on Nutrition Education (1983) *A Discussion Paper on Proposals for Nutritional Guidelines for Health Education in Britain*. Health Education Council.

Politics of Health Group (1979) *Food and Profit*. London, Politics of Health Group.

Rappaport, E B (1987) 'Iatrogenic Creuzfeld-Jacob Disease'. *Neurology*, Vol 37, pp1520–22.

Report of the Interdepartmental Committee on Physical Deterioration (1904). HMSO, Cmnd. 2175.

Southwood, R, Epstein, M A, Martin, W B and Walton, S (1989) *Report of the Working Party on Bovine Spongiform Encephalopathy*. Department of Health and Ministry of Agriculture, Fisheries and Food.

Tilly, L A and Scott, J W (1987) *Women, Work, and Family*. Methuen.

5 Assisted reproduction – usurping nature?

Eric Blyth

Introduction

> In pursuing techniques to provide children for the childless, we may, simply and commendably, be carrying out the task bequeathed to us from Aesculapius and Hippocrates, to use our God-given intelligence to improve the human condition. Or on the contrary, we may, in these attempts to impose human whims and wants on the most basic of life processes, be committing an intolerable trespass on domains best left to the working of God and nature; we may stand condemned with Prometheus for making off with the property of the deity
> (Lisa Newton, quoted in Bellina and Wilson, 1986, p343).

This chapter provides an overview and critique of assisted reproduction practices, and an analysis of the provisions of the Human Fertilisation and Embryology Act, 1990 as they affect services providers, potential recipients, donors of genetic material and those whose lives are established by assisted reproduction techniques.

Circumventing childlessness and infertility

Solutions to the problems of childlessness and infertility have exercised the endeavours of the human race from earliest times and several of the techniques currently practiced are far from new. Biblical accounts, for example, illustrate the opportunism of our childless ancestors who coerced their serving maids to act as surrogate mothers. The first recorded use of donor insemination for human purposes, a well-established practice in livestock breeding and animal husbandry, took place in the eighteenth century. More commonly many societies have utilised various adoption practices to provide children for childless adults.

More recent interest in assisted reproduction, particularly in the western world, centres around several contemporaneous developments: an increasing awareness of the prevalence of childlessness and infertility, a decline in the number of healthy white babies available for adoption, an increase in publicity concerning recourse to reproductive alternatives, the emergence of an organised, vociferous and articulate lobby representing childless people and the rapid pace of developments in reproductive and genetic technology.

Estimates of the incidence of involuntary childlessness in the western world vary between 10 and 15 per cent of the adult population of childbearing age (Mathieson, 1986) although these may well be underestimates. Some claim that involuntary childlessness has reached 'epidemic proportions' (Newill, 1986). Involuntary childlessness may result from conditions which tend to be labelled 'infertility', including readily identifiable physical pathology, 'unexplained' failure to achieve a pregnancy in spite of actively trying to do so and the possession of genetic disease which may be inherited by biological offspring. Alternatively involuntary childlessness may be a consequence of social practices such as leading a lifestyle which eschews heterosexual relationships.

Advocates of the provision and development of assisted reproduction promote its role on the basis that it helps the victims of reproductive dysfunction (especially women) 'fulfill their natural desire for parenthood' (Council for Science and Society, 1984). Patrick Steptoe, a prominent pioneer of reproductive technology, asserted:

> It is a fact that there is a biological drive to reproduce. Women who deny this drive, or in whom it is frustrated, show disturbances in other ways
>
> (quoted in Stanworth, 1987, p15).

Recognition of the social pressures on adults to become parents provides an alternative or supplementary perspective to that of 'biological destiny'.

> Reproduction (is seen as) a necessary criterion for personal fulfilment, social acceptance, religious membership, sexual identity and psychological adjustment
>
> (Daniluk *et al*, 1985, p75).

Failure to conform to dominant social pressures, for whatever reason or motivation, results in stigmatisation (Lasker and Borg, 1989; Pfeffer, 1987; Veevers, 1980). Whatever the source of pressures on childless people their 'desperation' is manifested in the, often costly and ultimately largely unrewarded, lengths they go to to achieve parenthood. The Warnock Committee, in endorsing the development of assisted reproduction services, considered that the experience of infertility could be so psychologically damaging as to warrant psychiatric treatment (DHSS, 1984), assisted reproduction, therefore, acting as a 'psychiatric prophylactic' (Pfeffer, 1990). From this perspective assisted reproduction acts in a supportive and remedial capacity when 'nature fails' to underwrite conventional beliefs about what is biologically and socially 'natural'.

However, despite assisted reproduction's claim to answer the problem of women's biological and social destiny, its benefits come with costs and by the early 1980s concern had risen to a level which compelled the Government to take action (Yoxen, 1990). Anticipating that public debate about assisted reproduction would raise controversial and potentially irreconcilable issues which would have an uncertain electoral impact the Government attempted to remove it from the party political arena, a venture that proved largely successful. In the first instance the Government established a Committee of Inquiry, chaired by Baroness Warnock, which published its report in 1984 (DHSS, 1984) and followed this with a Consultation Paper (DHSS, 1986) inviting comment on the Committee's recommendations. In the meantime, in response to the highly-publicised activities of commercial surrogacy agencies in Britain, the Surrogacy Arrangements Act, 1985 was passed with all-party support. This implemented several of the Warnock Committee's recommendations, prohibiting certain commercial activities associated with surrogacy, although not outlawing surrogacy altogether as the majority of the Committee had recommended. The Government subsequently issued a white paper (DHSS, 1987) and introduced legislation in Parliament in 1989. The Human Fertilisation and Embryology Act, 1990 is expected to be implemented during 1991.

Service provision

Currently assisted reproduction services are provided on an ad hoc basis within the NHS, and by private and charitable health organisations. 'Low-tech' methods which are not dependent on clinical skills and sophisticated equipment, such as donor insemination, are frequently utilised by individuals or groups on a self-help basis, whilst surrogacy is performed almost exclusively as a private enterprise without the intervention of medical practitioners or statutory agencies. 'High-tech' services such as in vitro fertilisation (IVF) and gamete intra-fallopian transfer (GIFT) and their variations are performed primarily in private health centres at considerable cost to recipients. Although IVF and GIFT are available within the NHS service provision is geographically patchy and recipients are charged in all but two centres. Furthermore, since assisted reproduction services are excluded from health insurance schemes, access to them is determined to a marked extent by ability to pay.

Accurate statistics concerning the use of assisted reproduction techniques in Britain are difficult to obtain because of the extent of undisclosed and unrecorded private arrangements. It is estimated that at least 2,000 children are born annually following DI (Snowden and Snowden, 1984; DHSS, 1987) and approximately 1,000 as a result of IVF (Interim Licencing Authority, 1990). National figures for the numbers of children born following GIFT are not available. The prevalence of surrogacy is also difficult to ascertain, although it is estimated that there have been between 29 and 70 surrogate births in total (Morgan, 1988; Ferriman, 1990).

High-tech treatments, though, are singularly unsuccessful, with overall failure rates of approximately 90 per cent, and some centres have yet to produce a live birth (Interim Licencing Authority, 1990). The reality for the vast majority of women who undergo these services is that they will not succeed in having a healthy baby. In stark contrast surrogacy provides an extremely favourable 'take home baby' rate of over 90 per cent (Lasker and Borg, 1989; Childlessness Overcome Through Surrogacy, 1990).

High-tech treatments are also responsible for high levels of fetal abnormality, spontaneous abortion, ectopic pregnancy, multiple pregnancy and birth, perinatal mortality and disability and maternal illness. Many of these are the direct consequence of multiple egg or embryo transfer (Howie, 1988; Interim Licencing Authority, 1990). In addition drug administration and some of the more recent techniques, such as cryopreservation of embryos and gametes requiring their freezing and thawing, may ultimately demonstrate longer-term effects which are not currently apparent.

IVF services have been subject to voluntary self-regulation since 1985 by the Interim Licencing Authority, a multi-disciplinary body formed by the Medical Research Council and the Royal College of Obstetricians and Gynaecologists as an initial, temporary response to the Warnock Committee's recommendation for the establishment of a formal licencing body. The ILA provides guidelines for both research and treatment services. However inadequate resources have prevented it from regulating GIFT services and its efforts to restrict multiple egg transfer have had limited success (Interim Licencing Authority, 1990).

Under the Act's provisions the ILA will be replaced by a statutory Human Fertilisation and Embryology Authority which will be responsible for licencing centres engaged in regulated research and service provision and for establishing minimum standards and codes of practice. The Authority will also be required to ensure that those centres providing licenced 'treatment services' offer potential recipients and donors of genetic material opportunities for 'proper' counselling. The Act's definition of 'treatment services' falling within the remit of the Authority as 'medical, surgical or obstetric services provided for the purpose of assisting women to carry children' serves to endorse a medical model of infertility and childlessness and, consequently, the central role of medicine in diagnosis and treatment. However the Act's exclusion of GIFT from the range of treatment services means that practices associated with GIFT which currently give cause for concern, such as multiple egg transfer, will remain outside regulatory control.

The overall effect of the Act in this respect will be to confirm medical intervention as the self-evidently 'obvious' route to overcoming involuntary childlessness (Franklin, 1990), whilst alternatives which do not rely on clinical expertise or which permit the bypassing of medical intervention and control become marginalised. Surrogacy arrangements present a particularly clear example of this. Currently they are made directly between childless people ('commissioning parents') and a surrogate mother who normally conceives following insemination of the commissioning father's sperm. Surrogacy has been subjected to considerable criticism not least because it exposes surrogate mothers to potential exploitation and surrogate children to stigma, and deliberately separates a mother from her child (BMA, 1987). However broadly similar objections could be made to other, less successful, forms of assisted reproduction which rely on 'donors' and which have, nevertheless, received formal sanction. What singles out surrogacy for such treatment is that, although as 'the last resort of the truly desperate' (Cotton and Winn, 1985) it may be perceived as providing ultimate evidence of commitment to the value of the family, it also subverts the ideology of the family. Surrogacy challenges conventional notions about the nature of motherhood by reducing the role of the surrogate mother to that of a 'breeding machine', whilst the pre-determined intention to hand the baby over to someone else undermines beliefs about the inalienable mother/child bond. Commercial surrogacy attracts additional censure because it is considered to 'violate the dignity of motherhood' by encouraging women to be paid for bearing a child 'by proxy' (Board of Social Responsibility, 1984) and one of the major ways in which the threat to perceptions of motherhood posed by surrogacy has been 'neutralised' is by questioning the inherent maternal qualities and psychological makeup of surrogate mothers (Cotton and Winn, 1985). Clearly the inclusion of surrogacy amongst the range of 'treatment services' covered by the Act would have afforded it formal legitimation – recognition that the majority of the Warnock Committee wished to avoid.

Furthermore the Act will have limited impact on the quality and quantity of service provision. Even though there is now recognition that at least some infertility is the result of potentially avoidable and controllable environmental pollutants, infections, and iatrogenic contraceptive and medical practices (Wilkie, 1984), preventive measures are currently under-resourced and it is unlikely they will be afforded higher priority under present proposals for the NHS. However expensive high-tech services will continue to be provided primarily by the private sector to those who can afford to pay.

Receiving assisted reproduction services

Until recently relatively little attention had been given to the experiences of recipients of clinical assisted reproduction services, and the lot of infertile and childless men has been largely ignored altogether. Historically clinical assisted reproduction services have developed from mainstream gynaecological and obstetric services where women's reproductive systems have been the focus of attention. Where medical interest in male reproductive systems existed at all, it focused more on terminating **fertility** than on remedying **infertility**. As a consequence, knowledge about male infertility and possible treatments is extremely rudimentary. First-hand accounts of male experiences are also rare, largely because there does not yet exist a male equivalent to the feminist movement which has done much in recent years to articulate women's experiences of assisted reproduction services.

Clinical services, particularly those within the NHS, have been found to be insufficiently consumer-responsive (Mathieson, 1986; Harman, 1990). Women have reported that administration of fertility drugs produces unwelcome side effects, whilst the regimen imposed on sexual relationships during fertility investigation and treatment may actually be counterproductive (Klein, 1989). The expansion of clinical indicators for the use of high-tech services from diagnosed female infertility to include male infertility, fetal sex selection, termination of 'abnormal' embryos and for diagnostic rather than exclusively therapeutic purposes means that painful and intrusive procedures with potentially eugenic implications are being used on healthy women with little evidence of success (Winston, 1989).

Apart from the sheer physical unpleasantness of being on the receiving end, Napier believes that routine IVF practice raises major ontological questions: 'You have to give your reproductive self away – a vital part of your self – and later have it put back. How do you make it belong to your self again?' (Napier, 1989, pp191–2).

At an ideological level too, assisted reproduction services reinforce dominant images about the biological and social roles of women. The use of pornographic magazines to facilitate masturbation for the production of sperm samples explicitly portrays women as legitimate objects of male sexual gratification. The very existence of assisted reproduction services perpetuates the image of women as mothers and increases the burden on infertile women to prove that they have tried sufficiently hard to achieve motherhood.

For feminists, in particular, clinical assisted reproduction practice provides a prime example of the imposition of alienating techniques on women, ostensibly for their own good, in order to subject them to the power and intrusion of a patriarchal medical profession. Spallone (1989) argues that since patriarchy has always identified women as 'close to nature' and regarded the exploitation of nature for its purposes as legitimate, it is no coincidence that reproductive techniques developed to improve the quality of agricultural stock have been unquestioningly imposed on women.

Whilst some feminists have seen pregnancy and motherhood as a biological and social straitjacket imposed by patriarchy others have regarded any interference in the 'natural' process between conception and birth as a threat to their individual autonomy and a degradation of the very notion of motherhood itself. Women have attempted to reassert their integrity and control through the rejection of increasing clinical and technological encroachment in obstetric practice and its substitution with 'natural' childbirth methods (Stanworth, 1987). They have actively resisted the scientific approach of assisted reproduction which 'imposes an aggressive confrontational relationship to nature . . . down plays reproductive rituals and up plays life risks other than those the technology makes' (Spallone, 1989, p187). Solomon (1989), an infertile feminist, urges the development of non-technological alternatives such as increased emotional and personal support to both men and women who find themselves involuntarily childless, as well as wider political and educational initiatives to challenge pervasive pronatalist attitudes and assumptions which stigmatise those who are childless.

However those women who do wish to receive assisted reproduction services have to satisfy dominant 'patriarchal moral norms' to establish their eligibility (Petchesky, 1986). Existing selection criteria for receipt of assisted reproduction clearly demonstrate the prevalence of assumptions both about the potential psychopathology of involuntarily childless people (Edelmann and Connolly, 1986) and about ideal child-rearing arrangements and family structures. In spite of limited empirical support such assumptions disadvantage homosexuals, people of limited means and people with disabilities (Golombok *et al*, 1983; Schaffer, 1988; Steinberg, 1986). Arguments regarding material status (except in so far as ability to pay acts as a form of social selection) and disability are less explicitly articulated than those relating to marital status and sexuality. Although the Warnock Committee recognised the impossibility of establishing sufficiently sensitive selection criteria to determine eligibility for receipt of assisted reproduction services, it concluded that it would be 'morally wrong' for the state to deliberately seek to create single-parent families (DHSS, 1984), reflecting a view that this poses a 'threat to normal family life' by failing to provide children with a 'nurturing father-figure' (Council for Science and Society, 1984). At an ideological level claims by single and lesbian women to 'family life' through assisted reproduction are invalidated on the grounds that their individual selfish 'right' to be a parent conflicts with the self-sacrificial image of motherhood (Haimes, 1990).

Whilst such views were close to those of the Government itself, which had already declared homosexuality to be a 'pretended family relationship' (Local Government Act, 1988), the Bill as originally drafted contained no reference at all to selection. During the parliamentary passage of the Bill, though, the Moral Right lobby sought to prohibit treatment for single and homosexual people, securing a Government concession requiring clinicians to take account of a child's welfare, including her or his 'need for a father', when considering for whom to provide treatment.

The probable implications of this measure are that discriminatory procedures against any potential recipient who does not meet the clinician's requirements of an 'adequate' or 'ideal' parent, for whatever reason, will be further encouraged. Those who fail to secure access to regulated clinical services are likely to seek alternatives which may place both themselves and any child at increased physical and psychological risk.

Donating genetic material

Assisted reproduction services would be severely limited without access to donated sperm, eggs and embryos. Supplies of genetic material for assisted reproduction purposes are in short supply, particularly for use by non-Caucasian recipients, and clinicians obtain it as best they can. In the recent past sperm donors have been suspected of possessing 'unnatural' or 'perverse' characteristics or 'unsuitable' motivation (Schellen, 1957; Feversham, 1960). Even today sperm donation, dependent on the still socially discreditable practice of masturbation, is performed as a secretive and furtive activity, whilst the motives and personal characteristics of surrogate mothers are called into question (Cotton and Winn, 1985).

According to conventional wisdom university and college students (particularly those in medical schools) have traditionally been the most readily available source of sperm for insemination even though this means for the most part that their fertility has not been proven (Winston 1989). Recent evidence indicates the use of a more socially diverse pool of donors, but also confirms that, for the most part, both male and female donors represent a 'captive' audience. Sperm donors include men visiting their partners on maternity wards following childbirth, men awaiting vasectomy who may 'be open to persuasion', and 'grateful' husbands whose own wives have been successfully treated for fertility problems (Humphrey and Humphrey, 1988). Some expedient clinicians have secured egg 'donations' by requesting 'surplus' eggs from women who have been superovulated for the purpose of IVF (Edwards, 1989). Women awaiting hysterectomy or sterilisation have been offered 'free' surgery in private centres, thus avoiding lengthy NHS waiting lists, in exchange for egg 'donation' (Interim Licencing Authority, 1990; Walby, 1990). The issue of coercing donations from women by the provision of unethical inducements has been the cause of concern and divided opinion amongst clinicians, resulting in substantive modifications to the ILA Guidelines in 1990 (Interim Licencing Authority, 1990).

Whilst selection of donors (the future child's genetic parents) has been characterised by largely pragmatic and opportunistic practice it does, of course, lend itself to eugenic application. Although in British practice this has remained an implicit possibility at least one American centre has been established with the overt intention to 'breed more intelligent human beings' (Lasker and Borg, 1989). The Repository for Germinal Choice, in California, stores sperm donated by Nobel prizewinners for the insemination of suitable mothers to produce a particular type of child (Lasker and Borg, 1989).

The Act provides clarity about the ownership of donated genetic material, the use to which it may be put and responsibility following its use. Donors' interests are recognised in provisions requiring that their informed consent to the future use of their gametes or embryos be obtained in writing after they have been provided with necessary information and offered the opportunity to receive counselling about the consequences of donating. The Act provides potential donors partial protection from improper inducements by insisting that no financial reward or other incentive should be offered except in line with directions issued by the Authority.

Under the Act's proposals donors who have given 'effective' consent to the use of their gametes or embryos will acquire no parental responsibilities for any child born following their use. However, they could still retain parental responsibilities if they have not given 'effective' consent, and parental orders in favour of 'donors' who intend to be the child's social parents may be requested from a court.

Although the Authority will be required to maintain records which would make it possible for the genetic parent(s) of a donor child to be identified, the Act specifically ensures donor anonymity. Clinicians have long argued that the guarantee of anonymity is essential to maintain an adequate supply of donated material, although empirical evidence indicates that such claims may be spurious (Blyth, 1990). However where a child is born with a congenital disability the Act will make it possible for the donor's identity to be made available to enable the child to initiate civil action for damages against a third party under the Congenital Disabilities (Civil Liability) Act 1976.

The use of donated genetic material and its implications is probably the most controversial aspect of assisted reproduction services. The two major sources of disquiet have been religious orthodoxy and the Moral Right. According to conventional religious views man (sic) should obey the will of God. Scriptural authority is employed to reinforce perceptions of the unity and sanctity of the procreative and conjugal relationship, with which man interferes at his peril. The use of donated gametes and embryos contradicts such directives, although some faiths have attempted to reach an accommodation with emerging 'real world' practices and attitudes. Others, however, have rejected dilution of traditional beliefs, holding firm to their convictions that the formal marital union provides the only acceptable basis for reproduction and that there should be no sex without reproduction, and no reproduction without sex (eg Congregation for the Doctrine of Faith, 1987).

The Moral Right is less concerned with infringing the laws of 'nature' or contravening the will of God than with preserving the status quo of interpersonal relationships and societal institutions:

There are three essentially 'biological' propositions which, in the light of human history, to make no higher claim for them, must command respect.

(1) That the conception of the child apart from normal intercourse, if widely practised, as a result of facilitating legislation, will ultimately produce a large and increasing category of children in whom the sense of identity and 'personhood' has been weakened and destroyed. A child's sense of identity derives primarily from its knowledge that 'X' is its father and 'Y' its mother.

(2) That the process will weaken and gradually destroy the unique biological 'blood' link between parent and child.

(3) That the process will weaken and gradually destroy the foundations of the almost-biological unity between husband and wife which is intimately bound up with the knowledge that the child, the issue of their relationship, is, in a sense, the product of their own two bodies, minds, beings.

In my view these are the biological and psychological bases on which both marriage and the family depend, far more than they do on the prescriptions of either civil or religious law

(Santamaria, 1985, p13).

From both perspectives, if for different reasons, not only is the conventional family seen as the 'natural' social unit for reproduction, but its very existence is threatened by the intervention of third parties for reproductive purposes.

Donor children

Assisted reproduction techniques may exert an impact on the children they create in a number of ways. The potential consequences of different methods of conception and selection of social and genetic parents have already been discussed. Other significant factors are determination of legal parentage, the significance of inter-generational genetic relationships and knowledge of genetic origins.

Defining parental relationships

Family breakdown and reconstitution, adoption and fostering arrangements have demonstrated the essential distinction between **biological** and **social** parenting, destroying the belief in an invariable relationship between inter-generational biological relationships and parental responsibilities in respect of children. However, as I have demonstrated, there is entrenched resistance to recognising and validating such distinctions. Traditionally a child's biological parents have been afforded recognition as the 'natural' or even the 'real' parents, at least implying that alternatives are 'unnatural' or 'unreal' (Bruce, 1990). It is only recently that alternative terms such as 'birth' or 'biological' parent have gained common currency in professional circles, and already these are proving anachronistic. The combination of fluid social relationships and various methods of assisted reproduction mean that the simple biological/social dichotomy is no longer adequate. Assisted reproduction has not only clearly demarcated the constituent parts of the parenting function, but also enables them to be performed by separate individuals.

> Reproductive technologies carry the threat (or the promise) of delegitimating genetic parenthood, and even of fracturing commonsense understanding of what 'the biological' is
>
> (Stanworth, 1987, p21).

It is now possible to identify a child's **genetic** mother, **genetic** father, **birth** mother, a **social** mother and a **social** father. In addition the birth mother may have a husband or male partner with some claim to a relationship with the child. Indeed under current British law if a married woman conceives following DI with her husband's consent, but intends to hand over the child at birth, ie to act as a surrogate mother, then she and her husband are regarded as the child's legal parents, irrespective of their 'genetic contribution' to the child or plans for her or his future care. Definition of parenthood under existing legislation in respect of a child born following the implantation in a surrogate mother of an embryo provided by a commissioning couple is less clear (Forrest, 1990).

If the child's social parents subsequently divorce and each remarries the child could acquire two **step-parents**. Sperm cryo-preservation could enable a woman to be inseminated with the sperm of her deceased husband. A child could be born an orphan following the use of a frozen embryo or gametes whose donors are both dead or unknown. At Bourn Hall clinic in Cambridge two twins conceived in vitro were actually born 18 months apart (Edwards, 1989). In South Africa a woman was implanted with an embryo from her daughter (who was unable to conceive because of blocked fallopian tubes) and son-in-law and subsequently gave birth to her own grandchildren (Reid, 1989).

The Act provides legal clarification of the ambiguous parent/child relationships created by assisted reproduction techniques. It is consistent with existing legislation in defining the legal mother as the woman who gives birth to the child. The determination of legal paternity has always been less certain, and this has usually been assumed on the basis of the birth mother's relationship with a particular male. The Act reinforces the definition of legal paternity of children born following DI previously established by the Family Reform Act, 1987. If a married woman conceives following DI then her husband will be the child's legal father, unless he can prove he did not consent to her insemination. If the woman is unmarried then the principles of common law apply. As a general rule donors of embryos or gametes will have no parental responsibilities in respect of any ensuing child. The difficulties caused for surrogacy arrangements have been addressed by a late amendment to the legislation. The Act introduces a new procedure for gamete 'donors' (ie the child's genetic parents) who also intend to be the child's social parents to seek a court order establishing their legal parental relationship with the child (and so avoiding the need to undertake adoption proceedings). The Act itemises strict criteria which must be met for such an order to be made, the most significant of which are that the 'donors' must be married, at least one of them must be the child's genetic parent, and the child must be living with them. In other words the arrangement must satisfy the ideological, structural and genetic elements of the conventional nuclear family.

The Act, however, still leaves some uncertainty over the paternity of donor children in certain circumstances (Morgan, 1990). The Act prohibits a man fathering a child posthumously so if a widow gives birth following insemination of her deceased husband's sperm or implantation of an embryo created jointly with him, the child will be born without a father. If a married woman receives DI and her husband is able to show he did not consent to the procedure then he will not be considered the child's legal father, but neither will the donor as long as his effective consent has been given. However if neither the husband nor the donor gave effective consent (as defined in the Act), then the donor might actually be the child's legal father.

Inter-generational genetic relationships

Bioethicist Leon Kass considers the importance of inter-generational genetic relationships for parents, children and for society itself:

> Clarity about who your parents are, clarity in the lines of generation, clarity about who is whose, are the indispensable foundations of a sound family life, itself the sound foundation of a civilised community.
> (Quoted in Grobstein, 1981, p65).

In most forms of assisted reproduction it is possible for the ensuing child to be genetically related to at least one of the social parents, and childless couples themselves have expressed a preference for such methods over adoption where the child would be genetically related to neither partner (Lasker and Borg, 1989; Owens, 1982).

Empirical studies of the experience of adoptees and, to a more limited extent, of those born following assisted reproduction have produced conflicting and contradictory conclusions about the importance of knowledge about genetic origins and relationships. Early research on adoptees identified the negative experiences of those who grew up with uncertain or total lack of knowledge about their genetic origins (Walby and Symmonds, 1990). Such people are said to experience 'genealogical bewilderment' which encompasses problems in social identity, personal security and self-esteem. Their active attempts to discover more about their genetic origins and seek out their birth parents gave rise to the assumption that only those adoptees with negative adoption experiences attempted to find their birth parents. However the significance of genealogical bewilderment on the experience of being adopted is now considered to be relatively modest and the search for genetic origins perceived as a legitimate and psychologically 'healthy' pursuit in determining a sense of personal identity (Humphrey and Humphrey, 1988). Snowden and Snowden (1984) found that ignorance of the identity of their genetic fathers seemed to pose few problems of personal or social identity amongst donor children, providing some evidence to suggest that a child's lack of knowledge about either genetic parent generates broadly similar (and apparently unproblematic) consequences.

Access to the truth about genetic origins

The structural normality of the two-parent family-by-donation facilitates the pretence of genetic normality and denial of the 'incomplete' genetic relationship between child and social parents. It has been customary for clinicians not only to encourage donor anonymity (Interim Licencing Authority, 1990) but also to advocate secrecy and deception, thereby deliberately separating a child from her or his genetic origins. Some DI practitioners have deliberately mixed donor sperm with that of the recipient's husband in order to preserve the possibility, however remote, that any ensuing child is a child of the conjugal relationship (Winston, 1989). Potential DI recipients are advised by the Royal College of Obstetricians and Gynaecologists: 'unless you reveal (DI conception) to your child there is no reason for him or her ever to know that he or she was conceived by donor insemination' (RCOG, 1987, p3).

Some clinicians have interpreted potential recipients' intentions to be open about recourse to assisted reproduction techniques as a contra-indication for treatment, whilst others have encouraged the deliberate destruction of medical records to ensure that donors cannot subsequently be identified or traced (Saunders, 1980). In consequence the needs and rights of donor children to have access to the truth about their genetic origins have been subordinated to the preservation of the myth of normality of the family-by-donation, and the maintenance of conventional images of acceptable family life.

Under the Act licenced centres providing assisted reproduction services will be required to keep records of the use to which donated genetic material is put and the outcomes of this. The records could, therefore, be used to establish the biological link between donors and their genetic offspring. However the guarantee of donor anonymity means that, for the present at least, donor children (except those born with a congenital disability) will not be able to learn the identity of the donor(s), although some limited information will be made available to them. Those intending to marry will be able to seek confirmation whether they were born following the use of donated genetic material and whether they might be genetically related to their proposed spouse. In addition those aged 18 or over will be provided with some non-identifying information about the donor(s). The nature of such information is to be specified in future Regulations, but is unlikely to include more than a 'pen-picture' of some of the donor's characteristics. A significant constraint on access to information is the knowledge of having been born following assisted reproduction in the first place. Those who have been kept in the dark about the true nature of their origins will certainly not know about such entitlement.

Conclusions

Assisted reproduction has been variously perceived as assisting nature, improving on nature or combatting nature. That such varying perspectives can be supported indicates that 'nature', rather than possessing an intrinsic reality, is a social construct, only making sense because it is attributed meaning by humans. On this basis it is possible to take a much broader view of 'nature' and its relationship with assisted reproduction than those presented earlier in this chapter.

Undoubtedly assisted reproduction has a contradictory message for conventional family-creation practices and social relationships. Methods which use donated genetic material simultaneously reinforce assumptions about family life and social relationships and challenge taken-for-granted 'truths' about the 'naturalness' of human procreation and genetic family relationships. The longer-term impact of the Human Fertilisation and Embryology Act in providing legitimacy to certain currently-novel assisted reproduction practices, particularly highly technological methods, will be to widen the definition of 'natural' family structures and methods of family-creation. At the same time the Act may be seen as an exercise in 'damage-limitation', reasserting dominant values about family forms and structures. Its measures determining legal parenthood following the use of donated gametes, provisions for the making of parental orders in favour of gamete donors and limiting the right of donor children to information about their genetic origins can all be perceived as attempts to contain the threat posed by assisted reproduction.

References

Bellina, J and Wilson, J (1986) *The Fertility Handbook: a Positive and Practical Guide.* Penguin.

Blyth, E (1990) 'Assisted reproduction: what's in it for children?' *Children and Society*, Vol 4, No 2, pp167–82.

Board for Social Responsibility (1985) *Personal origins*. CIO Publishing.

British Medical Association (1987) *Surrogate motherhood, Report of the Board of Science and Education.* BMA.

Bruce, N (1990) 'On the importance of genetic knowledge'. *Children and Society*, Vol 4, No 2, pp183–96.

Childlessness Overcome Through Surrogacy (1990) Newsletter No 8, March.

Congregation for the Doctrine of Faith (1987) *Instruction on respect for human life in its origin and on the dignity of procreation.* Vatican City.

Cotton, K and Winn, D (1985) *Baby Cotton: for love and money.* Dorling Kindersley.

Council for Science and Society (1984) *Human procreation: ethical aspects of the new techniques.* Oxford University Press.

Daniluk, J, Leader, A and Taylor, P (1985) 'The psychological sequelae of infertility'. In Gold, J (ed) *The psychiatric implications of menstruation.* American Psychiatric Press Inc.

Department of Health and Social Security (1984) *Report of the committee of enquiry into human fertilisation and embryology*, (The Warnock Report). HMSO, Cmnd. 9414.

Department of Health and Social Security (1986) *Legislation on human infertility services and embryo research.* HMSO, Cm. 46.

Department of Health and Social Security (1987) *Human fertilisation and embryology: A framework for legislation.* HMSO, Cm. 259.

Edelmann, R and Connolly, K (1986) 'Psychological aspects of infertility'. *British Journal of Medical Psychology*, No 59, pp209–219.

Edwards, R (1989) *Life before birth: reflections on the embryo debate.* Hutchinson.

Ferriman, A (1990) 'Doctors Scrap Surrogate Baby Plan'. *The Observer*, 24th. June, p3.

Feversham Committee (1960) *Report of the departmental committee on human artificial insemination.* HMSO, Cmnd. 1105.

Franklin, S (1990) 'Deconstructing desperateness: the social construction of infertility in popular representations of new reproductive technologies'. In McNeil, M, Varcoe, I and Yearley, S (eds) *The new reproductive technologies.* Macmillan.

Golombok, S, Spencer, A and Rutter, M (1983) 'Children in single-parent and lesbian households: psychosexual and psychiatric appraisal'. *Journal of Psychiatry and Psychology*, Vol 24, No 4, pp551–72.

Grobstein, C (1981) *From chance to purpose: an appraisal of external human fertilisation.* Addison-Wesley.

Haimes, E (1990) 'Recreating the family? policy considerations relating to the new reproductive technologies'. In McNeil, M, Varcoe, I and Yearley, S (eds) *The new reproductive technologies.* Macmillan.

Harman, H (1990) *Trying for a baby: a report on the inadequacy of NHS infertility services.* House of Commons.

Howie, P (1988) 'Selective reduction in multiple pregnancy'. *British Medical Journal*, Vol 297, No 6646, pp433–34.

Humphrey, M and Humphrey, H (1988) *Families with a difference: varieties of surrogate parenthood.* Routledge.

Interim Licencing Authority (1990) *The fifth report of the Interim Licensing Authority for Human In Vitro Fertilisation and Embryology.* Medical Research Council and Royal College of Obstetricians and Gynaecologists.

Klein, R (ed) (1989) *Infertility: women speak out about their experiences of reproductive medicine.* Pandora Press.

Lasker, J and Borg, S (1989) *In search of parenthood: coping with infertility and high-tech conception.* Pandora Press.

Local Government Act (1988) Section 28, Chapter 9. HMSO.

Mathieson, D (1986) *Infertility services in the NHS: what's going on?* House of Commons.

Morgan, D (1988) 'Surrogacy: giving it an understood name'. *Journal of Social Welfare Law*, No 4, pp216–37.

Morgan, D (1990) 'The Human fertilisation and embryology bill: the status provisions'. *Journal of Social Welfare Law*, No 4, pp120–22.

Napier, L (1989) 'The barren desert flourishes in many ways: from infertility to in-fertility'. In Klein, R (ed) *Infertility: women speak out about their experiences of infertility*. Pandora Press.

Newill, R (1986) 'Preface'. In Bellina, J and Wilson, J *The Fertility Handbook: a Positive and Practical Guide*. Penguin.

Owens, D J (1982) *Artificial insemination by donor: a report of attitudes of members of the National Association for the Childless*. Department of Sociology, University College.

Petchesky, R P (1986) *Abortion and women's choice: the state, sexuality and reproductive freedom*. Verso.

Pfeffer, N (1987) 'Artificial insemination, in vitro fertilisation and the stigma of infertility'. In Stanworth, M (ed) *Reproductive technologies: gender, motherhood and medicine*. Polity Press.

Pfeffer, N (1990) *An overview of the provision and delivery of infertility services in the private and NHS sectors*. Unpublished paper presented at the Northern England Study Day of the British Infertility Counselling Association, 29th October, York.

Reid, S (1988) *Labour of love*. Bodley Head.

Royal College of Obstetricians and Gynaecologists (1987) *Donor insemination*. RCOG.

Santamaria, B (1985) 'By whom begot?' *Salisbury Review*, January, pp11–18.

Saunders, D (1980) 'Assessment of the infertile couple for AID'. In Wood, C, Leeton, J and Kovacs, G (eds) *Artificial insemination by donor*. Brown Prior Anderson Pty Ltd.

Schaffer, H R (1988) 'Family structure or interpersonal relationships?'. *Children and Society*, Vol 2, No 2, pp91–101.

Schellen, A (1957) *Artificial insemination in the human*. Elsevier Publishing Co.

Snowden, R and Snowden, E M (1984) *The gift of a child*. George Allen and Unwin.

Solomon, A (1989) 'Infertility as crisis: coping, surviving – and thriving'. In Klein, R (ed) *Infertility: women speak out about their experiences of infertility*. Pandora Press.

Spallone, P (1989) *Beyond conception: the new politics of reproduction*. Macmillan.

Stanworth, M (ed) (1987) *Reproductive technologies: gender, motherhood and medicine*. Polity Press.

Steinberg, D L (1986) 'Research in progress: a report on policies of access to AID as a medical treatment in the UK'. *Women's Studies International Forum*, Vol 9, No 5, pp551–54.

Veevers, J (1980) *Childless by choice*. Butterworth.

Walby, C (1989) *Human fertilisation and embryology; a framework for legislation*. Note prepared for the Executive Committee of the Association of Directors of Social Services, Solihull, ADSS.

Walby, C and Symons, B (1990) *Who am I? identity, adoption and human fertilisation*. British Agencies for Adoption and Fostering.

Warnock, M (1985) *A question of life: the Warnock report on human fertilisation and embryology*. Basil Blackwell.

Wilkie, J R (1984) 'Involuntary infertility in the United States'. *Boldt Verlag Zeitschrift für Bevolkerungswissenschaft*, Vol 10, No 1, pp37–52.

Winston, R (1989) *Getting pregnant*. Anaya Press.

Yoxen, E (1986) *Unnatural selection? coming to terms with the new genetics*. Heinemann.

6 Caring for people: elegant model or flawed design?

Gerald Wistow and Melanie Henwood

Introduction

The white paper *Caring for People* (Department of Health, 1989b) is, by any standards, a watershed document. Implemented fully, it would be the vehicle for a radical transformation in both the outcomes for users of community care services, and also the means through which those services were delivered. The white paper was, of course, a long time in the making. Its immediate origins lie in the Social Services Committee Report on community care (House of Commons, 1985) and the subsequent studies by the Audit Commission (1986), the National Audit Office (1987) and Sir Roy Griffiths (1988). From another perspective, it forms the follow-up to Norman Fowler's Buxton speech and the long promised, but never published, green paper on the future of the personal social services (Fowler, 1984). Its lineage can also be traced back to both the Barclay (1982) and Seebohm (1968) Reports, as the Chief Inspector of the Social Services Inspectorate has noted recently (Utting, 1990).

Such 'official sources' should, however, be seen as markers of a more complex and inter-locking array of bottom-up as well as top-down influences which are reflected in the white paper. As Wistow has argued, *Caring for People* provides 'a welcome example of policy learning at the centre ... [that] legitimates and reinforces a set of ideas about good practice which have emerged from the field ... ' (Wistow 1990a p11). Those ideas, themselves, reflected 'the dissatisfaction of professionals and users with the appropriateness and quality of much of the community care provision currently available' (*ibid* p6).

In what follows, we explore the nature and extent of that learning as part of a wider analysis of the white paper's origins. In so doing, we consider how far it represents a radical departure from current policy and practice. Such a discussion must, however, distinguish between explicit and implicit intentions, on the one hand, and implementation capacities, on the other. We conclude, therefore, by considering how far the white paper anticipates and provides a basis for overcoming implementation difficulties which have hitherto impeded the realisation of community care objectives.

Caring for people: origins and background

The background to the publication of the white paper is complex and multi-faceted. While some of the major influences have been alluded to above, they may be summarised under five separate but related themes: policy failure; organisational and financial barriers; evolution of the policy base; commitment to needs and outcomes; and promotion of the mixed economy of care.

i) Policy failure

It is now 30 years since Richard Titmuss questioned, in a lecture delivered in 1961, whether community care was 'fact or fiction'. Anticipating Edelman's (1977) notion of 'words that succeed and policies that fail', he cautioned against 'the unfortunate consequences' which could arise if 'in the public mind, the aspirations of reformers are transmuted, by the touch of a phrase, into hard-one reality' (Titmuss, 1968, p104). Whether consciously or not, Sir Roy Griffiths was to echo Titmuss' prophetic concern about the potential gulf between intentions and outcomes. Thus he observed that:

> at the centre, community care has been talked of for 30 years and in few areas can the gap between political rhetoric and policy on the one hand, or between policy and reality in the field have been so great.
>   (Griffiths, 1988, para 9, piv).

The existence of what the Audit Commission (1986, para 18) more diplomatically termed 'slow and uneven progress' towards community care is now broadly accepted. Perhaps less well-noted, however, is the extent to which both the Griffiths and Audit Conmmission Reports represented a significant shift in the terms of the policy debate. Until the mid-eighties, much of the national debate focused on weaknesses in local implementation mechanisms and especially the failure of local agencies to create effective partnerships. Hence the 'care in the community' initiative (DHSS, 1983) principally sought to relax constraints on the transfer of resources from health to local authorities while also introducing greater flexibility into the joint finance arrangements. More far-reaching and fundamental options for organisational and policy change were explicitly rejected.

A Working Group on Joint Planning (1985), comprising officials from the DHSS and from health and local authority associations, spent some two years between 1983 and 1985 developing detailed recommendations for strengthening joint planning arrangements (Working Group on Joint Planning, 1985). Again, a more broadly-based review was resisted by Ministers and the Department (see Westland, 1988, pp29–30).

Already, however, the ground was beginning to shift with the publication of the Social Services Committee Report. This was critical of the outcomes of community care policies and advocated a number of radical organisational changes, including the transfer to local government of responsibility for mental handicap services and the establishment of a national development fund to support hospital closures. It was, however, the publication of the Audit Commission's Report *Making a Reality of Community Care* which finally shifted the policy debate into a new gear. As Wistow (1988, p74) observed, the report had two consequences:

> First, the Commission's general concern with effectiveness inevitably led it to question how far community care objectives were being achieved. As a result, the report shifted the spotlight from policy means to policy ends; from a narrow preoccupation with the technicalities of joint planning to a more fundamental consideration of the nature of community care objectives and the extent to which they were being achieved. Second, the Commission were statutorily required to investigate the impact of central government policies on local authorities. Consequently, the spotlight was also shifted from the failure of local agencies to collaborate effectively to the degree of central government responsibility for creating that failure.

From this point onwards, a substantial government response to the relative failure of community care policies became inevitable. The commissioning of the Griffiths' review was clearly intended to signal such a commitment to action (Wistow and Henwood, 1990).

ii) Organisational and financial barriers

As was noted above, the second half of the last decade witnessed a stream of critical reports about community care from governmental, parliamentary and non-governmental agencies. (See, in addition, Scott-White, 1985, and, Firth, 1987 on social security aspects.) The common threads linking them all are the identification of organisational and financial confusion. These well-documented barriers to fuller progress in community care were broadly encompassed in the five 'fundamental underlying problems' identified by the Audit Commission (1986); mismatched resources; lack of bridging finance; perverse effects of social security policies;

organisational fragmentation and confusion; and inadequate staffing arrangements. Griffiths accepted that this report, together with those from the Select Committee and the National Audit Office, contained 'the essential facts' and proposed changes to secure clearer patterns of responsibility and accountability at all levels:

- A Minister for Community Care responsible for specifying objectives and providing resources consistent with those objectives;

- Social Services Departments responsible at local level for identifying community care needs, planning and organising provision;

- Care Managers responsible at the level of individual users and carers for assessing their needs and arranging care packages tailored to meet them.

At the same time, Sir Roy considered the division of responsibilities between local authorities and the social security system for the funding of residential and domiciliary care to be a 'particularly pernicious split' (1988, para 4.21). Like the Audit Commission, he sought to eliminate the perverse incentive toward residential care which this produced. A key component of his solution was to prescribe a unified community care budget allocated to local social services authorities through a specific grant set at 40 or 50 per cent of agreed local spending. The grant was to be payable on condition that local authorities submitted community care plans which provided evidence of, *inter alia*, local needs, collaborative planning and the promotion of a mixed economy of care (see below). Griffiths' recommendations presented difficulties for Ministers both in terms of making explicit political accountabilities at the centre and also in according a lead role to social services departments locally.

Although they ultimately could find no feasible alternative to the local authority lead role, they did not accept the Griffiths package in its entirety. Significantly, the principle changes which they made concerned finance and the role of central government. With the exception of a relatively modest mental illness specific grant the link between local plans and earmarked resources was not accepted. The perverse incentive was to be removed by transferring to local authorities the care element of social security support to residential and nursing homes. Social Services departments were to be responsible for assessing the care needs of individuals and using those resources to provide whichever form of care most appropriately met their needs. However, these resources were not to be ring fenced but allocated through the general revenue support grant arrangements (see below).

The unwillingness to link planning with resource allocation processes also left the arrangements for inter-agency planning weaker than Griffiths had intended. The white paper seeks to create a new framework for collaborative working through a clarification of responsibility for health and social care, together with an emphasis on planning agreements rather than joint plans. However, it remains to be seen whether sufficiently different and adequate incentives are being put in place to secure a significantly different pattern of joint working. Indeed, the arrangements for planning and funding have been the most severely criticised elements of a white paper which has, in most other respects, been broadly welcomed (see House of Commons 1990a and 1990b on funding and planning issues).

iii) An evolving policy base

Alongside the need to clarify responsibilities and accountability arrangements, further influences on the white paper have been provided by developing understandings about the meanings and consequences of community care. The term was initially used to describe care provided in the community as an alternative to large-scale institutions for children or people with mental disabilities. Even in this initial form, it remained at best ill-defined and at worst the focus for inter-organisational and inter-professional competition or conflict. Titmuss (1968) was an early critic of its lack of clarity as a coherent policy across health and social service boundaries. Walker criticised the absence of any 'sustained attempt to define and measure the need for community care, to set policy goals and then relate the goals to the scale of need and the allocation of resources' (1982 p16). A DHSS review (1981a para 2.1) of community care also noted the lack of clarity surrounding the term which, it suggested, 'seemed to mean very different things depending on the context in which it is used'.

Thus, for example, the policy came to have different inter-pretations in the NHS and personal social services, respectively. In the former case, it historically implied shifting the balance from hospital to local authority residential services; and, in the latter, from residential to domiciliary and day care services (Webb and Wistow, 1982a; Hunter and Wistow, 1987). As a result, policy implementation has been shaped by the interplay of the organisational interests and priorities associated with each of the above perspectives. Similar and related conflicts have arisen in terms of the relative priority to be accorded to the 'direct' and 'indirect' routes to reducing the balance of hospital and other services (Wistow 1983 and 1987): that is, directly transferring patients from long-stay hospitals to the community, which most immediately benefits health authority budgets, compared with the more immediate local authority interest in supporting people already in the community and thereby preventing future hospital admissions.

Such differences of meaning have been overlain during the last decade by a redefinition of community care as 'care by the community'. This interpretation has combined both descriptive and normative components. On the one hand, there has been a growing recognition that the bulk of caring for dependent people is provided outside institutions by unpaid and frequently unsupported carers (see, for example, Moroney, 1976; Henwood and Wicks, 1984 and 1985; Henwood, 1990; Equal Opportunities Commission, 1982, Parker 1985 and 1990). On the other hand, the economic neo-liberalism of the New Right which infused all areas of government policy after the 1979 Conservative victory, stressed the virtues of self-help, personal responsibility and individualism as countervailing influences to a collectivist 'dependency culture' (Webb and Wistow, 1982b, McCarthy 1989). From this perspective, community or family care was a responsibility which the state was in danger of undermining.

At the same time, a feminist critique of community care came to emphasise the gendered and oppressive nature of a policy which, in effect, enforced and reinforced a rather different culture of dependency on women (Finch and Groves 1980, Ungerson, 1987; Dalley, 1988, Baldwin and Twigg, 1990; Henwood 1990). These descriptive and normative dimensions of community care policy are clearly reflected in both the white paper *Growing Older* (DHSS 1981b) and the Griffiths Report (1988). Thus the former asserted that:

> The primary sources of support and care for elderly people are informal and voluntary. These spring from the personal ties of kinship, friendship and neighbourhood . . . it is the role of public authorities to sustain and, where necessary, develop – but never to displace – such support and care. Care *in* the community must increasingly mean care *by* the community (para 1.9).

The Griffiths' framework has a broadly similar explicit starting point:

> Publicly provided services constitute only a small part of the total care provided to people in need. Families, friends, neighbours and other local people provide the majority of care in response to needs which they are uniquely well-placed to identify and respond to. This will continue to be the primary means by which people are enabled to live normal lives in community settings. The proposals take as their starting point that this is as it should be, and that the first task of publicly provided services is to support and, where possible, strengthen these networks of carers (para 3.2).

The white paper is no less explicit in its recognition that most care is provided through informal sources. It is, however, perhaps more emphatic about the role of the state in providing carers with 'help to be able to manage what can become a heavy burden', and in suggesting that 'their lives can be made much easier if the right support is there at the right time, and a key responsibility of statutory service providers should be to do all they can to assist and support carers' (para 2.3). Accordingly, the second of the white paper's six key objectives is to 'ensure that service providers make practical support for carers a high priority' (para 1.11). To this end, assessments of need are to take into account the carer's continuing ability to provide care, and services are to be offered which enable carers to make choices (para 3.2.6).

A key element in the feminist critique of care by the community has effectively represented the policy as one which substitutes the unpaid labour of women for formal services, collectively organised and funded. The challenge posed by, for example, Finch (1984) is whether a non-exploitative and non-sexist form of care in family or other domestic settings is, in fact, possible because of the gendered nature of relationships within families. Baldwin and Parker (1989, page 157) suggest that carers 'inhabit a strange Alice-in-Wonderland place where they are the main providers of community care but never the subjects of policy that deals with the provision of care'. It might be argued that such inferences can be drawn from the philosophy espoused by the *Growing Older* white paper, and other policy statements on community care from the early 1980s. However, the Griffiths report and *Caring for People* are successively more explicit about collective responsibilities for supporting and sustaining such care. While the latter justifies its approach as 'a sound investment' as well as being right in itself (para 2.3), it would be over-simplistic, if not misleading to represent its intention as being to substitute unpaid for paid care as part of a wider shift in the balance of collective and family responsibilities. Such shifts would not, in any case, be straightforward, the so-called 'demographic time bomb' means that the economic interests of the state and the role of women face increasing tensions and contradictions (Henwood, 1990; Kiernan and Wicks, 1990).

We should, of course, be wary of confusing intentions with outcomes: formal services may remain insensitive to the complex structure of carers' needs or may be simply inadequate in volume to meet the level of need revealed by extended assessment processes. Similarly, those processes may be dominated by provider definitions and understandings of need. In addition, the legitimacy of carers' ultimate choice not to continue with their caring role may not be recognised. We return to these and other issues below. Nonetheless, the placing of carers' needs at the heart of the white paper's core objectives does represent a degree of policy learning and development that should not be dismissed in advance of seeing its consequences for day-to-day practice and resource allocation decisions.

iv) Needs and outcomes

Traditional definitions of community care are notable for emphasising the location or source of assistance and support for dependent individuals (care in, and by, the community, respectively). They do not focus on either the needs of those individuals or the purposes and outcomes associated with interventions designed to meet them.

Wistow's review of community care planning arrangements revealed that they reflected and reinforced such service characteristics. Planning guidelines, he noted, were expressed as 'levels of service production (inputs and intermediate outputs) rather than outcomes for users' (Wistow 1990b, para 2.4). In addition, he suggested that the formulation of only a very limited number of such guidelines for each client group 'focused attention on a relatively narrow range and mix of service options, thereby discouraging innovation and the more flexible use of resources' (*ibid*). A further consequence was that the guidelines served as 'proxies for need' and that 'the purpose of producing those services (together with) their impact on outcomes and opportunities for users achieved relatively little attention' (*ibid*, para 2.6).

In these circumstances, providers had rather limited options available to them and their capacity to tailor services sensitively around individual needs was correspondingly restricted. Such inflexibilities may be criticised on cost-effectiveness grounds for their failure to achieve an appropriate match between needs and resources (see, for example, Audit Commission, 1986 and Davies and Challis, 1986). They are also open to the more fundamental criticism of not according due attention to the preferences of service recipients, including carers. Although planning guidelines were formally abolished in 1981, they continued to exercise an influence over health and local authority planning throughout that decade (Wistow, 1990b, Challis *et al*, 1988). However, they have been progressively overtaken by the twin forces of case management on the one hand, and 'ordinary life' philosophies on the other. The latter was derived from Wolfensberger's (1977) 'normalisation' principles and promoted in this country in particular by the King's Fund (1982). It has proved to be a strong influence in creating a more explicit value base for community care policies, particularly in terms of its emphasis on the rights of vulnerable and dependent people to participate in socially valued lifestyles which maximise opportunities for self-realisation and independence. As a result, it has contributed strongly to an emerging emphasis on the

importance of being explicit about the outcomes for users which
community care policies are intended to secure.

The white paper gives prominence to the importance of both
a needs-led and outcome-oriented approach to community care.
It also affirms the importance of systematic assessment and case
management procedures as a means for ensuring that services are
tailored to individual needs (Chapter 3). Its starting point, however,
is to make explicit the values which it seeks to promote. Hence it
argues that 'promoting choice and independence underlies all the
government's proposals' (para 1.8). These over-arching aims are
elaborated in terms of 'enabling people to live as normal a life as
possible . . . help them achieve their full potential . . . (and) give
people a greater individual say in how they live their lives and the
services they need to help them to do so' (*ibid*).

These statements strongly reflect the values-led approach to
community care which has emerged in recent years. As developed
in the white paper, they provide a clear sense of the outcomes
towards which community care provision is to be oriented, rather
than specifications of services to be provided at predetermined
levels and mixes.

In this respect, the document represents a significant break with
the recent past. Perhaps most substantial, however, is the extent to
which this approach signifies the return of need to the centre of the
stage. Thus, services are to be organised around the systematically
assessed needs of users and carers rather than those of services and
providers. Local authorities are also made responsible for assessing
community-wide needs and basing development plans upon them.
The phrase 'within available resources' is a constant refrain in all
of this discussion and it is unclear how the circle between needs
and resources is to be squared. However, both the assessment
and community care planning processes will make explicit the
extent to which the resources available are compatible with the
level of identified need. Thus the white paper is potentially of
major significance both in legitimating the centrality of needs
assessments (at the individual and community levels) and also in
providing mechanisms through which not only needs, but also the
gap between needs and resources are made more visible.

v) Promoting a mixed economy of care

A critique of the monolithic and unresponsive nature of state welfare
gained ground in the late seventies. From the voluntary sector, in
particular, the solution advanced was one of encouraging greater
'welfare pluralism' (Gladstone, 1979; Hadley and Hatch, 1981;
NCVO, 1980). The initial emphasis of the incoming Conservative
government was on the role of informal care, self help and

volunteering (Webb and Wistow, 1982a). However, the organised voluntary and private sectors have become more significant providers of formal care during the last decade (Knapp, 1989). Indeed, they now supply the majority of all residential and nursing home care, though they are considerably less well established in the day and domiciliary services sectors.

Although central and local government support to the voluntary sector appears to have grown substantially during the past decade (Knapp, 1989), support to the private sector has been less coherently orchestrated. Indeed, it was the apparently exponential growth of public financial support through the social security system to residential and nursing care that prompted the commissioning of the Griffiths Report. Proposals to 'cap' such social security spending formed a major objective of the White Paper, though a continuing expansion of private and voluntary sector provision was also intended.

This approach was derived from the distinction which Griffiths made between the funding and regulatory role of social services departments, on the one hand, and their role as service providers, on the other. Echoing Fowler's concept of the enabling role, Griffiths advocated a substantial recasting of the functions of social services departments. Thus they were to act as 'designers, organisers and purchasers of non-healthcare services and not primarily as direct providers' (Griffiths, 1988, para 1.3.4). In that capacity, they were to make the 'maximum possible use' of the voluntary and private sectors in order 'to widen consumer choice, stimulate innovation and encourage efficiency' (*ibid*).

In supporting the Griffiths case for the local authority lead role in community care, directors of social services emphasised that supply was already more diversified than sometimes appreciated and that the enabling role should be seen as an extension of their current activities rather than as a complete break with their existing style and mode of operation (ADSS, 1988, p4). By the time that ministers had determined their response to the Griffiths Report, they had already announced their intention to establish an internal market in the NHS based on a division of responsibilities for purchasing and providing health care (DoH, 1989a). Although unacceptable from some perspectives, therefore, the Griffiths case for the local authority lead role in community care was compatible with, and complementary to, the new purchasing role envisaged for district health authorities. Moreover, the extended purchasing and regulatory functions of social services departments could be secured at the price of reducing the scale of public sector provision. Hence, social services departments were required 'to stimulate the development of non-statutory service providers' (DoH, 1989b, para 3.4.3) and one of the 'six key objectives' of the White Paper was to 'promote the development of a flourishing independent sector alongside good quality public services' (*ibid*, para 1.11).

Caring for People envisaged that the statutory sector would 'continue to play an important role in backing up, developing and monitoring private and voluntary care facilities and providing services where this remains the best way of meeting care needs' (*ibid*, para 3.4.3). At the same time, the extent to which social services authorities were 'organising their move away from the role of exclusive service provider to that of service arranger and procurer' was to be one of the criteria against which community care plans would be judged and the need for ministers to intervene assessed (*ibid*, paras 5.6 and 5.10–5.11; DoH, 1990, para 2.21).

The grounds advanced in the White Paper for promoting a more mixed economy reflected those put forward by Griffiths: the extension of choice, more innovation and flexibility in meeting need; and better value for money through increased competition. However, the relationship between expanding the range of providers, on the one hand, and the range, flexibility and innovatory qualities of provision, on the other, is not a necessary or straightforward one. As Wistow (1989) argued:

> the move to unified (social care) budgets and single budget holders potentially leads to a concentration of power at both the authority level and that of the individual care manager. Add to this the possibility that service contracts could – but need not necessarily – tend towards standardisation, and the relationship between the enabling role and diversity in service provision . . . is less clearcut than it might appear
>
> (Wistow, 1989, p9).

Flynn and Common (1990) have also argued that the degree of choice and flexibility in provision is related to the degree to which purchasing responsibilities are decentralised:

> . . . if decisions on contracts are all made centrally, and the case managers have to rely on calling off from a centrally negotiated deal, this will reduce the element of choice and the flexibility of the packages. Only decentralised budgets and decentralised negotiations with a range of providers will produce a genuine increase in flexibility and responsiveness. Privatisation and transfer of services to large organisations will have no impact on market structure or price or the amount of choice facing a client
>
> (Flynn and Common, 1990, p27).

It might also be added that providing a wider range of service options from which case managers can choose is not necessarily to be equated with wider choice for users since the latter depends upon a significant recasting of power relationships between professionals and users. Nor can it be assumed that competition among providers will necessarily be on quality as well as price. A simulation of the NHS internal market resulted in standards being driven down in the face of resource scarcity. Greater diversity in the range of services available and offered to users and carers remains an important potential consequence of the White Paper's proposals. However, unless such objectives are central to implementation processes, there would appear to be no necessary relationship between such objectives and the growth of a more mixed economy of provision.

Implementation issues

We have argued that *Caring for People* can be viewed as a radical document. The white paper is, at one level, consistent with the long history of the development of community care policy, but in other respects it marks a significant departure. The framework for community care set out in *Caring for People* has enormous potential. It recognises that the needs of people – and of their carers – are central. The multi-disciplinary assessment of such needs, and the construction and management of individually appropriate care packages are proposed as the way forward.

There may, however, be a major discrepancy between the aspirations and intent of the White Paper on the one hand, and the practical achievements on the other. This is not to dismiss the policy as merely rhetoric, nor is it to call into question the integrity or motives of the architects of the policy. But it must be emphasised that in many crucial respects the plans are naive.

Over-optimistic rationality?

In its own terms the white paper – and the subsequent legislation – offered a 'sensible solution' to the problems of community care. The search for such rationality in policy making, and specifically rationality in terms of co-ordinating different aspects of policy, has a long and largely undistinguished history. It is a quest, Challis *et al* suggest, 'shaped by the assumption that there is such a thing as rationality in policy making independent of, and indeed opposed to, the rationality of politics' (1988, p1). The 'rational optimistic' model of policy formulation was exemplified in recent years by the work of the Central Policy Review Staff (CPRS), and in particular by the JASP initiative to operationalise the Joint Framework for Social Policy (CPRS, 1975). The plea for co-ordination in both policy and practice is the recurrent litany of the rational optimists, and it is one which is recited once more in *Caring for People*.

The model of the rational optimists is a consensus based one which sees governance not in terms of opposing interests and power-play, but as a realm in which problems are overcome through analysis and organisational adaptation – 'the triumph of administrative technique over the craft of politics' (Challis *et al*, 1988, p25). The barriers to effective co-ordination, according to this school of thought, can be overcome by restructuring organisations, and through co-ordinating policy and planning processes.

The white paper's analysis of the problems in developing community care is broadly correct, and, as we have argued, consistent with other critiques. It is, nonetheless short-sighted in its prescription, which seeks 'to establish the right financial and managerial framework which will help to secure the delivery of good quality local services in line with national policy objectives' (para 1.7). The model offered in *Caring for People* of matching individual needs and services is attractive. However, the apparent simplicity of the approach must lead one to ask why hasn't this happened before? The **implementation** of the new approach to community care – as opposed to merely the **policy** – is where doubts arise. In identifying what needs to happen, the white paper assumes implementation to be non-problematic. We argue that in at least four respects this assumption is wrong, and policy may be frustrated by these practical realities. Moreover, the assumption is wrong for precisely the same reasons as in the past when co-ordination has been invoked without reference to the interactive realities of practice, and process.

The particular issues of implementation are shaped by more general matters. The environment within which social services departments must operate is a changing one, and change itself may be disturbing. Certainly there will be a virtual revolution in the management culture; new skills will be required to meet the shift in role which is envisaged. The implications for information systems and for training and management development are extensive, yet relatively little support is to be provided by the Department of Health. The £2 million which has been committed for 1990–91 pales to insignificance alongside the development investment which accompanied the NHS reforms (£85 million in 1989/90 and more than £300 million in 1990/91).

Four problems of implementation

1   Whose needs have priority?

As we have indicated above, the emphasis on carers' needs represents a crucial shift in policy. While past policy statements have acknowledged the major contribution of carers, the underlying assumption has been that this is as it should be; as the 1981 white paper *Growing Older* stated, 'Care *in* the community must increasingly mean care *by* the community'.

Growing Older emphasised the responsibility for community care 'which must be shared by everyone'. While it also acknowledged that the role of public services was an enabling one 'helping people to care for themselves and their families by providing a framework of support' there was little attention to what this might mean in practice. The Griffiths report (1988) was significant in regarding carers not so much as **substitutes** for formal care, but as the focus around which complementary systems of formal services should be organised and delivered (para 3.2). The importance of supporting carers in their task has long been emphasised in the academic and research communities. Research has indicated that where such support **is** provided carers are able to continue to care for longer and that residential admission is less likely (for example, Levin, Sinclair and Gorbach, 1983). The second of the six stated key objectives of *Caring for People* is 'to ensure that service providers make practical support for carers a high priority. Assessment of care needs should always take account of the needs of caring family, friends and neighbours' (para 1.11). However, translating into practice this apparently good news for carers is far more problematic than the white paper appears to recognise.

How, for example, are carers' needs to be brought centre stage? There are two major difficulties, neither of which is acknowledged in *Caring for People*. First, very few services have been developed specifically for the support of carers. As Parker's review of the literature (1990) indicates, where services **have** benefited carers this has often been an incidental or secondary purpose.

> Consequently, carers' needs, or the way in which they might best be helped, are rarely taken account of in any systematic way. Despite the proliferation of accounts of services intended to support carers, instances of planned and monitored intervention are still comparatively scarce (1990, p95).

Parker concluded that domiciliary services are often of inadequate volume, and likely to be allocated by criteria which discriminate against carers, with services more likely to support those living alone than with others. The General Household Survey (GHS) of informal carers (OPCS, 1988) confirmed the minimal role played by services in supporting carers. On the very generous definition of 'regular visits' as at least once a month, the GHS found two thirds of carers with a dependant in the same household, and half of those with a dependant living elsewhere, received no regular help or visits from either health, social services or voluntary support. Rather than services being directed to complement and support carers, it appears in practice that carers are more likely to be treated as substitutes for services. There is also a tension between making practical support for carers a high priority while also ensuring that services are targetted on those in greatest need. Is it not likely that, as at present, scarce resources will be directed towards people with no available carers?

Targeting services on supporting carers also assumes that the best and most appropriate forms of care are both well known and unproblematic, but this is not the case. Parker's review of the research evidence indicated that 'much still remains to be discovered' about the most appropriate forms of relief and support, and particularly about the role of cash benefits vis a vis direct services. Moreover, such evidence as does exist about carers' needs and wishes may run counter to many of the assumptions made about the best ways of supporting carers. For example, the most useful help is often that which relieves carers of their responsibilities completely for a short period, rather than replacing their own 'normal' domestic labour, eg day care and respite care rather than home help or meals on wheels (Parker, 1990).

The second area which is problematic concerns the possible tensions between the needs of carers and those they care for. These needs will not necessarily be compatible, and this is an area where much remains to be known, yet *Caring for People* offers no guidance on whose needs should take precedence, nor how these competing interests are to be dealt with through assessment. For example, at what point should the objective of home or community based care be subordinate to the needs of carers which might actually indicate permanent residential care? Respite care or other support might enable carers to continue, but may not be what they really want. Informal care tends to be regarded as a self-evident good, when in fact the tensions and pressures in a caring relationship may be intolerable. Sustaining such a relationship may be deeply damaging both for the carer and cared for. While much is made of the importance of choice in the new community care arrangements. *Caring for People* does not allow carers the ultimate choice of whether or not to become, or continue to be, a carer.

2 Ensuring effective inter-agency and multi-disciplinary working

The multi-faceted nature of community care needs is well documented, as are the failures to provide correspondingly integrated services. As David Plank (1977) observed in studying provision for elderly people in London, 'because the "care system" is not a system but an unco-ordinated set of discrete and relatively autonomous parts, the care that any individual old person receives is to a major extent fortuitous' (1977).

While accepting that local authority social services departments should have the lead responsibility in developing community care, *Caring for People* emphasises the importance of other needs such as for housing and health care. The multiple needs of clients are to be addressed firstly through a multi-disciplinary assessment, and secondly through the construction and management of an individually tailored care package.

The interface between health and social care is the most significant. As *Caring for People* recognises, 'Community care is about the health as well as the social needs of the population.' However, the responsibilities of the health service 'remain essentially unaltered' by the community care reforms. Health authorities and family practitioner committees will 'be expected to make specific contributions to the new arrangements for community care' (para 4.7). Such contributions will include appropriate input to the assessment process, and, at the organisational level, authorities will be expected to work together – especially so in areas where 'it may well be difficult to draw a clear distinction between the needs of an individual for health and social care' (para 4.2).

The emphasis on co-ordination and collaboration is, as noted earlier, of long standing in health and social services. *Caring for People* acknowledges that the record of joint planning has been 'mixed' and has fallen short of earlier hopes. Wistow has argued (1990b) that the result is that 'there is currently no coherent framework for planning community care either within or between health and local government services.' (para 3.1). Whether the problems of the past are resolved by *Caring for People* is debatable. There are contradictions and ambivalence in the White Paper's stance on co-ordination. While largely rejecting old style collaboration which 'no longer fits well with the government aims . . . ', it nonetheless reiterates the mantra that 'further efforts are needed to improve co-ordination between health and social services' (para 6.1).

Wistow (1990b) has argued that 'there are, however, grounds for concern about the extent to which the white paper framework will make planning between health and local government services more or less difficult to achieve' (para 6.2). While *Caring for People* claims to offer a better approach for achieving effective joint working 'based on strengthened incentives and clearer responsibilities' (1989, para 6.1), it is by no means obvious that this will be achieved. The distinction between health and social care is not a black and white one, but in attempting to clarify responsibilities along such lines *Caring for People* may create incentives less for collaboration than for service differentiation and boundary defence. Wistow suggests that, far from collaboration becoming easier, conflict might be anticipated both around definitions of health and social care, and around the different priorities of the two agencies (1990b, Appendix 3). Similarly, the Select Committee (House of Commons, 1990a) has seriously questioned 'whether the new arrangements will provide any better framework or incentives for the two to work together' (p40). And that in such circumstances 'the risks associated with the introduction of community care will outweigh the benefits claimed for it by the Government' (*ibid*).

3   Integrated care packages

A related problem area concerns the delivery of care packages. The problems of co-ordination have not only been evident at a policy level (the issues around over-lapping and under-lapping responsibilities), but also in practice.

Whereas co-ordination in general is something which health and social services have not managed with great success, the specific co-ordination of care packages is an area of little experience. Health and social services rarely operate in a complementary manner. People who receive a high level of social support are also likely to receive significant health service inputs, yet it is likely that intensive home care and home nursing will be duplicating one another (Charnley and Bebbington, 1988). With some notable exceptions – such as the Kent Community Care project, the Gateshead scheme and other similar innovations – organisational fragmentation of health, housing, social services and income maintenance programmes (as well as between statutory, voluntary, private, formal and informal arenas) has made the construction of care 'packages' virtually impossible (Ferlie, Challis, and Davies, 1989). While much can be learnt from existing schemes, it would be mistaken to assume that any single model is amenable to wholesale replication. Even if care packaging **is** successful this still runs into the problems indicated above concerning the focus of the service and questions about **who** is the client. An emphasis on maintaining people in the community as long as possible may increase burdens on carers. Crucial questions also arise about the targeting of priority groups. If the very dependent are to receive intensive support, this implies reducing cover elsewhere.

4   Gap between needs and resources

The objectives of *Caring for People* are to be achieved 'within available resources', and it is this proviso which perhaps raises the greatest doubts about the viability of the community care reforms. The emphasis in *Caring for People* on meeting individual need was welcome. There was recognition that too often individuals are matched to (inappropriate) services, rather than services tailored to their needs. The stress on assessment and case management of individually tailored packages of care would seem to offer a more sensitive user-oriented approach, but if at the end of the day all this is subject to the same economic imperatives will it really be any different? It is impossible, of course, to conceive of a situation where resources would be sufficient to meet all needs. Nonetheless, the point at which the line is drawn, where resources are judged to be available and costs reasonable, is a critical one.

The 'availability' of resources raises questions about the mechanisms of resource allocation. As we have noted above, a crucial difference between the community care model advocated by Sir Roy Griffiths, and that set down in *Caring for People* concerned the ring fencing of resources. Sir Roy had persuasively put the case for protecting resources in this way. It would, he argued, provide recognition of the interdependencies of central and local government, and a degree of central influence and control; it would create a more stable basis for planning and service delivery; and it would ensure that transferred resources reached their intended destination, 'and do not end up in the general grant pool' (1988, para 5.13).

The Social Services Select Committee has continued to criticise the absence of ring fencing (House of Commons, 1990a and 1990b), and has emphasised the need for Central Government to assume responsibility:

> So long as the Government resists this recommendation, the Minister for Community Care in the Department of Health will be in an invidious position, answerable to Parliament for *services* provided by local authorities, but not responsible for the level of *resources* given to local authorities by central government in order to provide those services (1990b, p21).

We have identified above implementation difficulties which do not appear to have been fully recognised in the white paper, and which provide grounds for questioning whether the objectives and intentions of *Caring for People* are likely to be realised in practice. In addition the Government's commitment to implementing the white paper came into more immediate focus with its decision in July 1990 to delay the reform programme. Less than one month after the NHS and Community Care Act entered the statute book, the then health secretary, Kenneth Clarke, made a statement 'about the Government's policies for improving care in the community for elderly, disabled, mentally ill and mentally handicapped people' (Clarke, 1990). Instead of full implementation of the reforms from April 1991, these will now be phased in over two years. The transfer of social security funds, and the introduction of assessment and case management procedures will not take effect until April 1993. The delay in the implementation of the community care reforms appears to illustrate the inevitable consequences of need and resource incompatibility.

The reasons for the delay immediately confirm the tension between a needs-led approach, and resource constraints. The Government did not make known its estimates of the likely implementation costs of the community care reforms. However, the local authority associations estimated the total cost for 1991/92 would be £829 million, adding an average £15 to community charge bills (Henwood, Jowell and Wistow, 1991). For a Government which was coming under increasing criticism over the poll tax, this was toos risky. The phasing in would reduce the likely costs to charge payers, and would mean local authorities 'have longer to come to terms with the needs to discharge their duties efficiently and at a cost which their community charge payers can afford' (Clarke, 1990). In other words, local authorities appear to have been given the responsibility for finding some means of reconciling needs and resources, notwithstanding the tight constraints on their own overall levels of spending.

The delay announcement confirmed scepticism for other reasons. We have pointed out that in many ways *Caring for People* was unusual in its focus on needs, on carers, and on a clear espousal of normalisation values. It was also untypical for the apparent priority it was being shown. The white paper published in November 1989 was followed within six days by the NHS and Community Care Bill. The second reading, committee and report stages all followed in rapid succession, and it was intended that the new structure would be in operation within eighteen months of the legislation being introduced into the House of Commons. The contrast which this offers to the previous handling of community care is striking, with delay having been a recurrent feature since Sir Roy Griffiths was commissioned to review the policy area. The return to this familiar pattern could also be interpreted as a worrying 'business as usual' approach.

Conclusions

We have argued that the framework for community care set out in *Caring for People* has enormous potential. While the ethos and philosophy of the paper reflect the influence of the policy inheritance of the last decade in particular, other factors have also had a significant impact. Thus ideas about good practice and innovation, which have emerged from the field, have combined with the official and unofficial critiques to challenge the underlying concepts and approach to community care.

The essential difference between the world envisaged by *Caring for People*, and current practice is the central emphasis on assessing individual needs and meeting them with appropriate packages of care. The results of such a model would, it is believed, be apparent both in means and ends. More appropriate, flexible and responsive services would lead to improved outcomes as assessed against a number of criteria.

However, we have been cautious in accepting that the white paper's vision for community care will be attainable. Our optimism and enthusiasm for the principles of the new approach are tempered by a realistic awareness of the likely implementation problems which *Caring for People* ignores.

In many respects it is too soon to attempt to pass judgement on the relative success or failure of the new policy. Some of the problems may be reduced or eliminated with practice and experience, while others may become apparent. Of the four main problem areas which we identified, three are principally concerned with implementation issues around day-to-day practice. The fourth, however, is both more strategic and altogether more fundamental. While much of the day-to-day issues will be resolved (or not) at local level, resource issues are of a higher order and subject to a greater degree of central government control. As such, it is arguable, that it is treatment of these matters which is the most potent indicator of political will and commitment to the policy reforms.

In rejecting the arguments for a specific grant, the Government also rejected the Griffiths model which combined lines of account-ability and responsibility. The position of Minister for community care within the Department of Health also differs from that envisaged by Sir Roy. The result is an altogether weaker structure which both reduces the capacity of central government to steer local development, while also distancing it from direct responsibility for progress in achieving community care objectives. Without the linking of service objectives and resources at national level, the Select Committee argued, 'the accountability of central government will be much more difficult to secure' (House of Commons, 1990a, p22). Just how difficult this may be is perhaps indicated by the fact that central Government held local authorities responsible for the delay in implementation which it ordered.

No sooner, it seems, is a new and exciting approach up and running, than it is deliberately brought down at the first hurdle. The white paper claimed to offer 'a great opportunity to strengthen our caring services for the 1990s and beyond for the benefit of those most in need'. It would be a tragedy of enormous proportions if that opportunity were to be so casually tossed aside. While final judgements must be reserved, the delay in the implementation timetable is a highly ominous portent.

References

Association of Directors of Social Services (1988) *Community Care: Agenda for Action – response to Sir Roy Griffiths' report*. ADSS.

Audit Commission (1986) *Making a reality of community care*. HMSO.

Baldwin, S and Parker, G (1989) 'The Griffiths report on community care'. In Brenton, M and Ungerson, C (eds) *Social Policy Review 1988–9*. Longman.

Baldwin, S and Twigg, J (1990) 'Women and community care: reflections on a debate'. In Maclean, M and Groves, D (eds) *Women's issues in social policy*. Routledge.

Barclay Committee (1982) *Social workers: their role and tasks*. Bedford Square Press.

Central Policy Review Staff (1975) *A joint framework for social policies*. HMSO.

Charnley, H and Bebbington, A (1988) *Who gets what? An analysis of the patterns of service provision to elderly people living in the community*. Discussion paper 560, Personal Social Services Research Unit, University of Kent at Canterbury.

Challis, L *et al* (1988) *Joint approaches to social policy: rationality and practice*. Cambridge University Press.

Clarke, K (1990) 'Statement on community care'. *House of Commons Hansard*, 18 July, Cols 999–1014, HMSO.

Dalley, G (1988) *Ideologies of caring: rethinking community and collectivism*. Macmillan Education.

Davies, B and Challis, D (1986) *Matching resources to needs in community care*. Gower.

Department of Health and Social Security (1981a) *Report of a study on community care*. DHSS.

Department of Health and Social Security (1981b) *Growing Older*. HMSO Cmnd 8173.

Department of Health and Social Security (1983) *Health Service development: care in the community and joint finance*. Circular HC(6/LAC) 83 (5), DHSS.

Department of Health (1989a) *Working for Patients*. HMSO.

Department of Health (1989b) *Caring for People: community care in the next decade and beyond*. HMSO.

Department of Health (1990) *Caring for People: community care in the next decade and beyond, policy guidance*. HMSO.

Edelman, M (1977) *Political Language*. Academic Press.

Equal Opportunities Commission (1982) *Caring for the elderly and handicapped: community care policies and women's lives*. EOC.

Ferlie, E, Challis, D and Davies, B (1989) *Efficiency – improving innovations in social care of the elderly*. Gower.

Finch, J (1984) 'Community care: Developing non-sexist alternatives'. *Critical Social Policy*, Vol 3, No 3, pp6–18.

Finch, J and Groves, D (1980) 'Community care for the elderly: a case for equal opportunities?' *Journal of Social Policy*, Vol 9, No 4, pp487–514.

Firth report (1987) Report of a joint central and local government working party, *Public support for residential care*. DHSS.

Flynn, N and Common, R (1990) *Contracts for community care*. Caring for People, Implementation document CCI 4, Department of Health.

Fowler, N (1984) *The enabling role of social services departments*. Speech to the Joint Social Services Annual Conference, Buxton, 27 September 1984.

Gladstone, F (1979) *Voluntary action in a changing world*. Bedford Square Press.

Griffiths, Sir Roy (1988) *Community care: Agenda for action*. A report to the Secretary of State for Social Services, HMSO.

Hadley, R and Hatch, S (1981) *Social welfare and the failure of the State: centralised social services and participatory alternatives*. Allen and Unwin.

Henwood, M (1990) *Community care and elderly people*. Family Policy Studies Centre.

Henwood, M and Wicks, M (1984) *Forgotten army: family care and elderly people*. Family Policy Studies Centre.

Henwood, M and Wicks, M (1985) 'Community care, family trends and social change.' *The Quarterly Journal of Social Affairs*, Vol 1, No 4, pp357–71.

Henwood, M, Jowell, T and Wistow, G (1991) *All things come (to those who wait?): causes and consequences of the community care delays*. King's Fund Institute.

House of Commons (1985) *Community care with special reference to adult mentally ill and mentally handicapped people*. Social Services Committee, Second Report, Session 1984–1985, HC13–1, HMSO.

House of Commons (1990a) *Community Care: funding for local authorities*. Social Services Committee, Third Report, Session 1989–1990, HC277, HMSO.

House of Commons (1990b) *Community Care: planning and co-operation*. Social Services Committee, Eighth Report, Session 1989–1990, HC580, HMSO.

Hunter, D J and Wistow, G (1987) *Community Care in Britain: variations on a theme*. King Edward's Hospital Fund for London.

Kiernan, K and Wicks, M (1990) *Family change and future policy*. Family Policy Studies Centre.

King's Fund (1982) *An Ordinary Life*. Project Paper 24, King's Fund Centre.

Knapp, M (1989) 'Private and voluntary welfare'. In McCarthy, M (ed) op. cit.

Levin, E, Sinclair, I and Gorbach, P (1983) *The supporters of confused elderly people at home: extract from the main report*. National Institute for Social Work.

McCarthy, M (1989), 'Introduction: the boundaries of welfare'. In McCarthy, M (ed) *The new politics of welfare: An agenda for the 1990s*. Macmillan.

Moroney, R M (1976) *The family and the state: considerations for social policy*. Longman.

National Audit Office (1987) *Community care developments*. HMSO.

National Council for Voluntary Organisations (1980) *Beyond the welfare state*. NCVO.

Office of Population Censuses and Surveys (1988) *General Household Survey 1985: Informal carers*. HMSO.

Parker, G (1985) *With due care and attention: a review of research on informal care*. Family Policy Studies Centre (new edition 1990).

Plank, D (1977) *Caring for the elderly*. Greater London Council.

Scott-White, S (1985) Report of a joint central and local government working party, *Supplementary benefit and residential care*. DHSS.

Seebohm Commiteee (1968) *Report of the committee on local authority and allied personal social services*. HMSO, Cmnd 3703.

Titmuss, R M (1968) 'Community care: fact or fiction?' In *Commitment to welfare*. Allen and Unwin.

Ungerson, C (1987) *Policy is personal: sex, gender and informal care*. Tavistock.

Utting, W (1990) *The State of Social work*. The Third BASW Trust Annual Lecture, 15th November 1990, Birmingham, British Association of Social Workers.

Walker, A (1982) 'The meaning and social division of community care'. In Walker, A (ed) *Community care: the family, the state and social policy*. Basil Blackwell and Martin Robertson.

Webb, A and Wistow, G (1982a) 'The personal social services: incrementalism, expediency or systematic social planning?' In Walker, A (ed) *Public expenditure and social policy*. Heineman.

Webb, A and Wistow, G (1982b) *Whither State Welfare?*. Royal Institute of Public Administration.

Westland, P (1988) 'Progress in partnership: a case study'. In Wistow, G and Brooks, T (eds) *Joint planning and joint management*. Royal Institute of Public Administration.

Wistow, G (1983) 'Joint finance and community care: have the incentives worked?' *Public Money*, Vol 3, No 2, pp33–7.

Wistow, G (1987) 'Joint finance: promoting a new balance of care and responsibilities in England'. *International Journal of Social Psychiatry*, Vol 33, No 2, pp83–91.

Wistow, G (1988) 'Beyond joint planning: managing community care'. In Wistow and Brooks, op. cit.

Wistow, G (1989) 'Open Forum'. *Insight*, October 11, p9.

Wistow, G (1990a) 'Implementing "Caring for people": issues and perspectives'. Paper presented to the Association of Directors of Social Services, Blackpool conference, 3 May 1990. To be published by ADSS.

Wistow, G (1990b) *Community care planning: a review of past experience and future imperatives*. Caring for People implementation documents, CCI 3, DHSS.

Wistow, G and Henwood, M (1990) 'Planning in a mixed economy: life after Griffiths'. In Parry, R (ed), *Research highlights in social work 18: Privatisation*. Jessica Kingsley.

Wolfensberger, W (1977) *The principle of normalisation in human services*. National Institute on Mental Retardation Toronto.

Working group on joint planning (1985) *Progress in partnership*. DHSS.

7 Citizenship and frail old people: changing patterns of provision in Europe

John Baldock and Adalbert Evers

This chapter pursues two arguments. First, the role of the state in the provision of care for dependent old people is undergoing considerable change in most European countries. Frail old people are, incongruously, in the front line of social policy development. We look at Sweden, the Netherlands, Germany and the United Kingdom. Second, these changes amount to a renegotiation of the basic assumptions of social entitlement that have built up over the last half century. Put in the terminology of the moment, the meaning of citizenship for old people and their carers is under review.

In many industrial nations relatively predictable systems of support for the dependent (though sometimes predictably poor ones) are in a state of flux and uncertainty. This is partly because they have broken down under the weight of increased demand and partly because of changed social and political views as to what are feasible and appropriate. The Griffiths report and the white paper on community care have their counterparts in a surprising number of European nations. New definitions of state and private responsibility are being proposed and quite rapidly enacted. It is a little paradoxical that the frail elderly should find themselves in the vanguard of social policy change but that does appear to be the case. In the past old age may have meant falling into a form of partial, reduced citizenship, but at least one that was well understood and relatively predictable. Now radical improvements are promised but the likely balance of gains and losses is very uncertain.

In all four of the countries we have chosen to discuss, substantially new forms of social care for the dependent will come into operation during the first half of the 1990s. In each case this follows a period of debate and legislation. In Sweden, the Netherlands and the United Kingdom the legislation was linked to government – sponsored inquiries into the working of the care systems: the Dekker Report *Willingness to Change* was published in the Netherlands in April 1987, the Griffiths Report *Community Care: agenda for action* appeared in March 1988 and in May 1989 the Swedish parliamentary advisory committee on services for the elderly announced its conclusions. In what was West Germany the debate has been less focused round particular committees and reports but more generally round the *Pflegenotstand* (the 'care emergency') and has been no less vigorous. There discussion has been particularly concerned with finding a way of funding those whose need for long-term care makes them ineligible for support from the well-funded health insurance system. In 1988 legislation was passed by the Federal Government which for the first time allows the health insurance funds to pay for home care.

It is sometimes pointed out that it is a stigmatising mistake to associate old age with need and dependency (Freer, 1988; Taylor, 1988). The General Household survey shows that 36 per cent of the over 80s report no longstanding illness over the past year (OPCS, 1989). Those over 65 are an increasingly needed source of labour and skills. For example, they make a major contribution to caring, whether it be of grandchildren, less-able adult children or other old people (Green, 1988). However, here we are concerned with those amongst us who will spend at least a part of our old age dependent to some degree on others in order to get through the day. What sorts of help will we want in order to live in ways acceptable to ourselves and those around us – in order to remain full citizens of our society? This is a topic much discussed in the literature on disablement which deals with younger adults (eg Oliver, 1990). We are more concerned with the relatively larger numbers who, used to a life of full adult autonomy and self-responsibility, find themselves slipping into some degree of dependence on others.

The use of the idea of 'citizenship' to describe relations between the individual and the state is very much in vogue at the moment. Its resurrection has more than a little to do with the Left's search for a rationale for social policy which can compete with the rather brutal logic of Thatcherism and yet at the same time recognise that post-war universalism is dead. It would not be surprising to see the term appear in Labour's next election manifesto, unless the Conservatives manage to completely appropriate it first (eg Hurd 1988). The debate about citizenship is usually conducted at quite a high level of generality and it is hard to come by specific policy proposals. This, of course, explains the political attractiveness of the term but is less promising for those who may have to endure the social policies fashioned in its name. One such group is the growing number of dependent old people. Care of the elderly, as it is called, is a demographic pressure point in welfare provision and it is our hypothesis that the changes that take place in this area are portents of the redefinition of social entitlements in the rest of the system. In this article we attempt a classification of the policy changes affecting frail old people and to assess the implications for the content of their citizenship.

Citizenship is a malleable term and much of the discussion is complex (eg Plant and Barry, 1990; Deakin *et al*, 1990; Keane, 1988a; 1988b; Turner, 1986). It is often conceived of as a combination of political, legal and social rights. At other times it is more particularly tied to the social entitlements that complete that trinity (Marshall, 1950; 1981; Dahrendorf, 1988). In this view citizenship emerges ideally as the harmonious combination of liberal legal rights (civil liberties and the enjoyment and exploitation of private property), democratic political rights (a vote and freedom of political expression) and social rights (protection against poverty, illness and dependence).

Common to most accounts is the idea that by conferring rights and entitlements to at least some minimal welfare the state can enhance and equalise people's ability to participate in civil society, to exert their democratic and legal rights and to join effectively in a market economy. Indeed it has almost become a conventional wisdom that the development of the three institutional arenas of citizenship are mutually supportive of each other. Democracy produces welfare states which in their turn produce the political values and alliances which sustain democratic politics (Titmuss, 1968). Equally, the market economy, the ultimate manifestation of individual legal rights, is seen to have generated both the resources to finance the welfare state and the need for the health, skills and social security that social services produce (Marshall, 1965; George and Wilding, 1984). Thus has developed the pervasive view, often implicit and unargued that 'the three components of the modern state-citizenship relation in the West can be said to be the rule of law, representative democracy, and provisions for "civilian security" through the welfare state' and that these components are positively correlated (Offe, 1987, p502).

If this conception of the nature of citizenship is valid then one might expect a new area of social need, for that is what the substantial growth in numbers of frail elderly amounts to, to call forth additional state services compatible with this developed citizenship. There is indeed evidence of such developments which we summarise. On the other hand, there are new policy directions, quite meticulously argued in the documents we describe, which are at least ambiguous in their implications for the welfare of old people. They appear to signal a withdrawal of the state from accepted welfare commitments and an emphasis on selective and minimalist provision incompatible with earlier, broader conceptions of citizenship. We summarise some of these developments too.

How is this ambiguity in the development of social policies to be explained? The established forms of argument, between left and right or between those who would conserve and those who would reduce state services in the interests of welfare, do not seem sharp enough to distinguish the costs and benefits for the variety of interested parties. The advantage of using some conceptions of citizenship, and our reason for doing so, is that they allow one to tackle the ambiguity of the policy changes taking place. These are neither all bad nor all good: most have positive and negative implications simultaneously. The more sensitive models of citizenship permit one to begin to order these ambiguities because they recognise new differences of interest between citizens and the state, between one citizen and another, and even within each citizen as they perform their different social roles. For example, Claus Offe has suggested that the congruence between the legal, political and welfare components of citizenship may be less reliable than is presupposed and that the first two may now work to undermine the third. He argues, as have others, that there is significant evidence of a shift in the balance of emphasis in European politics away from traditional social entitlements and towards the values of the market, of consumer choice and freedom from public bureaucracy (Offe, 1987, pp505–8). Thus social policies defended in terms of some components of citizenship – freedom, self-determination, independence, variety, choice, flexibility – may serve to undermine others – equality, predictability and security.

Old age and retirement are perhaps when people might expect to enjoy the full fruits of citizenship and particularly the protection of the social components. Yet for many these are times of uncertainty and threat as the social policy most relevant to them comes under radical review. This is not helped by the fact that, whereas political and legal rights are often explicitly set-out, social entitlements are rarely stated in some permanent constitutional form but can change incrementally and almost unnoticed in the everyday processes of 'normal' politics. The slipperiness of the concept of social citizenship is not just an intellectual problem but a very practical one too. The assumptions upon which one has prepared for old age may be rendered outdated by the political exigencies and fashions of the moment.

Changing social policies for the elderly

The reasons why social policies affecting the elderly are the locus of pressure and changes are fairly simple and common to the countries we look at: Britain, The Netherlands, Sweden and the Federal Republic of Germany (including both East and West by the time this piece is published).

The demographic pressures are well-known. The numbers of over-80s, about half of whom will need some daily care, will have grown between 1980 and 2000 by 24 per cent in the United Kingdom, 37 per cent in Germany, 41 per cent in the Netherlands and 42 per cent in Sweden (OECD, 1988; de Jouvenal, 1989). Because absolute numbers are relatively small, these increases are certainly not insurmountable were there the will to divert resources to meet them (Lagergren *et al*, 1984). The over-80s will even by 2000 constitute only 3.2 per cent of population in the UK, 3.6 per cent in Germany, 3.0 per cent in the Netherlands and 4.4 per cent in Sweden. Throughout the period the proportions in the populations of those of working age and in the carer groups of the younger elderly (65–80) remain almost constant. It is not until 2020 and beyond that one sees substantial deteriorations in the dependency ratios and obvious shortages of people of working age (OECD, 1988).

Perhaps more important are the financial and ideological pressures. It is widely accepted that state expenditure on the old cannot grow at a pace to match the increase in numbers. New ways to provide for their needs will have to be found. This is essentially a political consensus which cannot be easily contested. At any one time the dependent old are too few to be electorally significant. What is needed is greater awareness amongst the rest of the electorate that the care of the old may be a small problem at the moment but over time is a very large issue touching us all. The cohort of people who are dependent in old age has almost by definition a very fast throughput. It is not a condition many people experience for very long but it is one that most will experience at some time. If one adds to that number those who at another time will find themselves bound to give care to the old rather than receive it, then the scale of the issue becomes clearer, to social scientists if not to politicians and their electors.

Neither is the debate about the care of the frail elderly one in which many people are deeply engaged. Changes in social policy that affect the old are generally argued about by a relatively small community of civil servants, professionals and researchers in health and welfare. The result, as we hope to show, is that almost any change can be sold to the electorate as progressive reform and political parties can adopt positions that have more to do with the prevailing rhetoric of care than its reality.

While there are important differences between the countries, their social care systems and the basic assumptions that lie behind them, a number of common themes are pursued in the reforms and it does appear reasonable to argue that not only do all the countries face broadly the same problems but that their governments are pursuing broadly similar solutions. A core, organising concept that is ubiquitous across this international policy debate is the idea of the 'enabling state'. This, an inherently normative or value-loaded term, captures most of the ideological rationale for the reforms. It is characteristically used to justify three principal kinds of new policy; the 'marketisation' of social care services, the encouragement of voluntary and private organisations, and the payment of informal family carers. These are the practical forms the idea of enablement takes and they generally involve a redefinition of the relationship between the individual and the state.

The 'enabling state'

The idea of the 'enabling state' contains much of the liberal conception of the right relationship between individual and government. The classic authorities from Locke and Hobbes to Hayek and Friedman are fundamentally concerned with setting out the conditions of a minimal state which will enable the citizen to pursue interests, make choices and enjoy property in a manner both unfettered and protected. The earlier authors did not need to consider what governments might do about the 'private' afflictions of ill-health and dependency since they did not conceive of state action that might alleviate them. The ability of modern medicine and nursing to sustain people over long periods spoilt the purity of the argument for the more contemporary neo-liberals. It became arguable that state protection in dependency and chronic ill-health were also necessary to the unfettered pursuit of life and liberty. Yet once the state does begin to guarantee care then the cost, the bureaucracy and the social control that follow begin to offend the more established components of citizenship. One solution is to permit some limited paternalism that defines the dependent, along with children and the insane, as less than full citizens (Friedman, 1962). This is not a very appealing solution. The 'enabling state' provides a more politically marketable idea. The government will not itself provide the care, except perhaps in the last resort, but it will create the conditions which will encourage the provision of care willingly by the market and the community.

The Netherlands provides one of the more explicit attempts to reconcile the need for care with the more established freedoms and rights of citizenship. The Dekker Commission states the issue at the very beginning of its report:

> Every citizen in the Netherlands has an entitlement to health care, but not to health. Since 1983 the constitution has contained an article under which the authorities are obliged to take measures to promote public health
>
> (MWHC, 1988, p33).

The report then describes the growth of the health and care system, arguing that it has become

> ... virtually autonomous and uncontrollable .... Traditional responsibilities and new challenges, combined with limited resources, have prompted a widespread search for solutions. The view has taken root that a regulatory, planning and paternalistic government will need to step back at all levels in favour of a system of control in which the state fosters and sets the framework, while the health sector regulates matters itself. Greater emphasis has to be placed on citizens' own responsibility for their health and the help that should be extended in this field by the community close to home.
>
> (*ibid* p35).

Very similar language is used in the British government's white paper on community care (Cm 849). Two words that appear with extraordinary frequency are 'enable' and 'promote'. 'Promoting choice and independence underlies all the Government's proposals' (1.8). 'The Government has endorsed Sir Roy Griffiths' recommendation that social services authorities should be "enabling" agencies. It will be their responsibility to make maximum possible use of private and voluntary providers, and so increase the available range of options and widen consumer choice' (1.11). Private (for profit) provision will be encouraged by a central government requirement of local authorities to draw up plans to make 'maximum use of the independent sector' (1.12) and by effectively restricting state subsidy to those below the poverty line (income support level). The white paper recognises 'the great bulk of care is provided by family, friends and neighbours' (1.9) and argues that 'helping carers to maintain their valuable contribution to the spectrum of care is both right and a sound investment' (2.3).

In fact the use of language is rather different in the Griffiths report than that which the white paper suggests. There is a considerable difference in tone which has not been much noticed. In Griffiths the principal diagnosis of what is wrong with the British care system is a lack of ultimate accountability for care, and the central recommendation is that the government clearly accepts this responsibility, appoints a minister to bear it publicly and establishes a financial system that 'ring fences' the money voted for social care. While recognising that the informal, voluntary and private sectors do indeed do most caring and that the state should encourage them, there is considerable emphasis on what the government should be responsible for and on what it should provide. 'The proposals take as their starting point . . . that the first task of publicly provided services is to support and where possible strengthen these networks of carers. Public services can help by identifying such actual and potential services, consulting them about their needs and those of the people they are caring for, and tailoring the provision of extra services (if required) accordingly' (Griffiths, 1988, para 3.2). In short, the difference in tone between the two documents is that while the Griffiths report is a sustained exercise in trying to pin down responsibility for care, the White Paper reads like an attempt to avoid and fudge that responsibility.

We have spent some time on the differences and similarities between the two British reports because they encapsulate the essential tension between the social protection component in citizenship and the civil and democratic components. The presence of this tension is at the heart of our argument. The Griffiths report lays a much more traditional emphasis on the role of the state in social protection, particularly on its ultimate responsibility to ensure and administer the care of the dependent, while the white paper is almost entirely devoted to elaborating dependent peoples' rights to choice, variety and autonomy. While these objectives are not intrinsically incompatible they are often difficult to reconcile in practice. The concept of the enabling state is notably useful for bridging, and often blurring, the gap.

In the Federal Republic of Germany it is fair to say that the issue of enablement has not reached the level of substantial policy documents or legislation. As is often pointed out, the principle of subsidiarity which informs social care in Germany, stresses rather the obligation of families and private resources to be the help of first resort (Jamieson, 1990). The process by which the state assesses people for public support consists in large part in checking first that these private sources have been used. At first glance there would appear to be considerable congruence between the concept of enablement and the principle of subsidiarity. A government that insists upon private obligation will surely soon come under pressure to support it? There is evidence, at least at the level of the Länder, that the growing body of research on informal carers and the burdens they bear, an area of study which has developed more slowly than in Britain or Scandanavia, is making it increasingly difficult for politicians to resist the path to enablement (Hummel, 1990; Steiner-Hummel, 1989). On the other hand, the principle of subsidiarity has its roots in a conception of citizenship that emphasises duty rather than entitlement. German social policy is built upon a conservative commitment, found in both the Catholic and Protestant churches, to strengthen 'natural' communities and sources of support, particularly the extended family and local charity. The state intervenes only when these organisations are exhausted (Esping-Andersen, 1990).

The Health Reform Act of 1988, which allows some financial help for caring relatives, has been much criticised for assuming that the problems of social care can be dealt with through the family when 40 per cent of the retired live alone, nearly 30 per cent have no surviving children and where for many of the remaining the post-war division of Germany and the pattern of economic development mean children live far from parents (Dieck, 1988). For these people care can only be obtained within the discriminating rules of social assistance and many choose not to endure the laborious means tests which precede the receipt of any kind of help (Regus and Trenk-Hinterberger, 1985). These contrast strongly with the generous and almost universal entitlements that are provided by health insurance. Here the presumption that medical 'cure' is a highly technical service that can only be provided by professionals has allowed a system of care to develop not within the conservative tradition of citizenship as duty but rather as part of the modern image of the citizen as an individual consumer. Thus the reformers have sought to either build social care into this medical system or to construct a parallel system of care insurance (Nesecker and Jung, 1988). The conservative rejoinder has been, in part, to argue that this would lead directly to consumerism undermining family obligations. The Federal Minister for Labour and Social Affairs, Norbert Blüm, argued recently that 'a son whose father has paid 40 years of social-care insurance will say "Use your contributions. Go to the that nice nursing home round the corner".' (author's observation).

This debate about the very principles of citizenship is now complicated, both materially and ideologically, by the unification of Germany. The communist party in East Germany sought to vest the traditions of family, community solidarity and duty in itself. The GDR Council of Ministers was vigorous in the adoption of resolutions on the welfare of the old (Schwitzer and Speigner, 1987). These emphasised the right of old people to be included in the organisational life of the community and to receive help from it. The local 'People's Solidarity Organisations' (*Volkssolidarität*) provided home help assistance and meals, at central canteens, at levels comparable with the UK. For example some 3 per cent of the retired still living in their own homes received home help in 1985 and 7 per cent attended the canteens (ibid). However, the quality of these services was often so low as to make them effectively a residual 'poor law' service where families could not provide better (Winkler, 1990; Arnold and Schirmer, 1990). This was alleviated to a degree by the fact that institutionalisation remained the dominant state solution to high levels of dependence. To the end the GDR was constructing old people's homes and nursing homes which in 1985 housed more than 5 per cent of the over 65s (Schwitzer and Speigner, 1987).

Although the new, united Germany offers no general citizenship right to care in old age, most of the formerly East German elderly are likely to fall within the eligibility criteria for public assistance, including social welfare payments for residential care. In the former West Germany, as in the Britain, an ad hoc way of dealing with the problem of financing institutional care had already led to huge public expenditure supporting over 70 per cent of the institutional population, some 260,000 people, in private and voluntary residential homes (Statistisches Bundesamt, 1988). Unification means that the German government will either have to expand this support for institutional care or greatly extend state financing of home care. Unification can only hasten the need to find solutions to the pressing uncertainty about the limits of state responsibility for the care of old people. The 'enabling state' offers a set of rationalisations that could potentially fill the yawning gap between the polar conceptions of the citizen as either supplicant or consumer that currently order the provision of care.

We have argued so far that the concept of the enabling state allows an apparent resolution between the conflicting need of a growing number of old people for care and the preference of the fit majority for as inexpensive a social welfare system as possible. This is done by arguing that the best interests of the old are served by maximising such citizenship rights as choice and autonomy rather than security and protection. In Sweden a similar language is in evidence but with quite different social policy implications. The Care for the Elderly Act passed in 1988 states that

> the elderly shall be entitled to choose to live at home even where the need for assistance is great. Elderly people who do not wish to or cannot remain at home shall be entitled to choose between different living and care arrangements – sheltered housing, old peoples' homes, group dwellings and nursing homes
>
> (MHSA, 1988)

A bill which voted an additional 540 million kronor for local authorities to finance the additional functions imposed left little doubt as to where the duty to provide lay. As Bengt Lindqvist, the minister then responsible, stated in a press release, 'Municipal responsibility for the care of the elderly, as advocated by the

Riksdag, will leave no doubt as to who is responsible and where the individual can turn for the care and attention which he or she is entitled to' (Lindqvist, 1989).

There is in Sweden little explicit attempt to minimise the state's role in the provision of care. This is based on more than a simple commitment to universalism. What distinguishes Scandanavian welfare from, for example, that available in Britain is not only the principle of equal care for those in similar need but, more fundamentally, a conception of rights to care. In Sweden these are made manifest in substantially more generous services – for example the availability of public home-help is relatively four times as great as in Britain (Kraan *et al*, 1990) – and social rights are actually stated in acts of parliament in a way that is rare in the United Kingdom. To British eyes, a remarkable feature of the key Swedish welfare legislation affecting the old (for example the Social Services Act 1982, the Health Care Act 1983 and the Care of the Elderly Act 1988) is that they contain explicit statements of welfare principles. These include: 'normalisation' – the right to live in as normal a setting as possible; 'participation' – a right to participate in society; and 'self-determination' in decisions affecting one's welfare. In addition the 1988 Act states two principles that any British parliament would regard as foolish hostages to fortune in a piece of government legislation, that it is 'the responsibility of the community to ensure that old people receive the services, care and attention they require' and that 'contributions by relatives should always be voluntary' (MHSA, 1988).

Nonetheless Sweden does face severe constraints on the provision of care for the growing numbers of frail elderly but these are more inescapably material than political or ideological. Not only does the country enter the 1990s with a crisis of growing inflation and foreign debt (Schierbeck, 1990) but Sweden simply does not have the spare labour capacity to carry out its planned care policies. Måten Lagergren has estimated for the Secretariat for Future Studies that, given present policies, by 2000 the care sector will require between 1.0 and 1.2 million employees out of a total likely labour force of 4.5 million (Lagergren *et al*, 1984). We discuss his proposed solution to this impasse in the section on informal care.

'Marketisation'

This is admittedly a rather clumsy word but it best describes the growing enthusiasm over the last decade or so for the use of the price mechanism in the allocation of welfare. 'Marketisation' is the means of enablement most commonly proposed. An almost ideal synthesis is achieved when that most basic of the liberal citizenship rights, the freedom to buy and sell and accumulate profit, is allied with the right to choose the care one needs. These days, of course, the popularity of the price mechanism cannot be entirely separated from the wider commitment to markets that is sweeping all before it across eastern Europe. Students of social policy seem almost cowed by these revolutionary circumstances. In Britain in particular, the discipline of Social Administration has traditionally conceived of its task as revealing the costs and disadvantages of market mechanisms (Mishra, 1989). Now these arguments, which are surely as relevant as ever and of particular significance to those managing the transformations of command economies, are uttered soto voce or not heard at all. Perhaps they have been blighted by the tendency their proponents had to regard all markets as intrinsically bad and welfare services as 'islands of collectivism' which would eventually link together to push back the seas of competition. However, that history appears to have shown how markets are often the most appropriate form of allocation does not necessarily mean that these islands are now unneeded.

As the textbooks point out, the use of the price mechanism can take many forms, from, at one extreme, the outright abandonment of any government role in the supply of a service, leaving it entirely to market forces, to situations where supply and payment remain solely a state responsibility but where internal markets are established within and between government bureaucracies (Judge, 1980; Le Grand and Robinson, 1984). The justifications for marketisation are usually one or both of efficiency and targeting. In principle efficiency gains are made because attaching prices to resources means they are used in the knowledge of their costs. Targeting means making those who can, pay.

Selectivity is at the heart of the hopes placed on the use of the price mechanism in welfare provision. Ideally the use of prices will control costs by selecting out the more cost-effective forms of provision and targeting subsidies on the most needy recipients. However the experience of the Netherlands and West Germany show that these outcomes do not readily follow. The insurance-based provision of much social and medical care in the Netherlands, and to a lesser extent in Germany, is already marketised in the sense that much provision is by non-governmental suppliers who seek at least to cover costs and quite often to make a profit. The systems are ordered by price mechanisms but not ones that achieve the goals usually claimed for them. In fact quite the opposite. Consumers are not particularly price-sensitive since their costs are largely, often completely, covered by insurance the price of which they have no control over – what economists call the problem of moral hazard.

The suppliers, on the other hand, often face incentives to use higher rather than lower cost forms of treatment and so maximise their incomes. These are the classic faults of insurance-based health care systems and are well-known and documented (Chambers, 1988). Now the growth in the numbers of old people who require long-term support has created the opportunity and the necessity to search for new remedies in both countries.

The chief difference for our purposes between the Dutch and the German systems in that in the Netherlands much of the longterm care required by frail old people can be obtained through the health insurance system whereas in Germany it cannot. Under the Dutch system, care is financed by a number of insurance funds and supplied by voluntary and private agencies. The advantage of this pattern, from the point of view of users, is that it guarantees care, but with a strongly medical and institutional bias. An exceptional proportion of the Netherland's mildly dependent elderly have found themselves in high cost nursing homes which are close to hospitals in their character (Kraan *et al*, 1990). The government and the insurance funds are anxious to encourage substitution downwards to cheaper and less-institutional forms of care. The principal remit of the Dekker committee was to advise on 'strategies for volume and cost containment against the background of an ageing population'. The solution they proposed was a 'shift from government imposed rules and regulations to regulation by the market' (MWHC, 1988).

Briefly, the changes proposed by Dekker involve a move away from the existing system in which health insurance premiums are largely income related and where the excess of supplier costs over the insurance funds' resources has effectively been made good by government subsidies. Under the proposed system a significant part of the health insurance premium paid by individuals will be flat rate one and the funds will compete to keep that as low as possible and to attract customers. Second the system of subsidies to service providing agencies will cease and they will contract with the insurance funds to supply services at fixed prices. The government role will become largely one of guaranteeing quality (MWHC, 1988). The Dekker report argued that it was proposing a system in which a balance could be struck between the competing principles that drive welfare systems. Quality, reliability and a basic level of equity would be guaranteed by the government and efficiency and choice will be generated by competition between the suppliers of care and by consumers being able to choose between insurers and service providers, presumably on the basis of cost.

This market logic can easily lead to a position where it becomes very much an individual's own responsibility as to the quantity and quality of care they will receive, beyond a basic minimum, in old age. This point has not yet been reached in the Dekker proposals under which home nursing services remain part of the compulsorily-insured benefits. Nonetheless such items as drugs for outpatients, artificial aids and appliances, physiotherapy and dental care, in all 15 per cent of the existing health services, would become insurable voluntarily 'as a whole, in part or not at all' (MWHC, 1988). In other words some will be left uninsured for what are basic elements in a care regime. An inevitable consequence must be more inequality of well-being in old age depending upon whether people have chosen to pay the premiums to cover these basic services.

In Britain the Griffiths report is quite explicit about the responsibility of individuals:

> Planning needs to take account of the possibility of individuals beginning to plan to meet their own care needs at an earlier stage of life. Recent changes in pension legislation have increased the opportunities to take more personal responsibility for planning pension provision. Moves to make provision for anticipated community care needs is a logical extension of such an approach
>
> (Griffiths, 1988, para 6.60).

Recent reports in the press indicate that the major British insurance companies are planning care-insurance schemes but are facing considerable difficulties in estimating the likely extent and costs of claims (Buckingham, 1990). That many, probably most, old people will be responsible for purchasing their own care is made inevitable by the basic assumption of both Griffiths and the white paper that henceforth state provision will be limited to those below the poverty line. The stipulation that charges will be made for the cost of services to all those that 'can afford them' does not receive a great deal of elaboration in either Griffiths or the White Paper but in fact is an assumption fundamental to how the whole system will work.

> Those able to meet all or part of the economic cost should be expected to do so. Moreover, effective costing and charging procedures can be valuable in achieving the best use of resources across the range of personal social services
>
> (Cm 849, para 3.8.1).

These twin emphases on charging anyone above a minimum income and contracting out a service wherever possible, taken literally, would substantially transform the public sector role in the provision of social care. There is much evidence that there is almost no service that cannot be provided substantially more cheaply by the private or voluntary sectors (though often at some cost to quality or the conditions of the staff) so contracting out should, logically, become the norm. At the same time 'those that can afford to' actually means, under the entitlement rules that currently apply in the United Kingdom, anyone with over £3,000 in savings. Those with more are obliged to spend down to that level. Thus what these proposals logically envisage, and the subsequent legislation provides for no more, is selective state provision for social care to the minority of old people who are officially in poverty. Furthermore, that care will be contracted out to non-statutory providers who can compete on costs within certain quality parameters, as yet unspecified but probably minimal. This is the reform of community care that the Labour Party is currently castigating the Government for not introducing more quickly. The fact that what is proposed is contrary to almost every principle of welfare espoused by the Labour Party since the war is not mentioned nor noticed by media or public.

Whereas in Britain the choices faced by politicians are somewhat eased by a public long-used to a welfare system generous in its self-image ('the best in the world') but brutally rationed in practice, in West Germany the problem is rather of a population accustomed to high standards of care, particularly medical care, which are seen simply as insured entitlements rather than the product of some grander conception of the welfare state. Insurance systems, though they may effectively be compulsory, are contractual arrangements which can be defined in legal terms outside a social conception of citizenship. However, the generosity of the German system has been largely confined to the provision of what can be defined as curative medical care or recuperation from it. Social care, either in one's own home or in an institution, must be purchased out of private resources and will only be paid for by the state where an individual is eligible for public assistance. A fifth of the social assistance budget now pays for the care of dependent people in institutions and, to a much smaller degree for the provision of home care services by voluntary agencies or the *sozialstationen* (Statistisches Bundesamt, 1988). As increasing numbers of elderly citizens require long-term social rather than medical care there are politically significant expectations that these too can be financed through the health insurance system. Yet contributions to the health insurance system already account for 13 per cent of gross wage costs, a 50 per cent increase since 1970 (Bundesminister für Arbeit und Sozialordnung, 1989). Extending insurance cover to the long term care of the elderly appears financially impossible without finding ways of containing potential consumer demand and limiting producer costs, the two unsolved weaknesses of the existing system. Amongst the solutions canvassed by academics is an insurance scheme that provides not a guarantee of care but vouchers that can be encashed for social care (Freier, 1989). Another solution advanced in the United Kingdom, and given brief mention in the Griffiths report, is 'social care maintenance organisations', modeled on American HMOs, where an insurer-manager basically controls the volume of demand for services by clients and bargains on their behalf with suppliers (Davies, 1989; Paton, 1990, p131). These kinds of solution are all essentially attempts to make market mechanisms more socially acceptable or to ration social commitments through a price mechanism.

The least emphasis on the use of prices is to be found in Sweden. Although consumer charges are made for some health and social services these charges are not a reflection of costs. Need and established social entitlements remain the core criteria of social service provision. Care resources appear to be allocated with very little idea of their costs, though with considerable concern about their scarcity. Over the last decade an absolute shortage of labour power led to a reduction in the provision of home care for the younger, less disabled elderly and tighter rationing of residential care. Inevitably some people are seeking to purchase the care they cannot get from the state by turning to private sources. Only 4 per cent of long-term care beds are currently in private institutions (Nordrup and Thorslund, 1987) but the number is growing as are sheltered housing schemes for private purchase. The fact that these schemes will inevitably draw resources away from the state sector has led to the beginnings of a debate, amongst academics at least, as to how the universal commitments of the Swedish system will either have to be deliberately modified or simply decay in an unplanned way. As one commentator has pointed out, 'Desperate staff in overcrowded hospital wards are undoubtedly going to encourage those patients with sufficient financial resources to use private sources of care in order to concentrate on those who cannot afford them' (Thorslund, 1991). It is a classic problem of universal systems that they must set standards that are acceptable to the most demanding or they start to fail (Esping-Andersen, 1990).

The most divisive effect that prices in welfare have upon citizenship is that they distinguish between those who can pay, or get paid for, and those who cannot. The latter may not be the poorest in society. The more positive effect is that prices allow choice and variety of response in a context where everyone's needs are often crucially different. It is this 'democratic' component that those who argue for citizenship rights often seek to add to more traditional forms of state welfare. They often appear to imply that choice is somehow a guarantee of supply and sufficiency, which of course it is not. What is more, feeble and frightened people cannot often act as effective consumers and are prey to the unscrupulous, who of course exist in any system.

The encouragement of voluntary and private organisations

Where enabling mainly means encouraging people to use alter-native, non-state sources of care, the question arises as to whether they are available, or can be made to become available. Need does not necessarily call forth a supply. That indeed was a basic reason for the evolution of state welfare services in the first place. In Britain the General Household Survey shows that, at least until recently, very few dependent old people used private, non-family sources of care. For example in 1985 no more than 1 per cent of the elderly living alone and unable to perform one or more basic domestic tasks used private paid help (OPCS, 1989, p207). Amongst those unable to prepare a meal the number was less than 1 per cent. The supply of private domiciliary care may be growing fast (Midwinter, 1986) but it certainly remains very tiny and insufficient to bear the considerable weight of government expectation implied in the White Paper. The voluntary sector too, though important, remains marginal. In terms of community care it features largely as the provider of day care, but only to about 2 per cent of the dependent at any one time (Kraan *et al*, 1990). While the Government makes much of its intention to encourage private provision little consideration has been given to the likely costs of purchasing privately-sourced provision sufficient to maintain people in their own homes. For some time now there have been press reports of the insurance industry preparing to market long-term care plans. So far none have actually appeared and it seems that the size of the necessary premiums will severely limit the market (George, 1990).

Similarly there is a considerable gap between rhetoric and reality concerning local authorities contracting out the provision of domiciliary care. The Griffiths Report argued that

> the responsibility of the social service authorities is to ensure that services are provided within the appropriate budgets by the public or private sector according to where they can be provided most economically and efficiently. The onus in all cases should be on the social services authorities to show that the private sector is being fully stimulated and encouraged and that competitive tenders, or other means of testing the market, are being taken.
>
> (Griffiths, 1988, para 24).

The white paper endorsed this in even stronger language: 'local authorities will be expected to make maximum use of the independent sector. The Government will ensure they have acceptable plans for achieving this' (Cm 849, para 1.12).

The current reality in Britain is very different. A recent survey of 109 local authorities found only 23 having contracts with independent suppliers for the provision of domiciliary services (Booth, 1990). Thirty-six contracts were involved, 17 with private organisations (of which 16 were for meal-on-wheels) and 19 with voluntary bodies (of which 13 were for day services). Only a third of the contracts had in fact been put out to a competitive tender (all of them meal-on-wheels). In no case had a voluntary agency actually had to tender, the arrangement was 'simply formalising a relationship previously based on grant-aid'. The researchers conclude, 'there is as yet no sign of a competitive market developing. Private suppliers are few and far between and their contribution is tiny. There must be some doubt about whether the private sector will, in the short term, be able to fulfil the role envisaged for it in a mixed economy of care' (ibid).

Comparison with the experience of the Netherlands and Germany shows that these doubts should not solely extend to the short term. In many ways the system of provision in the Netherlands exhibits the features the British Government wishes to attain. The vast bulk of the supply of care is by a great variety of private and voluntary contractors and there are many sources of finance. Yet it was this very pluralism that the Dekker committee saw as the source of rigidity and inflexibility. It argued that the diverse system of finance and supply means there is little substitution between one part and another of the care system. Once they use one form of care and supplier, dependent people find it difficult to shift to another as their needs change. In particular there are powerful obstacles to substitution downwards towards cheaper and less intensive forms. The suppliers are rarely likely to advise or facilitate such a move, just as a car salesman is unlikely to advise buying a cheaper model.

This is not to say that a care market cannot be constrained to produce more effective and efficient outcomes but that the technical problems of doing so are immense. The Dekker Report's complexity derives from its search for a regulatory environment that will make competition enhance welfare rather than detract from it. Competition on its own clearly has no necessary relationship with socially desirable outcomes. A government which seeks to withdraw from the direct provision of social protection must then fulfil its obligations to its citizens by regulation and in so doing will find itself just as accountable for the faults and deficiencies that result and for justifying the volume of resources that are consumed. A difference between the British Government's Community Care white paper and the Dekker Report is that the first appears to seek to reduce public accountability for social outcomes while the second merely searches for better mechanisms for fulfilling that accountability. It is not possible to supply the social components of citizenship simply by emphasizing the older democratic and civil rights. While there is indeed a balance to be struck between the different parts of citizenship, a government which fails to fulfil social expectations will be held accountable whatever the specific system of allocation. A government which seeks to re-emphasise such values as choice and competition in order to reduce its accountability for welfare outcomes is attempting to redefine the content of citizenship and to excise part of its social component.

The debate about integration of the voluntary organisations in the provision of social services, 'welfare pluralism' in the UK (Johnson, 1987), 'nonprofit federalism' in the US (Salamon, 1987), places strong emphasis on increased choice, flexibility in the face of rapidly changing needs and priorities, greater sensitivity to minorities and more room for innovation in service delivery. However, both Johnson and Salamon, for example, are sceptical of the nonprofits' ability to provide stable and reliable services. In principle they have the potential to reconcile or balance the conflicting components of citizenship. In practice they either enhance the liberal and democratic dimensions of citizenship at the possible expense of social protection or they provide uniform and standardised services in the manner of parastate organisations. This is very much what happened in the Federal Republic of Germany where five big voluntary organisations have come to dominate the provision of personal social services. Although these organisations have their own distinctive heritages – Caritas and Diakoni in catholic and evangelical roots, the Arbeiterwohlfhatr in working class social democracy – they now control the 'social' market in a corporatist manner without expanding choice. They combine monolithic immobility with managerial 'nonprofit amateurism'. There is an absence of democratic control and accountability over self-perpetuating boards of directors and financial scandals are common and are due largely to laxity rather that larceny. They play little part in what is often thought of as a central feature of voluntary provision, innovation. This has become the territory of the 'second voluntary sector', small scale, local, often self-help initiatives which must struggle for funding in competition with the established giants (Balke, 1987).

Inclusion of the informal sector

One trend that is very clear in all the societies we are discussing is the explicit inclusion of the informal sector, particularly family

carers, in changes in public policy for the dependent elderly. This
has involved a number of stages of policy development. First there
has been recognition everywhere that the state has never done most
of the work of caring for adult dependants. This has been followed
by public financing of research to document the amount and nature
of informal caring. This in itself is an instructive story which we do
not have space to analyse here. Much of the initial work was done
by feminist researchers who concentrated on the costs to women of
this work and analysed the economic and cultural forces that create
the informal carer (Parker, 1990; Twigg et al, 1990; Ungerson,
1987; Sundström, 1984; Johansson, 1985). In its most radical form
this analysis sees a thorough contradiction between the civil and
economic rights of women and the welfare needs of the old. Here
a traditional right of the elderly, to family care, ordained by custom
and tradition, finds itself in conflict with the developing citizenship
of women.

Next, and surprisingly rapidly at a time of constraint in welfare
budgets, have come new benefits and entitlements for informal
carers. In Britain expenditure on the Attendance Allowance (much
of which effectively subsidizes informal care) and the Invalid Care
Allowance has grown from nothing to almost a billion pounds a
year in less than a decade (DSS, 1989). In 1990 an additional £10
Carer Premium was introduced for those recipients of the Invalid
Care Allowance (carers of working age) whose total income leaves
them below the poverty line.

In West Germany during 1988 the government responded to
public pressure by passing some limited legislation which allows
health insurance to be used to purchase up to four weeks a year
of home nursing for the bed-bound. In addition, from the beginning
of 1991 the insurance system will pay for up to a maximum of 25
hours a month of professional home care or alternatively pay a
family carer up to 400 DM a month. So far this is the only way in
which funds from the health insurance system have formally been
allowed for care of the long-term dependant. The dependency
criteria are particularly strict and this has led to low take-up and
by the end of 1990 it can be estimated that less than 20 per cent
of potential expenditure will actually have been incurred (Haag and
Schneider, 1989).

In May 1988 the Swedish parliament passed the 'Care of the
Elderly Bill' which allowed carers to receive the equivalent of
up to 30 days a year income compensation from the health
insurance funds. The bill also allowed local authorities to make
cash payments to carers over pensionable age and encouraged
and strengthened the scheme under which local authorities can
treat carers as their full-time employees (MHSW, 1988). In the
Netherlands the health insurance funds have conducted substantial

'hospital at home' experiments which, though generously financed, allow considerable savings on the hospital costs which they are bound to pay. Relatives quickly become a key part of the care programme and have been paid for their work (Kraan *et al*, 1990).

The next step is to incorporate voluntary carers in some contractual way into care organised, or at least overseen, by state professionals. Thus appears the apparent contradiction of the 'paid volunteer', a significant feature of the community care experiments cited as best practice in the British governments White Paper (Cm 849, para 3.3.3). This is both a remarkably effective way of providing good home care and a remarkably cheap way. There are also indications that the workers recruited come from particularly disadvantaged sections of the labour market and the voluntariness of their contribution is at best ambiguous (Qureshi *et al*, 1989; Baldock and Ungerson, 1991).

Thus there does appear to be a trend in which governments are committing the welfare state to paying for people's social care needs in old age and to compensating those who find themselves bound to provide care for family members. However it is not easy to assess the character of this trend. Is it an example of the self-reinforcing congruence between democratic politics and welfare provision: a modern example of the process by which a democratic majority which feared the consequences of unemployment created protection against it? Now a majority which fears physical dependency and its consequences in old age is obliging governments to construct the necessary open-ended guarantees. An alternative interpretation is to see the trend as an example of the growing divergence between democratic politics and social policy. Both the frail elderly and those who care for them are marginal, powerless people. Public subsidies for their care can be kept to absolute minima per head and be made subject to very stringent needs and income tests. Thus this system, though it may be a substantial new form of public expenditure, is in no danger of becoming a core universal benefit to which all owe allegiance for one reason or another.

In this respect it is interesting to note how in those two of our societies where the support of all the frail old was for a time at least an accepted public responsibility, in Sweden and the former GDR, the solution was to build as many and as good old people's homes as possible. The Swedes interpreted this as the virtuous course through the 50s and 60s and are now left with the substantial physical consequences. Almost until the end the East Germans regarded the continuing construction of a system of old people's homes, relatively some four times as large as that available in Britain, as an achievement to be boasted about, even if towards the end a collapsing economy meant that some of the homes could no longer be operated (Arnold and Schirmer, 1990). In both cases it is perhaps important to distinguish the production of a care technology that turned out not to work acceptably from the universalist political consensus that created it. The intention was to replace the selective almshouse for the elderly poor with a high quality benefit that would be enjoyed by all. In contrast the selective subsidies for home care now being developed in the United Kingdom and in Germany may serve to create a marginal underclass of poor elderly and their carers existing in deplorable but hidden circumstances in their own homes.

In particular the implications for women, who do most though certainly not all informal caring (Arber and Gilbert, 1989), are very ambiguous. On one hand there is much evidence that there is a core of caring for the very dependent that cannot be done economically by professionals outside institutions and must therefore remain a voluntary, informal input if it is to happen at all. Paying the informal carers who do this work at least some compensation is surely a step forward. On the other hand, the amounts paid are too low to attract most men into a voluntary caring role and so serve to reinforce the traditional, lesser citizenship of women and even to confirm definitions of citizenship in terms of duty rather than entitlement.

In Sweden the search for solutions to the growing need for care in very old age is centred round ways of increasing the supply of resources available to the state to do the job. One solution suggested has been a form of 'social care conscription' (Lagergren, 1984, 1987). Måten Lagergren points out that 'the total time at work during life-span for the male population has decreased by around 1 per cent per year over the last 60 years, a trend which it is difficult to imagine will be broken' (1987, p109). This greater leisure and time spent in learning and retirement has had many advantages, not least the sharing out of employment. But, particularly in Sweden, it has meant that a ceiling has been reached in terms of both available labour and taxable capacity to fulfill the growing burden of care. 'One solution to this dilemma might be to think of the transferral in other terms – in terms of labour rather than of money. Solidarity with people in need can be expressed by way of personal action instead of impersonal tax-paying' (ibid). He doubts whether this transfer of leisure into more equitably borne care can be achieved voluntarily and so suggests a compulsory 'tax on time instead of income'.

This suggestion of Lagergren's has become well-known and is commonly greeted with a degree of derision. We do not wish to enter this debate except to say that there is a certain logic, if people are choosing free time rather than income that can be taxed, free time that is at least as unevenly distributed as income, to tax that time instead. What is significant here is the conception of citizenship that is encapsulated in this suggestion. It is one that rebalances the component parts and even redefines the content of the parts. Not only is social protection given a greater weight relative to democratic and legal rights but these earlier, more traditional forms of citizenship, are reinterpreted. The point is made that ones man's right to enjoy his leisure amounts to a restriction on another's (woman's). The care of the elderly is defined in part as a public good enjoyed by all, not entirely as a form of private consumption and private obligation. Once it is accepted that caring is a form of taxation generating a public benefit then democratic principles can be used to argue for its fairer allocation. Once it is accepted that time is a form of property then carers can demand that the state assist in the protection of it, just as it does physical property.

Conclusion

Caring for the still small but much increased numbers of the dependent elderly presents new challenges to social policy and to assumptions of citizenship. It questions the implicit contracts between citizen and state, and between citizen and citizen, particularly between citizens who are men and those who are women. The burdens of dependency fall unpredictably. It has always been possible to argue, not necessarily rightly, that people choose to have children, that they constitute a source of benefit as well as cost, and that therefore their care was largely a private matter. This is much less arguable in the case of dependent old people. Having a parent in need of long-term intensive care is as much a matter of chance as becoming ill. What is more, old people themselves can be argued to have as one of their citizenship rights an entitlement not to become dependent on particular people. If it is part of my citizenship that the state will assist me when I am ill why should it not assist me when I become dependent or when my mother does so? If, in return for taxes, the state contracts with me to protect my property and the enjoyment of my privacy, why should it not also protect my time and freedom from obligation? The very fact that the state does offer some assistance with the care of the dependent is a recognition that these claims exist. But the current direction of social policy almost everywhere does not amount to a clarification of these issues but largely an attempt to limit some central aspects of all our citizenship rights by claiming, in questionable ways, to extend or protect others.

References

Arber, S and Gilbert, G (1989) 'Men: the forgotten carers.' *Sociology*, Vol 23, No 1, pp111–18.

Arnold, M and Schirmer, B (1990) *Gesundheit für ein Deutschland*. Köln, Deutscher Ärzte-Verlag.

Baldock, J and Ungerson, C (1991) 'What d'ya want if you don' want money?' In McLean, M and Groves, G (eds) *Womens' Issues in Social Policy*. Routledge.

Balke, K (1987) 'Selbsthilfegruppen und Unterstützung: die Wohlfahrtsverbände besetzen ein neues Feld.' In Boll, F and Olk, Th (eds) *Selbsthilfe und Wohlfahrtsverbände*. Freiburg, Lambertus Verlag.

Booth, T (1990) 'Taking the Plunge: contracting out?' *Community Care*, July 6th.

Buckingham, L (1990) 'Insurers poised to offer free enterprise alternative.' *The Guardian*, May 26th.

Bundesminister für Arbeit und Sozialordung (1989) *Die Gesundheitsreform*. Bonn.

Chambers, G (1988) *The Health Systems of the European Community Countries*. Luxembourg, European Parliament Directorate General for Research.

Cm 849 (1989) *Caring for People: community care in the next decade and beyond*. HMSO.

Dahrendorf, R (1988) 'Citizenship and modern social conflict.' In Holmes, R and Eliot, M (eds) *The British Constitution: 1688–1988*. Macmillan.

Davies, B (1989) 'Financing Long-term Social Care: challenges for the nineties.' *Social Policy and Administration*, Vol 22, No 2, pp97–114.

Deakin, N, Jeffries, A, Meehan, E and Twine, F (1990) *New Perspectives on Citizenship*. New Waverley Papers, Social Policy Series No 3. Edinburgh, University of Edinburgh.

de Jouvenal, H (1989) *Europe's Ageing Population: trends and challenges to 2025*. Butterworth and Co.

Dieck, M (1988) 'Mehr Pflegehilfen? Oder: Demnächst Familiale Pflegepflicht wie im alten China?, *Theorie und Praxis der Sozialen Arbeit*, No 4, pp130–36.

Dieck, M (1990) 'Politics for elderly people in the FRG.' In Jamieson, A and Illsley, R (eds) *Contrasting European Policies for the Care of Older People*. Avebury.

DSS, Department of Social Security (1989) *Social Security Statistics 1989*. HMSO.

Esping-Andersen, G (1990) *The Three Worlds of Welfare Capitalism*. Polity Press.

Freer, C (1988) 'Old myths: frequent misconceptions about the elderly.' In Wells, N and Freer, C (eds) *The Ageing Population: burden or challenge?* The Macmillan Press.

Freier, D (1989) 'Soziale Dienstleistungen zwischen Reglementierung und Wettbewerb.' *Nachrichtendienst dzes Deutschen Vereins für öffentliche und private Fürsorge*, Heft 11, pp369–77.

Friedman, M (1962) *Capitalism and Freedom*. University of Chicago Press.

George, M (1990) 'An age-old concern: insurers aiming to fill the breach between the public purse and the rising cost of looking after the elderly.' *The Guardian*, October 6th.

George, V and Wilding, P (1984) *The Impact of Social Policy*. Routledge and Kegan Paul.

Green, H (1988) *Informal Carers*. General Household Survey 1985, No 15, supplement A. HMSO.

Griffiths, Sir R (1988) *Community Care: agenda for action. A report to the Secretary of State for Social Services*. HMSO.

Haag, G and Schneider, U (1989) 'Armut in Alter: Einkommen, Wohnen, Gesundheit und soziale Kontakte alter Menschen in der Bundesrepublik.' *Blätter der Wohlfartspflege*, No 11/12, pp321–30.

Hurd, D (1988) 'Citizenship in Tory democracy.' *New Statesman and New Society*, 29th April.

Jamieson, A (1990) 'Informal care in Europe.' In Jamieson, A and Illsley, R (eds) *Contrasting European Policies for the Care of Older People*. Avebury.

Johansson, L (1985) *Informell Kontra Offentlig Äldreomsorg: några data frå ULF-studien 1980/81*. Göteborg, Nordiska Hälsvådshögskolan.

Johnson, N (1987) *The Welfare State in Transition: the theory and practise of welfare pluralism*. Wheatsheaf Books.

Judge, K (1980) 'An Introduction to the Economic Theory of Pricing.' In Judge, K (ed) *Pricing the Social Services*. Macmillan.

Keane, J (ed) (1988) *Civil Society and the State: new European perspectives*. Verso.

Keane, J (1988) *Democracy and Civil Society*. London, Verso.

Kraan, R, Baldock, J, Davies, B, Evers, A, Johansson, L, Knapen, M, Thorlund, M and Tunissen, C (1990) *Care for the Elderly: significant innovations in three European countries*. Vienna, Campus/Westview.

Lagergren, M, Lundh, L, Orkam, M and Sanne, C (1984) *Time to Care*. Pergamon Press.

Lagergren, M (1987) 'Employment, economy and care in Sweden by the year 2000.' *Social Science and Medicine*, Vol 25, No 2, pp103–10.

LeGrand, J and Robinson, R (1984) 'Privatisation and the welfare state: an introduction.' In LeGrand, J and Robinson, R (eds) *Privatisation and the Welfare State*. Allen and Unwin.

Lindquist, B (1989) *Statement by the Minister of Family Affairs Concerning the Disabled and the Elderly*. Stockholm, Ministry of Health and Social Affairs, 22nd May.

Marshall, T (1950) *Citizenship, Social Class and Other Essays*. Cambridge University Press.

Marshall, T (1965) *Social Policy*. Hutchinson University Library.

Marshall, T (1981) *The Right to Welfare and Other Essays*. Heinemann Education.

MHSA (1988) *The Government's Care for the Elderly Bill*. Stockholm, Ministry of Health and Social Affairs.

Midwinter, E (1986) *Caring for Cash: the issue of private domiciliary care*. Centre for Policy on Ageing.

Mishra, R (1989) 'The academic tradition in social policy: the Titmuss years.' In Bulmer, M, Lewis, J and Piachaud, D (eds) *The Goals of Social Policy*. Unwin Hyman.

MWHC (1988) *Changing Health Care in the Netherlands*. The Hague, Ministry of Welfare, Health and Cultural Affairs.

Neseker, H and Jung, C (1988) 'Ist der Pflegenotstand Beseitigt: die Pflegeabsicherung in der Debatte um die Gesundheitsreform?' *Nachrichtendienst des Deutschen Vereins für offenliche und private Fürsorge*, Heft 10, pp317–22.

Nordrup, G and Thorlund, M (1987) 'Att bo på institution: en inventering av miljö och sociala förhålanden.' *Socialstyrelsen Redovisar*, No 2, pp12–59.

OECD (1988) *Ageing Populations: the social policy implications*. Paris, Organisation for Economic Cooperation and Development.

Offe, C (1987) 'Democracy against the Welfare State: structural foundations of neoconservative political opportunities.' *Political Theory*, Vol 15, No 4, pp501–37.

Oliver, M (1990) *The Politics of Disablement*. Macmillan Education.

OPCS (1989) *General Household Survey 1986*. HMSO.

Parker, G (1990) *With Due Care and Attention: a review of research on informal care*, 2nd edition. Family Policy Studies Centre.

Paton, C (1990) 'The Prime Minister's review of the National Health Service and the 1989 white paper Working for Patients.' In Manning, N and Ungerson, C (eds) *Social Policy Review 1989–90*. Longman.

Plant, R and Barry, N (1990) *Citizenship and Rights in Thatcher's Britain: two views*. Institute of Economic Affairs.

Qureshi, H, Challis, D, Davies, B (1989) *Helpers in Case-managed Community Care*. Gower.

Regus, M and Trenk-Hinterberger, P (1985) 'Armutspolitik und Krankheit im Alter: Deprofessionalisierung und Privatisierung der Pflegehilfe.' In Leibfried, S and Tennstedt, F (eds) *Die Spaltung des Sozialstaats*. Frankfurt, Suhrkamp-Verlag.

Salamon, L (1987) 'Of market failure, voluntary failure and third party government: towards a theory of government-nonprofit relations in the modern welfare state.' *Journal of Voluntary Action Research*, No 1.

Schierbeck, O (1990) 'The high price of life in Utopia.' *The Guardian*, 30th November.

Shchwitzer, K-P and Speigner, W (1987) 'The growing importance of care for the elderly in the GDR.' In Evers, A (ed) *Towards Better Links and Balances between Social and Health Services in Care for the Elderly*. Vienna, Eurosocial.

Statistisches Bundesamt (1988) *Sozialhilfe 1986*. Stuttgart.

Sundström, G (1984) 'De Gamla, deras anhöriga och hemtjänsten.' *Socialhögsklan*, Nok 22.

Taylor, R (1988) 'The elderly as members of society: an examination of social differences in the elderly population.' In Wells, N and Freer, C (eds) *The Ageing Population: burden or challenge?* The Macmillan Press.

Titmuss, R (1968) 'Trends in social policy: health.' In Titmuss, R *Commitment to Welfare*. Unwin University Books.

Thorslund, M (1991) 'The increasing number of very old will change the Swedish model of welfare.' *Social Science and Medicine* (forthcoming).

Turner, B (1986) *Citizenship and Capitalism: the debate over reformism*. Allen and Unwin.

Twigg, J, Atkin, K, Perring, C (1990) *Carers and Services: a review of research*. HMSO.

Ungerson, C (1987) *Policy is Personal: sex, gender and informal care*. Tavistock.

Winkler, G (ed) (1990) *Sozialreport 90: Daten und Fakten zur sozialen Lage in der DDR*. Berlin-Ost, Verlag der Akademie der Wissenschaften.

8 The making of European social policy: developments leading to the European Social Charter

John Ditch

The character of European social policy

It is worth reflecting on the reasons for the subordinate status of social policy within the European Community and for the apparent lack of progress in this area. The founding treaties are inherently laissez-faire in character and provide only a broad commitment to social progress. The Treaty of Paris, which established the European Coal and Steel Community in 1951, has a commitment to the improvement of living and working conditions for employees in each of the two industries and establishes a scheme for the resettlement and re-training of workers. The later Treaty of Rome, which established the European Economic Community, was even less interventionist. However Articles 3, 117, 118, 119 and 123–128 all related explicitly to social policy issues. Nevertheless, social policy activities during this time were structured around a number of central themes such as the promotion of economic growth, labour mobility, social security harmonisation, equal pay and the operation of the European Social Fund.

The decision-making process of the European Communities has always been complex and a necessary, but delicate, balance between national interest and common purpose. Given the institutional fragmentation in the 1960s, between Council, Commission,

Parliament, European Court, and Economic and Social Committee, it is hardly surprising that there was a tendency towards institutional atrophy. Specifically the Council of the European Communities, representing national interest, was reluctant to follow any lead shown by the Commission; the European Parliament was little more than an assembly without a real purchase on the policy agenda. Substantively, economic policy and economic objectives for the Community as a whole were deemed to have priority over other policy areas with the consequence that, insofar as there was any priority accorded to social policy at this time, it was as an adjunct to economic policy objectives.

Social policies derive from national experience, history and culture such that, for example, France has an emphasis on the family and Germany places emphasis on workers and the work ethic. In addition social policy is an area where the Treaties preserve considerable measure of autonomy for Member States. The European Commission was vested with the critical role of cultivating a coincidence of interest between Member States and did so by straight argument but backed its assertions with comparative and analytical studies and an annual report on the development of the social situation. To that extent the European Commission was and remains the dynamo for developments in the area of European social policy.

For many who encounter the European Community for the first time, and in particular discussions about its developing social policy, there is a rather baffling encounter with Euro-language. One of the more confusing aspects of this topic is that as the limitations of individual languages are revealed in the Tower of Babel (otherwise known as the Berlaymont Building in Brussels), so a whole new nomenclature has been developed for social policy making. Euro-speak is constantly referring to 'subsidiarity', 'convergence', 'harmonisation', 'partnership', 'observatory', 'exclusion', 'concertation' and 'dumping'. Elegance may have more to do with sartorial style than purity of thought in the context of the new Europe; indeed, many Community documents appear to have been translated by a machine (and in some cases written by one). An attempt is made in this chapter to explain their meaning in context but in some instances this must remain an ideal rather than a reality, such is the almost mystical nature of their explanation (Heidenheimer, 1986).

Throughout the early part of the 1960s there was a series of political difficulties within the EEC which impeded progress in many substantive policy areas: for example De Gaulle boycotted Community meetings throughout 1965. There was considerable disenchantment after the UK had twice been refused membership, first in 1963 and then in 1967.

Treaty provisions relating to European Social Policy were vague and imprecise and this led to ambiguity and provided ample opportunity for the deployment of delayed tactics by unenthusiastic Council representatives. Finally, in a period of relative affluence the reality of social problems in Europe may have seemed a little unreal and therefore not urgent (though this does not explain the turbulent situation in France or Germany in 1968). Had problems been perceived as being more real, and more importantly, the institutional framework of the European Community designed so as to facilitate maximum participation, it is possible that more progress in the area of European Social Policy could have been made.

Towards the end of the 1960s there was increased dissatisfaction with the apparent lack of progress with respect to a wide range of policy issues in the European Community. This change in attitude can be summed up as being somewhat more compassionate towards those with special problems (migrant workers, women, disabled people etc); and with criticism of the Community's ability to distribute the wealth equitably it was appearing to generate; an unwillingness to bear the costs and diswelfares of economic growth; and a concern to improve the image of the Community and thereby make it more acceptable to prospective new members including the UK, Denmark, Norway and the Republic of Ireland. Specifically the following themes were receiving more attention in both academic and policy literature:

Economic growth in the 1960s, although impressive at the aggregate level, had been uneven. Spatially, the lower Rhine conurbations had done well but the South of France, the Mezzogiorno of Italy and West Berlin had not done so well. Women, migrants, certain young and old workers and disabled persons (despite Treaty provisions and regulations) were receiving a disproportionately lower share of the employment market.

The social costs of economic growth in the form of pollution, health and safety at work, job security, work of participation and repetitive work processes were being increasingly recognised and publicised. Whereas the EEC did generate wealth it was at the expense of costs for individuals. Macro-economic processes to do with, for example, the restructuring of CAP and the associated move to more capital rather than labour-intensive agricultural production; technological developments resulting in firms becoming more efficient and less labour-intensive; structural changes associated with market completion and in particular the elimination of tariff and trade restrictions opening up sectors to acute competition with the result that some outmoded enterprises collapsed. Altogether these changes had great costs for individuals in where and how they were to be employed.

The EC needs a 'human face'

By the end of the 1960s the early and relatively easy phase of European integration has been concluded; the easy objectives had been attained and this had led to a decline in enthusiasm within and for the Community. There was consequently a need for the Community to be reinvigorated, which could be done by making it more attractive. Also opportunities had to be found for greater participation by social partners in Community policy and decision-making processes.

The resignation of President De Gaulle created an opportunity for new discussions about the composition and future of the EEC. The prospective members (UK, Republic of Ireland, Denmark and Norway) had electorates who were wise to both the strengths and the weaknesses of the Community and they therefore needed to be fully convinced that there were likely to be both material and social benefits flowing from membership. In this context a strengthened social policy was to be important. The image of the EEC as a businessman's club was no longer regarded as adequate or satisfactory; there was a need for the Community to develop 'a human face'. The political will to affect the necessary changes existed and was symbolised in the good personal relations between Chancellor Brandt, George Pompidou and Edward Heath in the very early 1970s, each of whom was secure politically, with sound domestic economies and committed to the European ideal.

The new commitment to the Community culminated in the Paris Summit of October 1972 at which agreement was reached to proceed towards economic and monetary union. In addition it was agreed to establish a Regional Development Fund and to promote a Social Action Programme concerned with the promotion of full and better employment, an increased role for the social partners in economic policy making and a commitment to the improvement of living and working conditions.

The lengthy and complex programme, full of good intentions, was not based on specific Treaty articles and this created juridical problems. Progress was dependent on political will which, although present in 1972, was to evaporate rapidly under the twin pressures of inflation and unemployment generated by the collapse of the US dollar, the Yom Kippur War, and the Miners' Strike in the UK; a process reinforced by the complete change of political leadership in France, Germany and the UK during the same period. Altogether these factors saw a significant reduction in commitment to the deepening of European integration. However the Council of Ministers did adopt the Social Action Programme in January 1974. It was, rather like the European Commission Charter of Social Rights adopted in December 1989, approval of a general idea, with specific measures being adopted on an individual basis at subsequent meetings of the Council of Ministers. As Michael Shanks, the then Director General of the relevant directorate of the Commission was later to write, 'its tone was pragmatic rather than ideological' (Shanks, 1977).

The remainder of the 1970s and early 1980s saw little progress in the area of social policy. A combination of economic problems and political indifference brought the EC to the verge of stagnation. It was in response to the institutional lethargy of this period that commitment to the Single European Act was sought.

The Single European Act

As early as 1981 the French had proposed a European revival involving the designation of a social area as an essential pre-condition for European development. Their specific proposal involved three principal objectives:

(i)   the placing of employment at the very heart of the Community's social policy by deepening co-operation and re-organising EC policies;

(ii) enhancing social dialogue at both Community and national levels within individual companies and elsewhere;

(iii) improving co-operation and consultation on matters of social protection.

The appointment of Jacques Delors to be the President of the European Commission, in 1984, gave new impetus to the process of reconstructing and developing the European Community. The Fontainbleau Summit of June 1984 was a critical turning-point in the history of the Community in that the difficult issues of the British contribution to the EC budget and the admission of Spain and Portugal to the Community were resolved and it was possible, with the imminent arrival of Jacques Delors, to move to a consideration of new policy areas. The incoming Commission of January 1985 identified a new programme consisting of four themes. First was the announcement of 1992, or more specifically 1 January 1993, as the goal for completing the internal market. The second objective was concerned to prepare and subsequently ratify a Single European Act (SEA) to complement the Treaty of Rome. The SEA was to add to the Treaty of Rome provisions especially with respect to working environment issues, social dialogue and the promotion of economic and social cohesion. The SEA entered into effect on 1 July 1987 after ratification in each Member State and is now regarded as being a part of the Treaty of Rome. The third element in the Delors package was a commitment to reform the CAP and revise EC finances. It also proposed both the reform and the doubling of the overall budget for the Structural Funds and the revival of social dialogue.

In addition certain institutional reforms associated with the SEA must not be overlooked. In particular the provision for introducing Qualified Majority Voting within the Council of Ministers was a highly effective and imaginative way of overcoming some of the blockages which had characterised debates at that level over many years. In addition there were to be an increased role and new responsibilities for the European Parliament. Taken together these institutional developments were to be of critical significance for the future of Europe.

The six key objectives of the Single European Act are:

1 the achievement of the Single Market by January 1993;
2 economic and social cohesion;
3 common policy of scientific and technological development;
4 strengthening of the European Monetary System;
5 introduction of a European Social Dimension;
6 co-ordinated action on the environment.

The social dimension of the process associated with the completion of the Single Market is to be seen as the product of two reinforcing tendencies. First, broad demographic and socioeconomic trends are necessarily and inevitably generating new problems, relationships and opportunities: these require new forms and levels of social intervention. Second, the legislative provisions and policy commitment associated with the SEA (as incorporated in the Treaty of Rome) are a partial response to the first trend but are also facilitating new social arrangements. Although it is considered highly probably that at an aggregate level there will be an increase in income, a reduction in price level and a boost to employment, it is increasingly recognised that costs and benefits will not be evenly distributed across regions or population groups.

To counter these anticipated consequences, and as early as 1987, a programme of action to assist the most vulnerable communities, regions and social groups had been adopted and regarded as entirely consistent with the economic objectives of the SEA. Specifically the intention was to create a citizens' Europe. As John Palmer has put it:

> The objective of the SEA, as the Commission put it at the time of the Brussels Summit, would be to ensure that the Single European Market brought wide benefits to all the people of the Community and specifically to help secure an improvement in the living and working conditions of Community citizens. This was particularly important for the poorer, mainly, though not exclusively, southern European countries

some of whom had feared that the abolition of national controls would place their industries at risk to the more powerful economies of the north.

(Palmer, 1989, p16).

The costs and benefits of the Single Market

The new commitment to the reinvigoration of Europe and in particular the attainment of a Single European Market had been based largely upon the need for a political solution to a series of particularly pressing problems. There was a remarkable absence of ·sound empirical evidence on the costs of not operating a complete, open and single market. It was only in 1986 that Lord Cockfield, the UK-sponsored Commissioner with responsibility for Single Market issues, invited Paolo Cecchini to organise a large and comprehensive study of the costs associated with the non-achievement of a Single Market. No less than 24 separate research teams, led by academics and consultants from throughout the EC, contributed to the production of a mountain of research evidence totalling over 20,000 pages of public material. Among their principal conclusions were that the total potential economic gain at an aggregate level to the Community would be in the order of ECU200 billion or more, expressed in 1988 prices. This would be equivalent to approximately 5 per cent of the Community's Gross Domestic Product. This represents savings due not only to the removal of trade, technical and physical barriers which directly affect intra-EC trade but also to the benefits to be gained from removing obstacles which currently hinder entry to different national markets and the free play of competition Community-wide. Downstream positive implications were thought to include the depression of consumer prices by approximately 6 per cent together with an increase in output, employment and living standards. Specifically, somewhere between 2 and 5 million new jobs, depending upon the micro-economic policies accompanying the 1992 programme, were projected.

However, even at this stage it was apparent that the aggregate benefits and the anticipated costs would not be evenly borne either socially or spatially. The completion of the internal market will make certain regions more attractive than others with the result that resources (human, material and financial) may move to areas of greatest economic advantage. The result could very well be that existing differences in levels of prosperity between regions will be exacerbated rather than reduced as the Single Market develops. The lower Rhine conurbation and the south-east of England may very well be better placed to benefit from economic expansion by virtue of their central location, good infrastructure and existing strengths in both industry and services. The Commission, being sensitive to the social and economic implications of such divergence, explicitly committed itself to the promotion of social and economic cohesion. The social dimension of the internal market must be seen, therefore, in this context.

The UK Government's view

The European social dimension is to be seen as an integral part of the programme established to achieve the Single European Market. However it must also be recognised that there are differences of emphasis between Member States and between, in particular, the United Kingdom Government and partners within the Council of Ministers, the Commission and European Parliament. Whereas the EC regard the social dimension as an integral part of the process which will achieve the Single Market, demonstrating that the Community has a 'human face', which in turn will help bind the social partners and in particular the Trade Union Movement to the process of market completion, the United Kingdom Government takes a somewhat different view. There can be no question but that the UK is committed to the achievement of a Single Market and believes in the social dimension to the extent to which new employment opportunities will be created. Moreover, and consistent with neo-classical economic principles, there is an assumption that the benefits of economic growth and employment opportunity will bring their own welfare rewards. However the UK Government is disinclined to support the EC to promote social programmes which are regarded as inhibiting the potential for economic growth and development. For example Mrs Thatcher in a speech at Bruges in September 1988 indicated her opposition to what she referred to as 'exercises in social engineering'. She elaborated by asserting that with the development of a European social dimension the European Community was becoming 'entangled in a network of rules and rigid regulations which would stifle enterprise.' Throughout, the British Government has been anxious to promote a partial conception of social policy, centred around labour market flexibility and deregulation. In the early 1980s the UK Government proposed, formally, the Action Plan for Employment Growth and succeeded in steering it to near the centre of the policy agenda. Despite having secured the joint sponsorship of the Irish and Italian Governments, and the endorsement of the Council of Ministers (following some supplementary drafting to include explicit reference to social dialogue) the document has only been referred to periodically. The UK Government's attempt to take the lead with anti-dirigiste measures has been outflanked by the Commission.

Real risks associated with the social dimension

Whereas the Cecchini Report anticipates a significant increase in aggregate levels of employment and income, more recent accounts have drawn attention to the regional imbalances that will inevitably follow. The Padoa-Schioppa Report notes:

> Regions tend towards an equalisation of incomes per head as a result of the mobility of capital and labour only under severe and unrealistic conditions, such as the absence of economies of scale or of specific locational factors influencing the investment decision. When these and other conditions are not satisfied the outcome in terms of regional convergence or divergence becomes uncertain. Any easy extrapolation of 'invisible hand' ideas to the real world would be unwarranted in the light of economic history and theory.

In this context a number of substantive risks may be identified: specifically, there will be spatial and sectoral impacts with peripheral and declining regions likely to be especially disadvantaged. Second, there is concern about conditions of employment which may deteriorate in the context of labour market fragmentation and increased flexibility. Employees in such situations are not so well protected as those in full time, primary sector, employment. Third, there is a concern about income levels particularly for those in vulnerable sectors and in the transitional period.

Economic and labour market restructuring has focused attention on a number of themes, many drawn together in the draft Commission Action Programme in Relation to the Implementation of the Community Charter of Basic Social Rights for Workers (1989). These include the legal position of workers (and new forms of contract); the recruitment and dismissal of workers; the reorganisation of working time and the protection/integration of vulnerable social groups. Again, the Commission expressed itself trenchantly:

> Solidarity with the least-favoured members of society is more essential than ever, particularly in our search for a more flexible labour market; this erosion of human resources must be stopped, for in the longer term it will undermine the flexibility of the economy as a whole and the stability of society in general: we have in fact a timebomb on our hands.

The idea for a platform of Fundamental Social Rights emerged during the Belgian Presidency of 1987 as a partial and rather opportunist response to the UK initiative: Action Plan for Employment Growth. The thinking was that not only would individual workers and citizens have rights incorporated in an EC document, but that it would, thereby, be a stimulus for further policy initiatives in this area. Specifically, it was felt that such protection would help prevent 'social dumping' by individual companies, sectors or states. The proposal is consistent with the recommendations of the Beretta Report (1987, Economic and Social Committee) which identifies social dialogue as the prime objective and a necessary precondition to the convergence or alignment of social security systems. Unsurprisingly there has been considerable opposition to the motion of a framework directive incorporating fundamental social aspects: Northern EC countries have resisted attempts to construct a rigid system of social legislation whereas the Southern EC countries are most concerned about the cost implications associated with the imposition of new standards.

Reformed European structural funds

The EC attaches considerable importance to the reformed Structural Funds and regards them as being, in the words of Commissioner Christopherson,

> ... one of the key components of the Community's economic and social cohesion so rightly advocated by the Single Act. Attainment of this objective necessitates the mobilisation of human resources, from now on facilitated by partnership, and of financial resources, now to be put to better use.
> (Into: Guide to Reform of The Community's Structural Funds, 1989).

A key element in the process which is designed to give effect to co-ordination is the principle of partnership, about which there is remaining dubiety in the relationship between the EC and the UK Government. The Framework Regulation for the reformed Structural Funds defines partnership as 'close consultation between the Commission, the Member States concerned and the competent authorities designated by the latter at national, regional, local or other level, with each party acting as a partner in pursuit of a common goal'. The principle of partnership is deemed to cover all elements of the process: preparation, financing, monitoring and assessment.

The principle of subsidiarity as applied to this area of activity ensures that Structural Fund activity is complementary to existing national and regional, measures. In addition to official dialogue between the Commission and the Member State (to 'increase efficiency through the sharing of tasks and a pooling of human resources . . .') there is an expectation on behalf of the EC (but resisted by the British Government) that dialogue and partnership should extend to 'the various economic and social partners (chambers of commerce, industry and agriculture, trade unions, employers, etc). This is a further aspect of partnership which can be fruitful and which should not be neglected' (Guide to Reform of Structural Funds, p15).

Social security and 1992

As far back as the Treaty of Rome, there was explicit recognition of the need to promote effective co-ordination in the area of social security. Article 51 refers:

> The Council shall, acting unanimously on a proposal from the Commission, adopt such measures in the field of social security as are necessary to provide freedom of movement for workers; to this end, it shall make arrangements to secure for migrant workers and their dependents . . . .

In the early days there was an assumption that harmonisation was to be the ultimate goal of Community policy making, and for two reasons: first, to minimise the opportunities for the distortion of competition, and second, to promote social cohesion and common standards. Indeed Article 117 explicitly calls for improved living and working conditions so as to make harmonisation possible.

Social expenditure in the EC increased significantly during the 1980s: from 559 becu in 1981 to 922 becu in 1987, representing a substantial proportion of individual Member States Gross National Products, ranging from 21.4 per cent in Greece to 39.9 per cent in the Netherlands. The scale of Member State Social Security expenditure amounts to 26 times the total EC budget and is financed by taxation of individuals and industry. As the House of Lords Select Committee expressed it: 'This must, at least in theory, carry implications for the working of the internal market, particularly for the free movement of labour' (HL Paper 12, Session 1987–88, p7).

The meaning of harmonisation

There is no legal definition and the concept is highly elastic. Sometimes the term approximation is used in lieu. But that merely begs a further question: is the approximation to be in the social or economic field? If it is to be the latter, that is to minimise distortions in competition, then the purpose is to reduce 'social costs' as a variable in the cost of labour. On the other hand, if the purpose is to being about better living standards (Article 117) by 'upward social harmonisation' then the focus is upon the level of social benefit.

Whereas the relationship between the two objectives is not, of necessity, mutually exclusive, it may in practice be impossible to pursue both objectives simultaneously due to the particular demographic characteristics and activity rates in particular countries.

The next step is to clarify the criteria according to which approximation will be pursued. Should there be reference to EC average benefit levels or contribution rates? or to the highest? or lowest? The consideration of such questions inevitably touches upon sensitive issues relating to national histories and values as they inform and structure different social security systems. There is no single model of income maintenance in the EC: some systems are universal (UK, Ireland, Denmark); some favour workers (Germany); some favour families (France). In addition, each national system is in the process of adaptation and reform: to cut across the trajectories of individual systems with an EC-wide programme would be to violate the development and sensitive adjustment of policy to local circumstance.

These appear, increasingly, to be insurmountable difficulties, such that harmonisation, as envisaged in 1957, no longer seems attainable – or, indeed, desirable. A more pragmatic tone has begun to permeate discussion about the future of European Social Security, with the EC cast in the role of agent-provocateur. Broad objectives are specified and new national programmes encouraged (if not by prescription, required) to converge. The policy emphasis has moved away from a concern with the means of social security, to one concerned with its objectives. In such circumstances greater co-ordination of social security should lead to greater social cohesion which, in turn should lead to more demands for more co-ordination of social security. In this context there is speculation that vox populi, at a European level, will encourage the pursuit of upward social harmonisation (See European Institute of Social Security, 1988.)

What impact will the completion of the Single Market have on social security?

A genuinely open, and unregulated, Single Market rekindles the possibility of a laissez-faire economy where the costs and benefits (being the inevitable and necessary by-product) of economic growth are unequally distributed. In such circumstances it is necessary to 'entail the re-establishment, at a higher level, of a system of guarantees – but a discipline as well – that no longer exists at the national level' (EISS, 1988, p39).

The EC's failure effectively to pursue the harmonisation of social security systems is in part the product of a deficient or ambiguous juridical base (as provided for in the Treaty). However another reason is the exaggerated concern with the mechanics of systems, schemes or the allocative mechanisms rather than an analysis of the principles and policies which underpin and inform such structures. The EISS paper (V/1653/EN-88) draws attention to the importance of this dichotomy and argues for a review of prospects for social security in the context of regulating the Internal Market.

Over the years the EC has moved to a position where mutual recognition (of diplomas and qualifications or technical standards) has facilitated greater openness. By extension, social security systems, being unique to each country, may be reciprocally recognised without their integrity being challenged: co-operation rather than co-optation is required. A part of this process and a precondition of further co-operation, is the appropriate, but extensive, exchange of information. The EC encourages this through its publications and networks of experts and national officials.

Contrary to general expectations the levels of migration have fallen over the past two decades. However, in the event of an increase in levels of economic activity and in particular a rise in the levels of employment, then the levels of migration will once again increase. Currently some 6 million citizens live and work in Member States other than their state of birth and 45 million workers live in frontier regions of Member States, either working in a different Member State than the one in which they reside or affected by the conditions in that neighbouring Member State.

The expectation is that the SEM will encourage a new wave of specialist migration (executives, researchers, consultants and other professionals). This migration will be complemented by EC programmes: Erasmus, Comett and Yes. Such migrants will tend to differential access to occupational or private pension schemes: this raises problems of pension portability.

Social dumping and the single market

There are long standing difficulties concerning its definition. It is, at heart, a problem to do with the costs and relative advantages associated with levels of social protection in competitive markets. Arguably, social dumpling is rather less to do with the actual level of social protection within Member States, than with wage costs, proportionate funding arrangements, and in particular the impact on employers.

The fear is that those countries with low wage costs (eg Greece and Portugal) will take competitive advantage of cost differential and attract mobile foreign investment. Conversely, it is argued, those with high wage and high protection economies, will be disadvantaged. The social charges borne by the employer represented 28.1 per cent of the worker's average wage cost in France and 33.5 per cent in Italy. However the actual cost (1735 Ecu per month in France and 1545 Ecu in Italy) is well below the total cost of 2008 Ecu in Germany, where the social charges are less, at 21 per cent. There is no coherent economic argument for the equalisation of social charges. Prediction in the light of such evidence is a most inexact science.

Labour cost is divided into direct costs (wages and salaries) and indirect costs (employers' social security contributions). Since the share of employers' contributions varies from country to country, so too does the total cost vary. However there is, according to

Eurostat, no significant correlation between unit cost of labour and structure of that cost. In other words, it would be presumptuous to '. . . infer from high rates of employer contributions in one country that the total cost of labour in that country will exceed the level of that cost in another country, where the rates of contribution are lower' (EISS, 1988 p71).

A frequently hypothesised scenario is one involving the Mediterranean countries taking advantage of their low wage costs to undercut the more prosperous (and generous) countries of the North. Indeed they might be encouraged to restrain the improvement of wages and social benefits, thereby effectively exporting unemployment to other EC countries. The response from the more prosperous countries might be to reduce their social and wage costs. As Teague has expressed it:

> Such retaliatory moves could trigger cost and price-reducing battles between the member-states, particularly in the more traditional product sectors which are price sensitive. An extensive price war would be highly destabilising for the Community's economy: effective demand would fall if governments restricted budgetary expenditure and adopted tight monetary policy, and the much needed drive to upgrade the quality of existing products, develop new products and master new production processes might be hindered as manager and government became more concerned with obtaining competitiveness through cost reductions. Overall, it is feared that there would be no winners from these policies, since all the member-states might experience a fall in employment.
>
> (Teague, 1989, p322).

There is an underlying fear that this trend would lead to a spatial division of labour and productive capacity: high-tech, high paid employment in the Northern countries and low-tech, low paid employment in the Southern countries.

However social dumping must be seen in the context of certain global trends, in addition to the completion of the Single Market, such as the introduction and use of new technology, effects of competition and world demand. In sectors likely to be affected by such macro-economic considerations, social dumping is unlikely to be a problem. But the same may not be said for labour intensive sectors such as construction, agri-foodstuffs, transport and public works. Employees recruited in one jurisdiction may be moved to fulfil the contractual obligations of employers in another jurisdiction.

But even if dumping proves to be a consideration, it remains to be seen which aspects of the social system will be most affected: wages, social security or health and safety? Most responsible argument, based on available evidence, does not consider social security as likely to be affected. Social costs, as a proportion of wage costs, in those most 'at risk' countries is on par with high wage economies.

Whereas the proportion of GDP assigned to social protection is low in Mediterranean countries, it is entirely comparable with such countries as America, Japan and Canada.

Differentials in wage costs are frequently offset by other factors such as level of productivity, geographical location, viability etc. As EISS report:

> The social dumping bogeyman gets trotted out when perhaps what we ought to be wondering about is how capable the less developed economies are of standing up to penetration by the big groups from the eighty industrialised countries. And lastly, even if their lower wage costs were to provide these poorer countries with development opportunities, isn't that a matter for rejoicing in the name of this 'economic and social cohesion' that everyone says they want? Wouldn't it be defeating the object of the exercise to create legal obstacles to their economic development at the very time when the decision is being taken to double the amount of structural funds?
>
> (EISS, 1978, pp76–77)

European Social Charter

Against this background, and over the past eighteen months, debate within the Community about the social dimension has focused down to the Commissions's Fundamental Charter of Social Rights, a document which has been consistently opposed by the United Kingdom Government. However, despite this opposition, the document was adopted by a majority of 11 to 1 at the Strasbourg Summit of December 1989 and the Commission is currently drafting individual proposals for consideration by Council over the next two years. The opposition of the United Kingdom Government will be insufficient to prevent the further development and deployment of the European social dimension.

The origins of the Charter go back to 1981 when the French President proposed the development of a 'European social area', a theme which was not adopted until 1987 when the Belgian Minister of Labour saw its potential within the framework of corporatist policy making strategy. He talked of the need to '. . . establish a platform of basic rights which would give the two sides of industry a stable, common basis from which they could negotiate to guarantee that the internal market has a real social dimension.' A year later, in a speech to the European Trades Union Confederation, Jacques Delors (President of the European Commission) underlined the importance of the idea's potential. He spoke of '. . . a minimum platform of guaranteed social rights with a view to the implementation of the single European market of 1992. This mandatory platform could be negotiated between the two sides of industry and then incorporated into Community legislation. It would serve as a basis for the social dialogue and for strengthening European cohesion.'

Successive European Council meetings (at Hanover, Rhodes and Madrid) accepted and ratified this objective, thereby confirming the legitimacy and importance of the social dimension of 1992. As a result the various components of the Community's decision making machine were brought into the process. In November 1988 the matter was referred to the Community's Economic and Social Committee which adopted an Opinion in February 1989 proposing that existing rights and obligations incorporated in conventions of the International Labour Organisation and the Social Charter and Code of Social Security of the Council of Europe be affirmed as part of EC legislation. Similarly, the European Parliament also advocated the formal adoption of existing Conventions but in addition wanted to establish a firmer legal base.

In the light of these background reports and opinions a draft Community Charter of Fundamental Social Rights was drawn up by the Commission, published on 30 May 1989 and considered by the Ministers of Labour and Social Affairs at their meeting on 12 June 1989, held in Luxembourg. Their conclusions, with the agreement of eleven delegations, became part of the conclusions of the Heads of State summit held at Madrid in later June 1989.

The UK Government did not/does not consider the Charter to be necessary, indeed that it will be likely to inhibit the creation and retention of jobs. Over the summer of 1989 further consultations (via a French Presidency ad hoc working party) took place which concluded in the adoption of a formal Draft Community Charter of Fundamental Social Rights in October 1989 (COM[89]471 final 2 October 1989). The key change was to restrict reference to workers' rights rather than citizens' rights. The UK Government continued to oppose the draft charter: Mrs. Thatcher was firmly of the view that job creation was being displaced as the top priority in Community policy, that competitiveness was being threatened and subsidiarity and diversity insufficiently respected. The thrust of the Draft Charter was deemed to run counter to the objectives of UK policy over the past decade. Moreover the UK questioned the legal competence and authority of the EC in this area of activity, for although the Commission had not proposed a legally binding document there was concern that it would entail legally binding consequences.

The Social Affairs Ministers met in Brussels on 30 October 1989 to discuss the Draft Charter: the UK remained in sole opposition as it was agreed that a (slightly amended) text should be considered by Heads of State at the Strasbourg summit in December 1989. Meanwhile it was agreed that the Commission would publish, in advance of the summit, a three-year Action Plan for the implementation of the Charter.

The debates which took place in the months preceding the Strasbourg summit resulted in some crucial amendments and compromises to the Charter. The German government was especially keen that binding minimum standards be incorporated within the Charter, as a bulwark against the possibility of social dumping. However, in general the document was weakened, with greater responsibility being placed on individual member states and the two sides of industry rather than the Commission: which was consistent with the application of the principle of subsidiarity which proclaims that no responsibility should be held by a superior authority if it can be more effectively and appropriately retained at a subordinate level. References to 'citizens' were restyled as 'workers' and a proposal that 'a decent wage shall be established, particularly at the level of the basic wage' was deleted, as was a proposal that 'every citizen of the European Community shall have a right to adequate social protection'. Nevertheless, the Charter as adopted by the Council of Ministers at Strasbourg in December 1989, is a 'solemn declaration' which identifies a number of principles including:

(i)   wide-ranging rights associated with freedom of movement for workers, subject to provisions relating to public order, public safety and public health. Family reunification is to be encouraged; the reciprocal recognition of qualifications facilitated; improvement of living and working conditions for frontier workers.

(ii)   an 'equitable wage' (sufficient to enable a decent standard of living) in each member state; right of access to public placement (employment) services free of charge;

(iii)   an improvement in living and working conditions; a limit on working hours in a week, night and shift work; right to annual paid leave and weekly/regular rest period, applicable to all workers whether full-time or otherwise; right to a contract for all workers;

(iv)   right to adequate social protection for all citizens including a minimum income for any workers who are not employed or entitled to benefit or who do not have adequate means of subsistence;

(v)   a right to belong (or not) to a trade union; freedom to negotiate and conclude collective agreements; right to strike (or not) without suffering personal or occupational damage;

(vi)   right to vocational training throughout working life; emphasis on the study leave and access to education on the same basis as nationals;

(vii)   equal treatment for men and women to be assured; emphasis on the reconciliation of occupational and family responsibilities;

(viii)   a right to information, consultation and participation for workers especially concerning new technology, company restructuring and collective redundancies;

(ix)   health and safety at the workplace;

(x)   a minimum age for employment of 15; a guarantee of training during working hours for all under 18 years;

(xi)   the elderly, at the time of retirement, to have resources sufficient to provide a decent standard of living;

(xii)   measures to facilitate social and professional integration of the disabled.

Conclusion

The Action Programme, presented by the European Commission, and representing the core of Community social policy activities for the foreseeable future, was presented (in late 1989) in the form of thirteen separate chapters being concerned with the various aspects of the Social Dimension and the attainment of social and economic cohesion within the EC. Each chapter summarised progress to date and proceeded to outline intended work and the form of legal instrument (Opinion, Recommendation, Directive or Regulation) proposed. Throughout there was an emphasis on the principle of subsidiarity (in response to representations from the UK Government), but the Commission declined to specify the legal base for action, ie whether to proceed on the basis of those Treaty Articles which will require Qualified Majority Voting as opposed to Articles requiring unanimity at Council meetings. The programme mostly concerns those measures likely to promote social cohesion by developing, for example, social security arrangements for migrant workers, freedom of movement, working conditions, vocational training and health and safety in the workplace. Each proposal will be considered by the national governments, employers' representatives and the trades unions: progress will be slow but, notwithstanding the reluctance of the British Government, the place of social policy within the Single Market project is firmly assured. Increasingly and inevitably there will be a need for social policy analysts and policy makers to take greater and greater cognisance of developments throughout the European Community. The frame of reference is now clearly and firmly beyond the boundaries of the nation state: the age of comparative social policy has arrived.

References

Brewster, C and Teague, P (1989) *European Community Social Policy.* Institute of Personnel Management.

Cecchini, P (1988) *1992 The European Challenge – The Benefits of a Single Market.* Gower.

Collins, D (1975) *The European Communities. The Social Policy of the First Phase.* Vols 1 and 2. Martin Robertson.

Commission of the European Communities (1986) *Social Europe: Special Edition on the Social Dimension of the Internal Market.*

European Institute of Social Security (1988) *The role of Social Security in the context of the completion of the Internal Market by 1992.* Report for the Commission of the European Communities (V/1653/EN-88).

Heidenheimer, A J (1986) 'Politics, Policy and Policy as concepts in English and continental languages: an attempt to explain divergences.' *Review of Politics.* Winter, pp3–30.

House of Commons Employment Committee Draft Community Charter of Fundamental Social Rights. Minutes of evidence 17 October 1989 HC 577-i.

Marin Report (1988) *The Social Dimension of the Internal Market.* Commission of the European Communities.

Padoa-Schioppa, T et al (1987) *Efficiency, Stability and Equity.* Oxford University Press.

Palmer, J (1989) *1992 and Beyond.* Commission of the European Communities.

Select Committee on the European Communities. *A Community Social Charter with Evidence.* Session 89–90 (HL Paper 6).

Shanks, M (1977) *European Social Policy Today and Tomorrow.* Pergamon.

Teague, P (1989) 'European Community Labour Market Harmonisation.' *Journal of Public Policy*, Vol 9, No 1, pp1–33.

Venturini, P (1988) *1992: The European Social dimension.* Commission of the European Communities.

9 European Community social policy and the UK*

Martin Baldwin-Edwards and Ian Gough

*We are indebted to Simon Bulmer, University of Manchester for his helpful comments on an earlier draft of this manuscript.

Introduction

The prime task of this chapter is to present an 'audit' of the impact of EC membership on the UK in various fields of social policy. This immediately raises an issue of definition since 'in the Community and generally in continental Europe the term "social policy" has a much wider content than in Britain, covering not only social security and welfare issues but also, critically, industrial relations and collective bargaining' (Grahl and Teague, 1990, p185). Here we treat it in the narrower, British sense, yet even so several social policy areas, such as occupational health and safety and initiatives on poverty and disability, are excluded. 'Impact' is assessed using a crude counterfactual, of Britain not having acceded to the EC. Essentially we present here a positivist exercise, but a necessary preliminary one if the implications of '1992' for social policy are to be properly assessed. However, we conclude with some more speculative analysis as to why the UK is so often at odds with EC developments in the domain of social policy.

European Community policy

The Treaty basis

We begin with a brief survey of the bases and nature of EC interventions in the domain of social policy thus defined. The Treaty of Rome establishes a common market; that is, in addition to a customs union, there must be free movement of the factors of production. Relatively unimpeded freedoms of movement of persons, capital, services and goods constitute the 'four freedoms' of the EEC Treaty.

Certain social policy considerations follow logically from this. The principle of non-discrimination on the grounds of (EC) nationality is embedded in EEC Article 7 and more precisely in Article 48(2). Furthermore, there are specific measures for the achievement of integration goals. These include the co-ordination of national social insurance schemes (Article 51) for the benefit of migrant workers; the exchange of young workers (Article 50); and promotion, by the Commission, of co-operation in the fields of employment, labour law and working conditions, vocational training, social security, occupational health, and rights of association and collective bargaining between employers and workers (Articles 117/8). The European Social Fund is established by Articles 123–127, and is charged with the task of promoting employment opportunities, along with geographical and occupational mobility within the Community; Article 128 requires the Commission to promote a Community vocational training policy.

Article 119 establishes the principle of equal pay (of women) for equal work; this is the only policy without an obvious 'integrationist' rationale. In fact, its inclusion was at the insistence of the French, who feared lower economic competitiveness owing to their own higher female pay (Brewster and Teague, 1989, p54).

The Single European Act, 1987 amends the Treaty of Rome, and makes several changes to social policy provisions. In particular, new powers are conferred in the areas of health and safety in the workplace (Article 118A), social dialogue and collective agreements (Article 118B), and reform of the Structural Funds (Article 130A to 130E). The new Co-operation Procedure is established by Article 149, whilst Articles 8A and 8B allow for majority voting for the purpose of attaining the Single Market. Derogation is made in Article 100A for fiscal measures, free movement of persons and 'the rights of employed persons'.[1]

Community legislation and policy implementation

The principal sources of Community law are the Treaties, secondary legislation, international agreements entered into by Community institutions, and judicial legislation (ie the case law of the European Court of Justice). Basically, secondary legislation is needed to flesh out Treaty provisions and can take the legally-binding forms of Regulations, Directives or Decisions. Regulations have 'direct effect' (ie can be invoked by individuals), Directives are addressed to member states requiring implementation by national legislation, and Decisions are addressed to states or legal personalities. Although theoretically very different, these forms have considerable overlap owing to the Court's interpretations, some of which we examine below.

The EEC legislative policy process is well-known, and we

shall not repeat it here (see eg Nugent, 1989, pp54–207). The **implementation** process is less clear, especially with regard to the evolution of social policy considerations. There are four types of Community institution which have played significant roles in the implementation and interpretation of Community legislation: the Commission, the European Court of Justice (ECJ), various administrative bodies and certain advisory committees.

The Commission's function includes guardianship of the Treaties, that is, a role of 'legal watchdog', whereby it can under EEC Article 169 bring action against member states for non-compliance with Treaty obligations.

The **European Court of Justice** is not responsible for day-to-day enforcement of Community law: this is the responsibility of domestic courts. However, there are two circumstances in which its role is crucial. These are Article 169 references (see above) and preliminary rulings made under EEC Article 177, whereby national courts can request guidance on interpretation of Community law. Rulings made under the latter provision have three functions.

> First, they help to ensure that national courts make legally 'correct' judgments. Second, because they are generally accepted by all national courts as setting a precedent, they promote the uniform interpretation and application of Community law in the twelve member states. Third, they provide a valuable source of access to the Court for private individuals who cannot directly appeal to it, either because there is no legal provision or because of inadequacy of funds. (Nugent, 1989, p160).

The judicial legislation of the Court has been remarkable, since it has acted as a more ardent promoter of supranational powers than even the Commission. One commentator concludes that the ECJ 'has accomplished a pervasive substitution of litigation for legislation and for formal constitutional amendment' and that 'the impasse resulting from . . . inactivity of the political processes is remediable by judicial activism' (Rasmussen, 1986, pp377 and 381). The evolution of EC policy has been intricately bound up with far-reaching judgments of the European Court of Justice (Brewster and Teague, 1989). Nowhere has this radicalism been more apparent than in the areas of EC migrants' rights and sex equality: the ECJ has consistently prioritised individuals' rights and the upholding of Treaty 'freedoms'. The principles of direct effect[2] and of the primacy of Community law[3] are now well established, and accepted by all member states.

The main **administrative body** in the field of social policy is the Administrative Commission for Social Security. This consists of one representative from each member state, with Commission representatives taking an advisory role. It has delegated authority from the Council to determine rules supplementing the social security co-ordinating regulations (see below), though there is some doubt about the legitimacy of a legislative body not established by treaty. Its functions are to establish model forms and documents, to provide a clearing system for social security payments and reimbursements, and to promote co-ordination and co-operation between social security agencies.

Various **advisory committees** exist in the area of social policy. They include Social Security – Migrant Workers; Free Movement of Workers; European Social Fund. These are basically corporatist advisory bodies. The Council appoints, for a two-year term, two government representatives, two trades' union representatives and two representatives of employers' organisations from each member state. Their purpose is to examine general Treaty principles in their policy area, to formulate opinions and to propose amendments to the secondary legislation.

Policy areas

Let us now examine the role of the EC and its impact on the UK in the following policy areas: non-discrimination of (EC) migrant workers, social security co-ordination, sex equality legislation, the European Social Fund and vocational training, and general provisions in the area of health. Even so, several areas of social security and health are not covered, including occupational health and safety (the subject of major initiatives in the Social Charter), and initiatives on poverty and disability. In each case we attempt to construct a counterfactual (of not having acceded to the EC) in order to make some sort of assessment of the impact of Britain's membership.

Non-discrimination of migrant workers

The free movement of workers is probably the most outstanding concession to supranational authority in the entire EEC regime. Not only are member states obliged to admit all EC workers, self-employed persons and tourists – subject only to a tightly-defined derogation of public health, morality and state security policy – but governments are answerable to the courts with respect to impeding free movement. Furthermore, the ECJ considers that any measure discriminating directly or indirectly against migrant workers is in breach of Treaty obligations and secondary legislation.

The principle of free movement of workers is laid down in EEC Article 48, and for the self-employed in Articles 52 and 59/60; EEC Article 7 forbids discrimination on the grounds of nationality generally. For workers, this is elaborated in Regulation 1612/68. The 'social advantage' rule of Article 7 states:

1 A worker who is a national of a Member State may not, in the territory of another Member State, be treated differently from national workers by reason of his nationality in respect of any conditions of employment and work, in particular as regards remuneration, dismissal, and should he become unemployed, reinstatement or re-employment.

2 He shall enjoy the same social and tax advantages as national workers.

3 He shall also, by virtue of the same right and under the same conditions as national workers, have access to training in vocational schools and retraining centres.

4 Any clause of a collective or individual agreement or of any other collective regulation concerning eligibility for employment, remuneration and other conditions of work or dismissal shall be null and void in so far as it lays down or authorises discriminatory conditions in respect of workers who are nationals of the other Member States.

Regulation 1612/68 applies to all EC migrant workers (but not to those in search of work) and their families, regardless of nationality (Forcheri, Case 152/82). It has been held to extend to housing rights, social assistance, trades union rights, and family members' social and employment rights. Where the provisions of 1612/68 have been seen by the ECJ as deficient, it has extended its scope by relying on EEC Article 7.[4]

The Court has determined that direct, indirect and reverse discrimination can be unlawful impediments to the free movement of persons. Indirect discrimination is that which achieves the effect of discriminating on nationality grounds by some other means; reverse discrimination is the situation in which a national's own country accords him less favourable treatment than it would another EC national. In this latter case, where a situation is entirely internal to a state then Treaty provisions cannot usually be invoked. Other legislation with some impact includes Reg 1251/70: this allows a worker to remain in a member state after retirement, incapacity or involuntary unemployment.

In the UK, several major areas have been affected by these provisions (Baldwin-Edwards, 1991). State subsidised housing is now available equally to EC workers; study grants must be awarded on the same terms as to nationals to EC migrant workers and their families, and college tuition fees cannot discriminate between UK and EC students. British immigration policy has been substantially modified: not only is there an obligation to admit all EC workers and their families (the latter regardless of nationality) for purposes of employment or tourism, but also an invalidation of the 'no recourse to public funds' provision applied to non-EC immigrants. Thus, involuntarily unemployed EC workers in the UK generally have unrestricted access to social assistance (ie Income Support), with no possibility of deportation.

A counterfactual for this area is relatively straightforward. First, there were no special provisions in the UK for immigration rights or non-discrimination of EC citizens prior to EC Accession. Second, we can posit an 'ex post' counterfactual of the rights, within the UK, of citizens of EFTA and Council of Europe states. These rights are minimal, and in no way compare with the EC situation. Thus the impact of this aspect of EC policy has been substantial.

Social security co-ordination

EEC Article 51 states that:

> The Council shall, acting unanimously on a proposal from the Commission, adopt such measures in the field of social security as are necessary to provide freedom of movement for workers; to this end, it shall make arrangements to secure for migrant workers and their dependants:
> a) aggregation, for the purpose of acquiring and retaining the right to benefit and of calculating the amount of benefit, of all periods taken into account under the laws of the several countries;
> b) payment of benefits to persons resident in the territories of Member States.

This is embodied in the current Regulation 1408/71 (as amended) and implemented by 574/72 (as amended); for the self-employed, 1390/81 implemented by 3795/81. These Regulations are co-ordinating measures, and do not constitute any attempt to harmonise different national social security systems; rather, they aim to encourage labour mobility by preserving social security entitlements for migrants within the EC.

The Regulations apply to all general and special security schemes, whether contributory or not. A wide range of benefits is covered: sickness, maternity, invalidity, old age, survivors', occupational hazard, death, unemployment and family benefits. Social and medical assistance, along with war victims' and civil servants' special schemes, are excluded. In practice, the ECJ has frequently included social and medical assistance by using a 'double function' test, whereby a legal right to even a means-tested benefit leads to its assimilation to a social security benefit. This generous interpretation suggested that only discretionary payments counted as 'social assistance' and were thus excluded. More recently, the ECJ has tended to use the 'social advantage' rule of Regulation 1612/68 (see below). On the other hand, only state or state-nominated general insurance schemes are included: occupational pensions schemes are not affected by the Regulations.

Four principles are embodied in these Regulations:

Non-discrimination on grounds of nationality Persons covered by the Regulations are 'subject to the same obligations and enjoy the same benefits . . . as the nationals of that State'. This prohibits covert as well as direct discrimination (see eg Palermo, Case 237/78).[5]

Exportability Acquired rights are retained when living in another member state. Residence in a state other than the 'competent' one does not disqualify or reduce benefits relating to invalidity, old age, survivors', occupational disease or death. Sickness, unemployment and family benefits are not covered by this principle: alternative, more restrictive arrangements exist for these.

Aggregation Where necessary[6] account must be taken by the competent state of periods of contribution, employment and residence in all member states in order to determine eligibility and the amount of benefit. This provision applies to most, but not all, benefits; those covered are sickness, maternity, old age, death, unemployment, family and orphans' benefits. Rules exist to prevent overlapping of benefits, or in certain cases to provide for apportionment of costs borne by the competent institutions.

Applicable law For different categories of workers (eg frontier workers, temporary workers, diplomatic services) Article 13 either defines the national law to which they are subject for social security purposes or allows a choice of the state in respect of compulsory insurance. Generally, this is the state in which the individual is employed; however, social security rights can be acquired through voluntary insurance elsewhere and through residence.

The Regulations apply to any employed or self-employed EC national, or immediate family, who has at any time been subject to the relevant social security legislation of any member state. This includes part-time work, even where earnings do not reach subsistence level, and previous work. Coverage is based on the fact of insurance, although it does not extend to the insured unemployed (eg as in the UK). The immediate family or survivors are covered, regardless of nationality, as are stateless persons and refugees. Not covered are those who have never been employed, including students. Perhaps most important, third country migrants are **not** covered by Regulation 1408/71 and are dependent on bilateral and multilateral conventions for freedom of movement and any social security rights.

Old Age and Death Pensions are calculated according to complex rules for aggregation and apportionment, without detriment to any claim under national law where that benefit would be higher. Unemployment Benefits can be 'exported' for a maximum of three months (under Article 69) subject to stringent conditions; if the claimant returns after three months, entitlement to benefits under national law are not retained (Testa, Case 41/79). Sickness Benefits are available in two situations. First, when resident in another state, benefits in kind are provided in accordance with the law of the state of residence – the cost is borne by the competent institution (ie the institution to which contributions have been paid). Second, while visiting another state, if the insured's condition (or that of a family member) necessitates immediate treatment. The unemployed can claim sickness benefits, if entitled to them with the competent institution. Pensioners also are entitled, but costs are borne by the competent institution to whose legislation the pensioner has been subject for the longest period of time.

What has been the actual impact of all this? One index is the extent of cross-national payments of benefits within the EC. Table 9.1 shows a small part of this: UK payments of old age pensions in member states. The total cost of pensions paid in 1987 amounted to £100m for 99,300 recipients. The outstanding feature is the size of payments made in Ireland, and the rapidly rising payments in Spain.

However, before we can gauge the impact of the EC on the co-ordination of social security for migrants, we obviously need to

Table 9.1 Payment of UK old age pensions in EC members states

	Annual payments (£m)			Number of recipients (000)		
	1986	1987	1988*	1986	1987	1988
Belgium	2.2	2.4	2.7	2.8	3.3	3.6
Denmark	0.3	0.3	0.4	0.2	0.3	0.3
France	3.9	4.1		5.1	5.6	6.1
Germany	7.4	8.3		9.1	10.6	11.7
Greece	0.6	0.7	0.9	0.8	0.9	1.0
Ireland	53.5	56.6		44.0	48.0	51.0
Italy	9.1	10.2	12.7	8.1	9.5	10.6
Netherlands	1.6	1.8		2.0	2.4	2.6
Portugal	1.0	1.2	1.4	1.4	1.7	1.8
Spain	12.6	15.1	18.1	14.9	17.0	18.5
Total	92.3	100.7		88.5	99.3	107.3

*1988 payment figure not available for some countries
Source: Gough and Baldwin-Edwards (1990)

consider what would have been the case had Britain not acceded to the EC. Prior to the formation of the EEC, there had been a proliferation of bilateral agreements, multilateral agreements and ILO Conventions, which have continued to accumulate right up to the present. On this basis, we argue elsewhere that EC membership has materially affected only arrangements with Greece (Gough and Baldwin-Edwards, 1990).

Nevertheless, the EC has made a positive contribution to the social security rights of migrants from member states in several respects. First, the EC arrangements cope reasonably well with movement across three or more member states, something that conventional multilateral schemes never satisfactorily resolved. Second, the EC regulations establish a coherent body of law common to all states; despite great complexity and innumerable derogations, this is still a great advance on previous arrangements. Third, this body of law is automatically directly applicable in all member countries and must be enforced by national courts. This is a significant change in the UK, where previous agreements had to be incorporated into domestic law by Orders in Council, and were therefore strictly controlled by government. Fourth, and perhaps most important, this body of law is interpreted by a novel institution – the ECJ. It has adopted a Community-wide approach, removing many of the previous legislative barriers to the free movement of persons, including social security barriers. The one dark and massive cloud in this picture remains the rights of non-EC migrants.

Sex equality

This is one area of EEC social legislation where rights are granted to all EC nationals, rather than to just migrants. Thus it is to some extent harmonising legislation, although the instruments used (directives) leave the implementation to national laws. However, owing to unsatisfactory implementation of directives by many national governments, the ECJ has ruled that direct effects can occur (see above).

EEC Article 119 provides for equal pay for equal work – a rather narrow definition. Nevertheless, it was one which many governments were originally reluctant to implement. In Defrenne no 2 (Case 43/75) the ECJ ruled that Article 119 has direct effect; in the two other Defrenne cases (80/70; 149/77) it was determined that the Treaty provision did not pertain to retirement age or occupational pension schemes.

The Equal Pay Directive (Dir 75/117) extends the provision to 'equal pay for work of equal value', outlaws discriminatory clauses in collective agreements and requires the introduction of national legal mechanisms for individual petition. Equal treatment in employment, vocational training and working conditions is enshrined in the Equal Treatment Directive (Dir 76/207), which defines equal treatment as 'the absence of all discrimination whatsoever on grounds of sex either directly or indirectly by reference in particular to marital and family status'. Further, the directive requires states to protect employees from dismissal via enforcement procedures, and also to ensure that employers are aware of the Directive and any national measures.

Directive 79/7 on Equal Treatment in Social Security outlaws discrimination in statutory social security schemes, effective from 1984. Included are schemes for sickness, old age, accidents at work, occupational health, and supplementary schemes; not included are survivors' benefits, pensionable age and spouse's contributions. All occupational social security schemes are affected by Directive 86/378. Both direct and indirect discrimination are prohibited, including a scheme's scope, conditions of access, level and conditions of contributions, and the calculation of benefits. The Directive is to be implemented by 1993; however, the amended text allows different actuarial data on life expectancy to set lower benefits for women.

The Self-employed Directive (Dir 86/613), effective from 1989, aims at equality of access to financial services and contributory social security schemes, particularly with respect to married women. Also, states are directed to examine methods of providing maternity services and temporary replacement workers during pregnancy.

According to Meehan (1988, p56), 'Anticipated membership of the EC was one of the spurs hastening the advent of the Equal Pay Act of 1970.' The Act includes the concepts of victimisation and indirect discrimination, departing to some extent from UK traditional practices. However, the Act's formulation of equal pay was found defective by the ECJ in 1982. Under the Equal Pay (Amendment) Regulations of 1983, the wording has been changed to 'equal pay for work of equal value', and is not solely dependent upon a job evaluation scheme; also, workers now have a statutory right to demand independent job evaluation.

In 1983, the ECJ ruled that exemptions of employment in private households and in businesses with fewer than five employees were in breach of the Equal Treatment Directive and that the UK had taken insufficient measures to abolish discrimination in collective agreements. The Sex Discrimination Act of 1986 amended these defects, as well as repealing all protective legislation for women on factory night-shifts (Mazey, 1990, p14). The latter Act also made women's retirement at 60 non-compulsory, following the case of Marshall (Case 152/84); there, the Court held that retirement ages were covered by the Equal Treatment Directive, although state pensions and statutory retirement ages were not. Another significant change is the right of British married women to receive a carer's allowance, formerly paid only to married men or single men or women (Drake, Case 150/85).

Most recently, the British government has been required to amend legislation to make provision for EC rulings. First, in the Social Security Act 1989 the 1986 Directive on Occupational Social Security Schemes is implemented; however, it does not cover pensionable age or survivors' pensions, as permitted by the Directive. (A draft directive is intended to cover these and other areas of discrimination.) Second, the Employment Act 1989 repeals much legislation restricting the employment of women, in line with the 1976 Equal Treatment Directive and the direct effect of Article 119. Since January 1990, any provision of existing legislation is void if it imposes a requirement constituting direct or indirect sex discrimination in employment or vocational training. This is a major shift from the provision of the 1975 Sex Discrimination Act. One review concludes that the Employment Act 'illustrates the profound effect of EC legislation on UK employment law' (EIRR, 1990).

Since the Social Security Act 1989 was passed, the ECJ has ruled that occupational pensions fall within the scope of EEC Article 119. In Barber (Case 262/88) the Court ruled that a man denied a retirement pension upon compulsory redundancy, whereas a woman would have received such, suffers discriminatory practice contravening Article 119. Thus it appears that occupational pensions schemes must set common pensionable ages and benefits: the SSA 1989 now needs revision. State pension schemes are not affected by this ruling, however. Another recent ruling (Ruzius-Wilbrink, Case 102/88) outlaws discrimination of part-time workers' benefits, accepting that a different basis of calculation for benefits was indirectly discriminatory since the majority of claimants were women.

The EC measures promoting sex equality have been seen as significant enough to be cited by some Labour MEPs as a sufficient reason for the UK to remain in the EC (Mazey, 1988, p82). Between 1972 and 1986, nine (out of an EC total of 20) preliminary rulings were requested by UK courts (Meehan, 1988) and 1,742 claims in 1976 were made in the UK under the Equal Pay Act (Mazey, 1990). The UK weakened the Directive on Occupational Social Security Schemes and the Self-employed Directive; also, it vetoed the draft directives on part-time work and parental leave. There can be little doubt that British equal opportunities policy has been dragged along by the EC, not only in terms of coverage but also of enforcement mechanisms. It is unlikely that such changes would have occurred had Britain not been a member. However, it has been suggested that the reason, at least for the large number of ECJ hearings, 'lies not . . . in any greater reluctance, or even a greater failure on our part, to observe Community law, but rather in the different styles of drafting and interpretation prevailing under the two legal systems' (Steiner, 1988, p205).

The European Social Fund and vocational training

The European Social Fund has undergone numerous substantial revisions since its establishment, and for some time has been far removed from its original Treaty objectives. We shall examine its activities over two periods – immediately prior to, and after, the reforms introduced in the Single European Act.

In 1983, the Council decided to focus the Fund on two objectives: young people under twenty-five, in particular those with reduced employment activities, and the 'most disadvantaged regions'. Though only Northern Ireland qualified for the latter category in the UK, the 'priority regions' which attracted the bulk of remaining monies embraced much of Scotland, Wales, the English North and Northwest, Yorkshire and parts of the West Midlands. Table 9.2 shows how this targeting has benefited the UK.

Total Fund expenditure is a small proportion of the total EEC budget, but Britain's receipt in 1987 of mEcu 593 (about £400m) amounted to 19 per cent of the total – slightly higher than its population alone would warrant.

Though its purpose is to improve employment opportunities, the European Social Fund increasingly overlaps, or substitutes for, social security schemes; in Britain, as elsewhere, schemes to prevent unemployment by training the unemployed increasingly overlay programmes to compensate them with benefits. The Youth Training Scheme, now part of Employment Training, has been the major beneficiary; indeed, the ESF rules appear to have shaped the YTS programme. In this way, EC employment policies may have had an impact on UK social security for the unemployed,

Table 9.2 European Social Fund Expenditure Approvals, 1987

	UK		EC	
Category	mEcu	%	mEcu	%
Young people, priority regions	68	11.4	1063	33.7
Young people, other regions	451	76.1	1298	41.2
Adults, priority regions	11	1.9	308	9.8
Adults, other regions	53	8.9	384	12.2
Specific operations	10	1.7	97	3.1
Total	593	100.0	3150	100.0

Source: Gough and Baldwin-Edwards (1990)

by encouraging the development of youth training and work experience as a *quid pro quo* for the receipt of unemployment benefit.

The Fund has possibly had a marginal impact on British social policy in three ways. First, the Fund's contribution to the MSC programmes has been of the order of 10–20 per cent throughout the 1980s, although Teague (1989, p49) has concluded that the monies were simply fiscal transfers for nationally-determined labour-market policies. Second, he links the Fund with the emergence of the MSC's 'New Training Initiative' in 1981. Third, European monies via the Fund have slightly mitigated the financial squeeze and loss of autonomy by British local authorities in the 1980s.

In the 1987 Single European Act the European Council agreed to reform and integrate the Structural Funds (EEC Article 130 D). Under this reform, the different Funds (European Social Fund (ESF), European Regional Development Funds (ERDF), European Agricultural Guarantee and Guidance Fund (EAGGF) and the European Investment Bank (EIB) are to act in tandem in order to promote co-ordinated regional initiatives on a medium-term basis. They now have five objectives (Regulation 2052/88):

1 Promoting the development and structural adjustment of the regions whose development is lagging behind
2 Converting the regions, frontier regions or parts of regions (including employment areas and urban communities) seriously affected by industrial decline
3 Combating long-term unemployment
4 Facilitating the occupational integration of young people
5 with a view to reform of the common agricultural policy:
    a) speeding up the adjustment of agricultural structures
    b) promoting the development of rural areas

The ESF must prioritise vocational training and employment aids for objectives 3 and 4, also supporting 1, 2 and 5(b). The ERDF must provide support for objectives 1 and 2, and also 5(b). The EAGGF (guidance section) is confined to objectives 1, 5(a) and (b). The European Council agreed to double the funds to reach mEcu 13,000 in 1992 – a likely increase in the proportion of total EC budget from 18 per cent in 1986 to over 30 per cent by 1993 (Teague, 1989, p54). The Council has also agreed to devote 75 per cent of the ERDF to objective 1, thus doubling those areas' allocation.

In the UK, as stated above, only Northern Ireland is in the objective 1 category. Objective 2 areas (Decision 89/288/EEC) in the UK now include parts of Scotland, NE and NW England, Wales and the Midlands. Yet is seems likely that the UK will benefit still

more under the new arrangements. In August 1990 the Commission
announced that the UK is to receive bEcu 1.0 (£0.7b) out of a total
ESF allocation of bEcu 2.5 (Financial Times, 3.8.90) – an increase
from 18 per cent for 1987 to 40 per cent for 1990.

Under the auspices of EEC Article 128, the Commission has also
enacted some notable measures in the area of vocational training.
The European Centre for the Development of Vocational Training
(CEDEFOP) was established in 1975. It is run as a corporatist
body attempting to raise standards of, and access to, vocational
training and to ensure mutual recognition of qualifications between
member states. Council Decision 87/569/EEC of December 1987
established a five-year programme of vocational training initiatives;
in particular, it requires member states to provide school-leavers
with access to a minimum of one year, and preferably two or more,
of vocational training.

Health

Apart from occupational health and safety, health and health policy
are absent from the Treaty of Rome. In recent years, however,
initiatives have been taken (under the auspices of EEC Articles
117/8 supplemented by Articles 135, 155 and 235) on cancer,
AIDS, drug abuse and a European health card.

The 'Europe against Cancer' programme emerged from the 1985
Council meeting and is being pursued by an advisory group to the
Commission. The aim is to reduce mortality from cancer by 15
per cent by the year 2000. It commits the EC to action on several
fronts, including campaigns to reduce smoking and improve diets.
As part of the former, the EC pledges to align tobacco taxes upward
– notwithstanding the substantial increases in tobacco prices this will
occasion in southern Europe, to harmonise the labelling of cigarette
packets, to eliminate duty-free sales of tobacco products and to
protect children against their sale. Apart from a disagreement with
the UK government on health warnings on cigarette packets, this
programme will on the whole bring southern countries more into
line with current practice in the UK and other northern member
states. It signals an innovatory policy of collaboration on health
prevention, but will have a minimal impact in the UK.

Resolutions in the European Parliament concerning AIDS in 1984
and 1986 were followed by a Council Resolution in 1986 asking
the Commission to investigate the scope for Community action.
In 1987 it called for, *inter alia*, increased exchange of experience
in health education and medical research (for which mEcu 5.5
has been allocated). In 1986 the Council approved a Resolution
permitting the voluntary carrying of a Euro health card for use in
medical emergencies in member countries. In these small ways the

EC is taking tentative steps towards involvement in health policy, but its impact on national policy is miniscule.

More important in the immediate future are the implications of the Single Market in labour and goods for the provision and delivery of health care. First, the freedom of medical personnel to practise in member countries has been progressively established since the late 1960s. Directives have been adopted to co-ordinate training and to ensure the mutual recognition of diplomas and doctors, including general practitioners (75/362, 75/363, 82/76, 86/457), nurses (77/452, 77/453), dentists (78/686, 78/687), midwives (80/154, 80/155) and pharmacists (85/432, 85/433). The effect so far on the movement of health personnel has been minimal, but this may change as a result of the '1992 factor'. Secondly, the effect of an internal market for medical equipment and pharmaceutical products may be profound. These are two sectors where present non-tariff barriers are high and intra-EC trade is low, hence where 1992 should provide substantial scope for substitution and cost-saving.

Third, and perhaps most important, the mobility of retired people within Europe is growing fast, as more buy houses and retire or winter in the sunnier climes of Spain and the other Mediterranean countries. This will redistribute the demand for medical and social care between member states, and increase the redistribution undertaken via the health compensation mechanisms. Where there are no bilateral agreements, entitlements are determined by the 'competent institution' and reimbursed to the 'state of residence' providing the service. This could cost the NHS a rising sum in the future, although it appears that bilateral waivers are being negotiated between the UK and Greece, Spain and Portugal (Gough and Baldwin-Edwards, 1990).

Summary

In two domains of social policy EC membership has had a major impact on the UK: sex equality and non-discrimination of EC nationals. Equal treatment of EC migrants, along with rights of admission, quite clearly would not have occurred outside the EC; neither, of course, would the correlative rights of UK nationals in other EC countries. In practice, there are relatively few EC nationals in the UK, so that at present this is of little practical consequence (although the legal requirement of non-discrimination seems to have shifted the burden of college fees onto non-EC students, since EC students can only be charged at UK rates). The other major policy impact has been to encourage equal treatment of women. Even if our counterfactual admits the possibility of equivalent action having been taken, it is clear that the implementation would have been very different.

In other policy areas the effects have been in the same direction, but weaker. External funding for local authorities has mitigated slightly the 1980s trend of centralisation of government; the advent of MSC training policy is linked with the ESF; and social security co-ordination rights have required some extra degree of government accountability. In three policy areas – social security, equal treatment for women and non-discrimination of migrants – the ECJ's judgments have extended coverage to part-time and very low earners. This is perhaps a significant gain in the context of 1980s Britain. Only in the area of health, where EC activity has been highly constrained anyway, has there been little or no impact.

Generally, the imposition of EC legal requirements has led to an increase in the fundamental rights of citizens to challenge the state, to demand a hearing, and to have legitimate expectations fulfilled. These are significant inroads into the concept of Crown prerogative. Nevertheless, the core areas of national social policy making remain unruffled by the existence of the EC.

Towards a Social Charter

The aim of the 1992 Single Market and the Single European Act have given renewed impetus to the idea of a 'Social Dimension' and its centrepiece – a European Social Charter. However, what started out, under the Belgian Presidency in 1987, as a charter of workers' social and employment rights has been modified and diluted to such an extent that it is now no more than a vague political affirmation. (Even the original proposals contained little beyond the Council of Europe's 1961 Social Charter, ratified by nearly all member states – though, ironically, not by Belgium). Opposition to the 1988 draft for the Charter came principally from three directions: the employers' union, UNICE; the lower wage countries of the Mediterranean; and the UK government, pursuing labour market deregulation and flexibility (Rhodes, 1991). Alone of the twelve member states, the UK Government refused to sign even this weak non-binding declaration in 1989. Its veto is in line with previous UK vetos of proposals relating to part-time working and parental leave.

The prospective impact of the Social Charter on the UK is unclear, mainly because the precise legal measures which will be enacted are unknown. If measures are passed by majority voting, however, there are possible implications for the UK. A major area affected could be the rights of part-time and other 'atypical' workers, who in the UK are disproportionately low paid and under-protected. The new provisions would bring more workers under national insurance coverage and into company pensions schemes.

However, despite the insistence otherwise of the European Parliament, the Charter remains relevant largely only to workers. Furthermore, in its deference to national traditions the Commission has lost the opportunity to establish a baseline of fundamental rights in the EC. The immediate future may hold some dramatic changes, though. The Italian Presidency in its European Council summit of December 1990 intends to push for a new treaty, extending EC competence to workers' rights, health, citizens' rights and common policies for non-EC nationals. Such a radical modification of the EC would indicate transformation from a mere economic arrangement to some kind of political union; it is unclear whether Europe, let alone the UK, is ready for this.

Towards an explanation

What explains the conflicts and lack of congruence between the EC and the UK in the field of social policy? Of course this is a daunting question which can be addressed only cursorily here. We contend that underlying the surface explanations, invoking for example 'Thatcherism' and the contrast between deregulatory and corporatist strategies, there are deeper institutional patterns. These reveal profound contrasts between the **social policy** regimes and the **legal structures** in Britain and the founder EC states. Let us consider each in turn.

Social policy regimes

Esping-Andersen (1990) has done much to clarify the nature of social policy systems, moving beyond simple contrasts of expenditure levels which tell us little about the principles underlying social programmes. He distinguishes three 'welfare state regimes': the conservative (or, as we would prefer to call it, the 'Christian Democratic'), the liberal and the socialist (or, our preference again, the 'social democratic'). He argues that countries' social policy systems cluster into one or other of these regimes, though he analyses only social security and employment programmes and excludes health and education. Nevertheless, his model highlights the incompatibilities between social policy in Britain and the bulk of EC countries.

The welfare state regimes of five of the founder EC nations (Germany, France, Italy, Belgium and Luxembourg) are 'conservative', with only the Netherlands clearly exhibiting some differences. Features of this model include:

- law-based rights to a wide range of social benefits
- social insurance as the central mode of organisation and delivery of benefits (including, in most cases, medical services in kind)

- the principle of subsidiarity alongside a limited role for autonomous
  private agencies
- occupationally differentiated benefits delivered by separate corporatist bodies.

We noted above that the social policy of the European Community is predominantly employment-based. This has had the effect
of reproducing a markedly Germanic, Bismarckian or conservative
policy regime. Since all of the original EC six nations exhibit similar
welfare state structures, the EC regime has been accommodated
relatively easily by them. These same principles underpin the
European Commission's most recent social policy initiatives, although this cannot be demonstrated here.

The UK social policy regime is harder to place, but appears to
combine elements of the liberal and the social democratic, with
the former predominating in the last two decades. This means
that it forms an almost polar contrast with the above principles
and practices:

- rights to social benefits in law are non-existent or weak
- a rising proportion of benefits are income-related on an assistance
  principle, whilst medical services in kind are supplied on a universal
  basis via a quite distinct NHS
- state organisation is centralised, yet runs alongside an extensive
  private sector, in pensions for example
- occupational and status differentiation is low

Table 9.3 illustrates these patterns for eight member states
using the two of Esping-Andersen's indicators of 'welfare state
stratification' which display the most marked contrasts. It shows that
the UK scores low on the measure of 'corporatism', as specifically
defined in Table 9.3, and high for its reliance on income testing.
Denmark, the Netherlands and Ireland are close to the UK in the
first case, but not in the second. Here it is France and Italy which
have more in common with Britain. Nevertheless, the British regime
stands in marked contrast to the dominant principles and structures
informing the social policy innovations of the EC. It is not just
the beliefs of the Thatcher administrations, nor the whole-hearted
endorsement of neo-liberal policies which explain the divergent
social policy paths of Britain and the EC.

Legal structures

Similar contrasts are observable in the principles and structures of
the legal systems of the founder EC nations and Britain. Arnull
(1990) identifies four general principles of law which have informed
the ECJ's judgements (see also Steiner, 1988, pp40–50):

Table 9.3 Comparative indicators of welfare state regimes, 1980

Country	'Corporatism'	Means-testing
Belgium	5	4.5
Denmark	2	1.0
France	10	11.2
Germany	6	4.9
Ireland	1	5.9
Italy	12	9.3
Netherlands	3	6.9
UK	2	13.8
EC8	5.1	7.2
EC8 – UK	5.6	6.2

Notes:
Corporatism: number of major occupationally distinct public pension schemes
Means-testing: expenditure on poor relief (including general means-tested schemes, but excluding service-related schemes) as percentage of total public social expenditure. Our own estimates for UK derived from Social Trends.
Sources: Esping-Andersen, 1990, Table 3.1
        Social Trends no. 12 (1982), Table 5.7

Legal certainty – the effect of the law must be clear and therefore predictable. This is derived from German, French and Belgian law, and is concerned that Community measures should not violate legitimate expectations.
Equality – the prohibition of discrimination, frequently covered by specific Treaty provisions. There is also 'a general principle of equality which is one of the fundamental principles of Community law' (Ruckdeschel, Cases 117/76, 16/77) and is at least partly derived from French law.
Proportionality – measures are weighted according to the severity of the issue. This too is derived from Germanic code, and imposes limitations upon Community and national authorities in the exercise of their EC powers.
Right to a hearing – within which are subsumed also the duty to give reasons and the right to due process. The latter was established recently in Johnston (Case 222/84) whereby the right to judicial process, for persons who consider themselves wronged, was pronounced

> a general principle of law which underlies the constitutional traditions common to the member states. That principle is also laid down in Articles 6 and 13 of the European Convention for the Protection of Human Rights and Fundamental Freedoms . . .

These four principles[7] are derived from Germanic and civil legal traditions, doubtless reflecting the original membership of the EC. Britain and Ireland of course have a quite different Anglo-American legal system, whilst Denmark exhibits a third, Nordic form. However these latecomers to the Community, notably Denmark, the UK and Ireland, have had little impact upon the already-developed substantive law of the EC. Although these ECJ principles exist in English law, most judicial activity is concerned with the literal interpretation of statutes or with common law precedents. The Continental, and in particular the ECJ's, approach is less literal and more prepared to engage in legal construction. Thus, the ECJ guiding principles fit uncomfortably alongside UK practices.

Moreover, the structure of the English legal system is 'dualistic', ie international treaties are not directly incorporated into domestic legislature. This, again, is a feature of Anglo-American and Scandinavian systems, as opposed to most Continental countries which grant greater or lesser degrees of 'direct effect'. The outcome of this difference is that treaties ratified by the UK, such as the European Convention on Human Rights (ECHR) and the Social Charter, are not part of UK law. Direct incorporation of these would probably lead to major policy shifts. Thus the UK has been isolated from international norms rather more than most EC countries: only Ireland, Denmark and the UK have consistently opposed EC ratification of the ECHR (Betten *et al*, 1989, pp119–20).

The dominant characteristics of European Community social policy are its Treaty basis, which is largely employment-oriented, and interpretation by the ECJ, which is rights-based. These characteristics enable us to define the EC social policy regime as 'conservative' and its legal system as 'Franco-Germanic'. The UK welfare regime and legal system represent a stark contrast with both patterns in most other member states and with the EC regime itself. Such institutional barriers impede not only Britain's full incorporation into the European Community but also the development of a genuine EEC social policy. Increasingly, it seems that social-economic reform and closer integration with Europe will require constitutional reform in the UK – but that is another story!

Notes

1 The term 'derogation' refers to specific exception to a general legal measure. The arrangement for 'rights of employed persons' is ambiguous, although Vogel-Polsky suggests that unanimity will be required 'only for drafts concerned exclusively with the rights and interests of workers alone' (Vogel-Polsky, 1990, p72).
2 van Gend en Loos (Case 26/62); Grad (Case 9/70) where even a Decision was given direct effect.
3 Simmenthal (Case 106/77).

4 The ECJ has frequently extended the provisions of the social security co-ordinating provisions of Regulation 1408/71 by reinforcing them with Regulation 1612/68 (Inzirillo, Case 63/76); where even that is insufficient, EEC Article 7 is extremely potent (eg Forcheri, Case 152/82).

5 Recently, the ECJ has effectively annulled a specific article excluding French family benefits for children resident elsewhere (Pinna, Case 41/84). However, if a state's social security scheme requires insurance periods in that state as a condition of affiliation, then a worker cannot cite covert discrimination in order to qualify on the basis of insurance in another state (Vigier, Case 70/80).

6 In Petroni (Case 24/75) the Court decided that although the regulations limit the relevant legislation to one member state, a migrant may retain benefits under two states' laws if the regulations have not been invoked to acquire those benefits. Subsequently, this ruling has been extended to allow payment outside the competent state (Giuliani, Case 32/77). Thus the regulations do not perfectly co-ordinate social security schemes.

7 With regard to international conventions, strictly the ECJ is obliged to consider only those entered into by the Community. However, in Nold (Case 4/73) the Court held that 'international treaties for the protection of human rights can supply guidelines which should be followed within the framework of Community law'. Subsequently, the ECJ has cited the 1977 Joint Declaration, by the Parliament, Council and Commission, on respect for the European Convention. Also, the Preamble to the Single European Act affirms adherence to the European Convention and the Social Charter; in 1989 the Parliament adopted a declaration of fundamental rights, based on constitutional traditions, international instruments and ECJ case law, and requesting the other Community institutions to endorse it. (See Collins, L, 1990, pp8–15; also Cappelletti, 1985, p300 et seq.)

References

Arnull, A (1990) *The General Principles of EEC Law and the Individual.* Leicester UP.

Baldwin-Edwards, M (1991) 'Migration policy'. In Bulmer, S (ed) (1991, forthcoming) *European Community Membership under Scrutiny: UK Study.* Pinter.

Betten, L *et al* (1989) *The Future of European Social Policy.* Deventer, Kluwer.

Brewster, C and Teague, P (1989) *European Community Social Policy.* Institute of Personnel Management.

Cappelletti, M *et al* (eds) (1985) *Integration through Law*, Vol 1, Bk 3. De Gruyter.

Collins, L (1990) *European Community Law in the United Kingdom.* Butterworth.

Esping-Andersen, G (1990) *The Three Worlds of Welfare Capitalism.* Polity Press.

European Industrial Relations Review (1990) no 196. May 1990.

Gough, I and Baldwin-Edwards, M (1990) 'The effect of EC membership on UK social security and health'. In *The Implications of 1992 for Social Insurance*. Cross-National Research Papers, London School of Economics.

Grahl, J and Teague, P (1990) *1992 – The Big Market*, Lawrence and Wishart.

Mazey, S (1988) 'European Community action on behalf of women: The limits of legislation'. *Journal of Common Market Studies*, Vol XXVII, pp63–84.

Mazey, S (1990) *Women and the European Community*. Polytechnic of North London Press.

Meehan, E (1988) 'Women's equality and the European Community'. In Ashton, F and Whitting, G (eds) *Feminist Theory and Practical Policies*. Occasional Paper 29, School for Advanced Urban Studies, University of Bristol.

Nugent, N (1989) *The Government and Politics of the European Community*. Macmillan.

Rhodes, M (1991) 'The social dimension of the Single European Market'. *European Journal of Political Research*, March 1991.

Rasmussen, H (1986) *On Law and Policy in the European Court of Justice*. Dordrecht, Nijhoff.

Steiner, J (1988) *Textbook on EEC Law*. Blackstone Press.

Teague, P (1989) *The European Community: the social dimension*. Kogan Page.

Vandamme, J (ed) (1985) *New Dimensions in European Social Policy*. Croom Helm.

Vogel-Polsky, E (1990) 'What future is there for a social Europe following the Strasbourg Summit?' *Industrial Law Journal*, June 1990.

10 One in ten: lone parent families in the European Community

Jo Roll

Introduction

As the number of lone parents and, among lone parents, the numbers dependent on benefits for most of their income, have inexorably risen (Family Policy Studies Centre 1990), policy makers in this country have become increasingly concerned to do something about it. Indeed, this concern has been so great that it sometimes appears to have elbowed out the issues which affect other types of family; and much heralded statements about policies towards 'the family' have frequently turned out to be statements about policies for lone parent families.

Former Prime Minister Mrs Thatcher's Pankhurst lecture to the 300 Group in July 1990 is a case in point. Although she mentioned other issues, the only policy proposal was a child support agency to extract higher levels of maintenance from absent fathers. Such a policy had been hinted at in speeches by Government Ministers during most of the year and when, in October 1990, the Government eventually announced details of its plans in a white paper (Lord Chancellor's Department, 1990), it followed a long period of speculation about what was in store for lone parents.

This speculation was not only about the kind of child support policies that might emerge but also whether lone parents on benefit would be encouraged, expected or required to seek paid employment. The Social Security Advisory Committee, which advises the government, commissioned an independent report on the issue (Brown, 1989) and when the white paper was published, it also contained proposals designed to affect the incentive to take part time work.

Is this country unique or is this concern widely shared? Although Denmark is the only European Community (EC) country where the proportion of families with children who are lone parents is as high as in Great Britain[1], France, Germany and the Benelux countries are not far behind, and many of the countries where the proportion is still low have recently started to experience the same social changes which have led to the growth of lone parent families in this country.

Lone parents therefore already are, or are likely to become, a policy issue in most EC countries. The form which this takes, however, is likely to depend not only on the size and composition of the group but also on existing policies and on existing patterns of employment among women, women with children in general and lone mothers in particular, all of which vary enormously between countries.

As a result of recent trends, the European Commission has also taken an interest in the situation of lone parents. Its first major report on the subject was published in 1982 within the framework of the anti-poverty programmes (EC, 1982). Much of it was based on information relating to the early or mid-1970s which, given the pace of recent developments, was already out of date by the time a second report, this time within the framework of the 'Equal Opportunities for Women Programme', was under consideration at the end of the 1980s.

Naturally the ultimate aim of a policy-making body is to develop policies. But in the case of lone parents, as with many Community-wide issues, the facts on which to base the policies were missing as there are no regular official statistics on the number of lone parent families, let alone more elaborate details about them.

The Family Policy Studies Centre was asked to produce the second report[2]. Its major purpose was therefore to document the situation of lone parent families in the European Community, bearing in mind that the information was intended to serve to develop policies consistent with the equal opportunities for women programme and also bearing in mind the conclusions of the previous report, that lone parent families are at greater risk of poverty than two parent families. This paper sets out some of the facts and issues arising.

A new phenomenon? Background trends

Lone parent families are one of the most obvious consequences of wider family trends, such as the increase in the proportion of births outside marriage and the breakdown of marriages where there are children. Although they are not the only result – for example, many babies born outside marriage are in fact born to cohabiting couples and not to a mother on her own – they are undoubtedly one of the results over which there has been most concern.

In response to this concern, it is sometimes argued that lone parents are nothing new and that the attention they have received in recent years is out of proportion to the size of the phenomenon. There is a sense in which this is true. Widows and widowers with dependent children are certainly not a new development. On the contrary, their numbers are generally static or declining.

What is new is the recognition and growth of new types of lone parent resulting from divorce or separation and, to a lesser extent, from a rise in births to unmarried mothers, coupled with the view that, in spite of their diversity, these family situations have something in common which warrants a common label.

It is only possible to understand this development in the context of wider family and population trends, in particular some of the more dramatic changes of the last 25 years which have both contributed to, and resulted from, changes in the situation of women. However, the proportion of lone parents who are women – nine out of ten in most EC countries – illustrates clearly the limits of these developments. Whatever else may have changed, women are still the ones chiefly responsible for bringing up children.

When viewed at one point in time, variations between EC countries appear to be enormous, although, viewed from a historical perspective, the extent to which countries have experienced the same trends is striking, even if the rate of change and the sequence of events are not the same in all cases.

Table 10.1 Divorces per 1,000 existing marriages

	1960	1970	1980	1988
Belgium	2.0	2.6	5.6	8.4
Denmark	5.9	7.1	1.2	13.1
FR Germany	3.6	5.1	6.1	8.8
Greece	n.a.	n.a.	n.a.	n.a.
Spain	n.a.	n.a.	n.a.	n.a.
France	2.9	3.3	6.3	8.4
Ireland	0.0	0.0	0.0	0.0
Italy	–	1.3	0.8	2.1
Luxembourg	2.0	2.6	6.5	n.a.
Netherlands	2.2	3.3	7.5	8.1
Portugal	0.4	0.2	n.a.	n.a.
UK	2.0	4.7	9.6	12.3

Notes: The latest figure for Germany relates to 1987
The pre-1983 figures for the UK relate to England and Wales only.

Source: Eurostat: Demographic Statistics, 1990

Divorce laws, for example, have been introduced or liberalised in most countries since the 1960s and even in Ireland, which is now the only EC country where divorce is still prohibited, the number of separations has increased. Table 10.1 shows the rise in divorce rates experienced by many countries.

It should be noted that the figures in Table 10.1 understate the number of relationship breakdowns in countries such as Denmark and the UK, where cohabitation is relatively common, and in countries such as Italy and Spain, which require a 'two stage' divorce, that is, a period of formal separation before the divorce can take place. In Italy, for example, the number of legal separations has recently been higher than the number of divorces.

As for the proportion of births outside marriage, although they vary substantially, from 45 per cent in Denmark to 2 per cent in Greece (see Table 10.2), all countries apart from Greece, where the figure is too low to represent much change, have experienced a substantial rise. Even the 'Catholic' countries, such as Spain and Italy, have had rises from about 2 per cent in 1960 to around 8 per cent and 6 per cent respectively in the mid to late 1980s.

The same applies to some of the broader trends, such as falling family size, which are not directly – or even indirectly – the cause of lone parent families but which have contributed to the changing pattern of family life of which lone parents are a part. The long-term decline in the overall birth rate, as measured by the Total Period Fertility Rate, is another example. At the time the report was being written, Ireland was the only EC country with a birth rate high

Table 10.2   Births outside marriage as percentage of all live births

	1960	1970	1980	1988
Belgium	2.1	2.8	4.1	7.9
Denmark	7.8	11.0	33.2	44.7
FR Germany	6.3	5.5	7.6	10.0
Greece	1.2	1.1	1.5	2.1
Spain	2.3	1.4	3.9	8.0
France	6.1	6.8	11.4	26.3
Ireland	1.6	2.7	5.0	11.7
Italy	2.4	2.2	4.3	5.8
Luxembourg	3.2	4.0	6.0	12.1
Netherlands	1.4	2.1	4.1	10.2
Portugal	9.5	7.3	9.2	13.7
UK	5.2	8.0	11.5	25.1

Note: The latest figure for Belgium relates to 1986 and the latest figure for Spain to 1985

Source: Eurostat: Demographic Statistics, 1990

enough to replace the population. Yet in terms of its own history it was experiencing the lowest rate since records began and last year, there too, the rate fell below replacement levels.

What is a lone parent? Issues of definition

As there are no official EC statistics on the subject, there is also no official EC definition of a lone parent. It may seem strange to have to ask, 'What is a lone parent?' but, before attempting to collect comparable information, it is necessary to ask if there is a national definition in each country and if so, what it is.

Choosing a definition is not simply a technical matter. It raises the fundamental issue of what it is that is distinct about a lone parent and why it is of concern. In some countries the debate appears to have reached a more refined level than others, however. The French contribution to the EC report, for example, was accompanied by a paper entitled, 'Les familles monoparentales existent-elles?' (Lefaucheur, 1987)

In practice, not only do definitions vary between countries but in many there is no generally recognised single definition. However, three broad areas generally seem to arouse the most controversy, that is the marital status of the parent, the household situation and the definition of a dependent child.

In relation to marital status, it is sometimes argued that the analogy between divorced and widowed lone parents is a false one; a child of divorced parents still has two of them and these should each count as a lone parent. This definition has largely been rejected on practical grounds but there are also arguments against including in the same definition both the absent parents who may have nothing to do with their children, financially or otherwise, and the parents who have to bear the everyday financial costs and provide the day-to-day care.

However, this perspective does usefully focus attention on the fact that many children in lone parent families do have two living parents who often have legal and/or moral and obligations towards the children, even if these do not always operate in practice. The distinction between unmarried and divorced fathers in this respect has, at least on practical grounds, now also been rendered unnecessary by 'genetic fingerprinting' to establish paternity.

If alternate or joint physical custody of divorced children were ever to become commonplace, however, then it would be difficult, if not impossible, to decide who was the lone parent. But in that situation the concept itself of a lone parent might have to be abandoned and the analogy with widowed parents dropped altogether.

Another issue concerns new partners. If a lone parent cohabits, is s/he still to be regarded as a lone parent? Most definitions in use assume that the answer is 'no', although this raises the issue of the extent to which cohabitation really does resemble marriage and, in practice, it may be hard to categorise relationships, particularly if they are not stable.

A similar question arises in relation to second marriages. A major Italian survey, for example, treats remarried lone parents as lone parents, thus raising again the fundamental question of what it is that is being measured and why. However, even if the approach is adopted that natural parents have a responsibility toward their children for life, it can still be argued that the parent who has custody of the children is in a significantly different situation if living in a new marriage rather than living without a partner.

The question can be extended further to first marriages if it is thought that resources and caring responsibilities are not generally shared in a fair way, that is, to what extent are the disadvantages faced by lone mothers different from those faced by mothers married to the father of the child? However, while doubt exists on these matters, it is of concern to policy makers to know how many people are bringing up children while not living as a couple.

There are other issues relating to household status, for example, whether only those parents who live entirely on their own (that is, not only those without a partner, but also those living without any other adult) are 'real' lone parents.

Although the people with whom a lone parent lives may affect living standards, such people do not usually have legal responsibilities towards the child and may or may not choose to 'help out' with baby-sitting, finance etc. Lone parents may also be sharing out of necessity and not out of choice. Excluding sharers may therefore exclude many of those whom government policies need to reach.

In relation to the definition of dependent 'children', there are many issues, for example, should a simple age dividing line be used and, if so, which one? Should those living at home without an independent income still be considered dependent even if they are beyond the age at which their parent is legally obliged to maintain them? And should the definition relate to the education status of the child, as it does in this country, for example?

In summary, recent changes have given rise to a multiplicity of situations: unmarried mothers, divorced mothers, cohabiting couples (separated and together), step-families, absent fathers, a higher proportion of young people continuing in education and training and a high proportion unemployed, etc.

From the point of view of monitoring changes in family and living patterns, all these situations are of interest. However, for comparative purposes one definition has to be chosen and there does seem to be a case for focusing on lone parents with day-to-day responsibility for children. For this, and a number of pragmatic reasons, the following standard definition is used here, that is a parent who:

- does not live in a couple (married or cohabiting)
- may or may not live with others (eg friends, parents)
- lives with at least one child under 18 years old.

Nevertheless it is clear that the more fluid and flexible living arrangements become and the more situations are formed which do not fall into any of the traditional categories – eg partners who do not live together but have a close relationship which may involve sharing of financial resources or vice versa – the harder it is likely to become to distinguish a lone parent family.

Comparing like with like? Sources of information

In practice, many of the national figures are not based on definitions which have been chosen because anyone considers them desirable but are simply by-products of information collected for other purposes.

The figures presented here are mostly based on specific surveys, sometimes combined with Census data. As not all countries have a survey like the British General Household Survey which collects information about lone parents every year, most of the results have to be treated with caution. They are tentative and do not all relate to exactly the same year, although all are up to date at least to the mid-1980s.

There is perhaps a case for a separate European-wide household survey but, in the meantime, the most appropriate potential, but existing, European source is the Labour Force Survey. This is carried out at regular intervals on a comparable basis in each EC country under the terms of a Regulation derived from the Treaty of Rome. But the published volumes do not include information about lone parent families.

However, as Table 10.3 demonstrates, a great deal more information is collected than is actually published and this does include some information about lone parent families. Although the Labour Force Survey by no means provides all the information that might be relevant to lone parent families, if there were enough pressure for this to be done, it could be adapted to provide such basic information as their number, marital status, ages of children, education and labour market status of the children, and of the parent, as well as trends over time.

Table 10.3 Percentage of all mothers and of lone mothers with children aged 0–4 in full-time and part-time employment, 1988

| | Full-time | | Part-time | | Total empl. | |
	All %	Lone %	All %	Lone %	All %	Lone %
Belgium	37	32	16	10	53	42
Denmark	46	39	29	31	75	70
Germany	16	26	18	15	34	41
Greece	33	41	6	6	40	47
Spain	24	44	4	6	28	50
France	38	45	14	8	52	53
Ireland	19	13	6	4	25	17
Italy	35	53	5	5	40	58
Luxembourg	27	73	9	2	36	75
Netherlands	4	7	25	11	29	18
Portugal	54	56	6	9	61	65
UK	11	6	25	12	37	18

Notes: The definition of a lone mother is not the same as that used in the EC report. It only includes those who are householders and does not exclude all those who are cohabiting.

The part-time category varies in scope from country to country. In some, eg Denmark, part-timers tend to work much longer hours than others eg the UK.

In countries where the number of lone mothers is very small, the sample sizes in each category are likely to be very small.

Source: Figures from the Labour Force Survey, 1988 provided by Eurostat to the European Childcare Network, published in Cohen, B (1990) *Caring for Children.* Family Policy Studies Centre

How many? Numbers and characteristics

On the standard definition described above, the number of lone parent families as a proportion of all families with children in the EC appears to be at least 10 per cent. The country figures are shown in Table 10.4.

Those countries which have used a relatively consistent definition over time and which have used a definition close to the 'standard' one all show an increase in the proportion of lone parent families since about 1970, that is, Denmark, Germany, France, the Netherlands and Great Britain. Indeed, latest figures for Great Britain show that the proportion rose to 17 per cent in 1989 – from 14 per cent in 1987, which was the latest figure available at the time the figures were collected (OPCS, 1990).

Over the longer term, a useful way of looking at the situation may

Table 10.4 Lone parent families as a proportion of all families with children

%	Country
14	Denmark, UK (GB)
12–13	Germany, France
10-12	Belgium, Luxembourg, Netherlands
5–10	Spain, Ireland, Italy, Portugal
Under 5	Greece

Source: Family Policy Studies Centre (1989). Report to the European Commission, *Lone Parent Families in the EC*

be to see it in terms of a U curve, due initially to a decrease in the number of widows and then to a rise in the number of divorced and separated people. It may be that different countries are at different points on the U curve, although without further information it is not possible to say for certain whether it does apply to all countries. It is likely that stages of development may be combined in some countries.

Although the degree of detail available about lone parents varies from one country to another, some generalisations are possible, although not all of these are based on information from all countries:

- The overwhelming majority are women, that is between eight and nine out of ten.
- The unmarried category is the smallest – at most one in five is unmarried. The largest group consists of divorced and separated people.
- Very few are aged under 25. In most countries, the proportion is less than one in ten, although it is higher than that in Great Britain.
- They have fewer children than couples do. Most have only one child.
- Their children are on average older than those in two parent families, although this does not apply to the 'never-married' category of lone parent.
- Most live on their own but the proportions doing so vary from country to country, for example, the figure was 96 per cent in Denmark and 80 per cent in Italy.

An important question concerns the length of time that a person remains a lone parent. Very little information is available on this subject but evidence from four countries suggests that over half leave the lone parent state within five years, either through remarriage or because the children leave home or reach the age beyond which they are no longer considered as children.

These figures may vary over time as marriage and remarriage rates have been tumbling, although, in countries where the information is available, this appears to some extent to be offset by a rise in cohabitation. The age of the lone parent and of the children are also likely to affect the issue. Younger mothers may generally be more likely to marry or remarry but if their children are young and they do not remarry, they potentially face a longer period as lone parents.

However, as far as policies are concerned, even two years on a subsistence income or struggling to make ends meet could be important for a child's development, and another implication of taking a dynamic view is that many more people are likely to pass through a phase in a lone parent family than the 'snapshot' numbers presented here.

Where does the money come from? Sources of income

Information about income is very patchy, but it is possible to draw some broad conclusions about the three main sources of income that lone parents are likely to depend on, that is, maintenance payments from a former partner, employment and social benefits.

Information from seven of the EC countries illustrates the fact that maintenance payments are usually very low, often non-existent and frequently paid irregularly or not at all. For example, in one Belgian survey, lone mothers' average share of disposable income from maintenance was only 10 per cent. In Great Britain, only 4 per cent of lone parents had maintenance payments as their main source of income in 1987 (House of Commons Hansard, 1990).

This general conclusion applies even in those countries which have guaranteed advance maintenance payments schemes, although the figures do vary. For example, according to one major German survey, only 15 per cent of lone mothers have maintenance as their main source of income, and, in France, according to one French survey, the share of revenue from maintenance or a pension in the father's name was on average 13 per cent.

In most EC countries laws distinguish between maintenance for spouses and children. The presumption in the former case tends to be that no maintenance should be available unless one of the spouses has good reason not to be able to support themselves, whereas the presumption in the case of children usually is that the absent parent should provide maintenance unless his (her) income is too low.

In those countries which have a set scale or clear guidance for awarding maintenance payments the amounts are related to the ex-partner's income, a factor which is also taken into account in other countries. The level of the ex-partner's income and commitments is crucial either because it determines the level of maintenance payments awarded or, if the maintenance payments are not realistic, it is likely to influence the amount, if any, that is actually paid. In France, for example, money was not recovered from half the debtors pursued in 1986, either because they could not be found or because they did not have the money.

In several countries, for example, Denmark, France and Germany, the problem is shouldered by public institutions through a system of guaranteed advance payments where money is advanced to the custodial parent and the relevant public body takes responsibility for recovery from the absent one. This is not the same as paying social assistance and then chasing the 'other' parent for the money. Nor is it the same as the scheme of child support proposed in this country and mentioned in the introduction to this paper.

Although the role of employment as a source of income for lone parents varies dramatically from one country to another, in general it is undoubtedly a more important source of income than maintenance payments. As Table 10.3 shows, the variations between countries for mothers with a child under five are substantial, and there are similar differences in the employment of mothers with older children.

It is interesting to note that in some countries lone mothers are much less likely to be employed than other mothers; in some there is little difference; and in some lone mothers are much more likely to be employed than other mothers. The availability of social security benefits is likely to be part of the explanation as, in countries where these are not widely available, lone mothers may have no choice but to take employment.

However, the overall level of mother's employment does not appear to be related to a single factor, even the availability of childcare services, which may nevertheless be crucial for enabling mothers to take employment in countries where their employment is now low (Moss, 1988).

The role of social security benefits as a source of income varies enormously between countries. In some, they are like maintenance payments in that they play a very minor role; in others, while employment predominates, they are an important secondary source; and in yet others, they are the major source of income for lone mothers.

In only one country is there a benefit aimed directly at lone parents which is designed to provide them with a basic living income and that is the French A (Allocation de Parent Isole). This means-tested benefit is paid by the family allowance authorities to lone parents with a child under the age of three or for one year after becoming a lone parent. In practice only about 10 per cent of lone parents receive API.

Widows' benefits are long established in most countries. They are often related to the contributions paid by, or the employment record of, the husband under social insurance schemes. Widows may also be entitled to occupational pensions from their husband's employer. They have therefore been relatively well provided for, although this may change in the future. For example, in Denmark there is no distinction between widows and other lone parents and in one or two countries widows' benefits have recently been cut back or restricted to those with children. The Danish pattern may therefore become more common.

The Deserted Wives Benefit in Ireland is the only social insurance benefit for women in case of marital breakdown, although several countries provide benefits in one form or another for deserted children. In order to receive the benefit 'desertion' has to be proved. As many as half of the applications for this benefit (and the parallel Deserted Wives Allowance within the mans-tested scheme) are refused and about half of the refusals are either because the husband was not deemed to have left of his own accord or 'reasonable efforts' had not been made to obtain maintenance from him.

Variations in the level and coverage of family allowances are enormous although every country provides some form of family allowance for some families. For example, an employed lone parent, or other family, with three children in Spain would have received about £4 a month whereas a similar family in Belgium would have received about £160 a month in 1988.

Pro-natalist family allowances, which pay higher rates the more children there are in order to encourage families to have more children, exist in several countries and work to the disadvantage of lone parents because lone parents rarely have three or more children and very often have only one child. Maximum rates are, in many countries, paid for three or four children, and in France the basic allowance is not paid at all for the first child.

In some countries family allowances are only paid to those in employment or in receipt of a social insurance benefit. This and other benefits provided through employment, such as medical care in many countries, disadvantage lone parents because it is generally much rarer for both parents in a two parent family to be out of the labour force. It also provides a very strong incentive for lone parents to take employment even if they cannot make satisfactory arrangements for the care of their children.

In some countries substantial proportions of lone parents rely on social assistance (used here to mean benefits similar to Income Support) while in other countries there simply is no such benefit.

The rules also vary a great deal. For example, some exempt lone parents from the requirement to seek work but in some cases this only applies to those with children below a certain age.

In spite of the diversity of employment patterns and social benefits, the evidence presented by most countries confirms previous findings about the standards of living experienced by lone, as compared with two, parent families: their average standard of living is lower and they are far more likely to be living in poverty, whatever the measure of poverty used. This also applies to other indicators of lifestyle such as home ownership, car ownership, and going out in the evenings.

Lone parents are not a homogeneous group, however. A divorced mother in her late 30s, working full-time, with a university education and who has only briefly, or never, left the labour force is in a very different position from a young 'never-married' mother, with little education and a child below school age, struggling to balance child care and a part time job.

Those countries which had information on the differences between lone mothers and lone fathers also showed that lone mothers generally have lower incomes than lone fathers and are less likely to be employed. This may, to some extent, be due to the fact that, in the few countries where the evidence is available, lone fathers tend to have older children than lone mothers, as well as to fathers' stronger position in the labour market.

Conclusion

A recurring question in much of the literature about lone parents, and in particular lone mothers, is the extent to which the cause of their low income lies in the fact that they are lone parents and the extent to which the roots of the problem need to be traced further back to the division of labour within families where men are the primary breadwinners and women the primary carers – a division which leaves a parent particularly vulnerable when s/he has to combine both roles (Millar, 1989).

Policies which assume the former would concentrate on lone parents in particular whereas policies which assume the latter would include families in general as well. This is not to say that, even if gender equality were achieved within couples, there might not be a case for providing lone parents with some compensation for the time and money which a partner would spend on the child.

A fourfold classification of policies which would incorporate this distinction has sometimes been suggested (Kammerman and Kahn, 1989) and, slightly adapted, it provides a useful way of analysing policy strategies.

Given the diversity of policies – or lack of them – in different countries at the moment, the short-term response in each would need to be different even if they were all following a common strategy and, in practice, these diverse policies are frequently not the result of deliberate strategies but *ad hoc* responses to changing circumstances or simply the result of neglect.

Nevertheless, the adapted fourfold classification of strategies, which are not necessarily mutually exclusive, provides a useful basis for discussion. Strategies three and four could be regarded as primarily designed to help all families, strategy two is by definition specific to lone parents and strategy one would treat lone parents as one of the larger group of poor people.

1   An anti-poverty strategy

Supporting lone parents as part of a more general concern with the needs of poor families – a strategy which could permit them to remain 'at home' while rearing their children.

The British Income Support is often cited as an example of this kind of strategy, and although 'social assistance' in several countries plays a similar role, the extent to which it does enable lone parents to remain 'at home' varies; as described above, some countries require lone parents with a child over a certain age to be available for work.

Unless all the causes of poverty have been eliminated and employment opportunities improved, some 'safety net' benefit for those out of work is probably necessary for the economic security of lone parents as well as others and it is interesting to note that, in France, where 'social assistance' was little more than local charity, a national minimum income scheme, in some ways similar to Income Support, was introduced at the beginning of 1989.

However, in countries where large numbers of lone parents are dependent on such a benefit, there has been some concern both from governments anxious to keep public expenditure under control and from those who do not think that bare subsistence minimum benefits are suitable as a way of living for several years.

2   A categorical strategy

Special benefits for lone parents which could permit them to stay out of the labour force while rearing their children.

The drawbacks of social assistance have led some to suggest a special benefit for lone parents. The French API mentioned above is the only existing benefit in EC countries for all types of lone parents designed to provide a living income but it is of very limited duration.

A possible objection to such benefits is that they can trap lone parents in the home rather than provide them with choice. In this respect, there is a crucial difference between non-means-tested and means-tested benefits as the former more readily allow lone parents to combine receipt of benefit with earnings (see strategy three).

Another objection to specific benefits for lone parents is that they might encourage the formation of such families. If this is considered a problem, a solution, but a costly one, would be to pay a similar child carers' benefit to married mothers or fathers. A benefit of this kind exists in France and Germany, although it is only payable for a short time, and in France only to certain families. This solution might also meet the objection that the needs of mothers within two parent families are similar to those of lone mothers.

An important question is whether such a benefit should only go to those who are out of the labour force or whether it should also be paid to those in work to enable them to pay for childcare. The answer to this depends not only on attitudes to whether the caring parent should work but also on the availability of publicly provided childcare services.

3   An active family strategy

Policies directed at all families which could include additional assistance for lone parents.

In countries where there is an explicit family policy, it is often linked to goals which are unfamiliar in this country, such as increasing the size of the population, and the structure of family allowances often reflects this. Countries which have the most generous family allowances therefore tend to gear them towards larger families. But (see above) lone parents tend to have smaller families on average and very often have only one child.

So, although family policies, such as family allowances, could be of considerable help to lone parents, they need to be designed with lone parents as well as other families in mind. A policy which would give equal weight to each child whatever the number in the family seems most likely to meet that objective; and an increment for lone parents might provide an acceptable compromise to the objections to a specific benefit for lone parents.

If paid at a rate that covered, or made a major contribution towards, the subsistence costs of a child, they could greatly ease movements into employment and would make part-time employment a more viable option. They could therefore be combined with strategy four, particularly if, like Child Benefit, they were not means-tested.

This is not to say that means-tested benefits cannot be combined with employment, as Family Credit is designed to be in this country, but, of their nature, means-tested benefits create problems because of the way that benefit is withdrawn as more money is earned and because take-up tends to be low. They are also complicated to administer and delays are common. In this respect they are of least help to those whose circumstances, like lone parents or the unemployed, are most likely to change.

Systems for advancing maintenance payments in respect of the children could be part of an active family policy which would at least make a small contribution to the income of lone parents. But they can take many different forms, some of which are likely to have a greater impact on the income of lone parents than others.

In practice the different schemes in existence reflect the different pressures which have led to their establishment, for example, concern to provide income security for lone parents and to relieve them of the burden of chasing their ex-partner through the courts; belief in the moral duty of both parents to provide for their children; and governments' desire to keep public expenditure under control.

Depending on which motive predominates they can be more or less punitive in the amount of money extracted from the absent parent and in the conditions to which the custodial parent is subjected; and more or less benefit the lone parent. Their success in alleviating poverty is also likely to depend on other policies pursued at the same time.

The proposals in the White Paper mentioned at the beginning of this chapter, for example, are designed to help those lone parents who are in employment, not those on Income Support. The extent to which other policies really do facilitate employment is therefore crucial.

4 An integrated labour market and family strategy which would promote gender equality at work and in the home

Policies designed to facilitate mothers' employment, which need to be distinguished from those which would simply drive mothers into low paid jobs, are particularly associated with the Scandinavian countries and, within the EC, with Denmark; and the availability of good quality, free or reasonably priced childcare facilities for children of the relevant age has been one of the most important elements in such a strategy (Moss, 1988, 1990).

Although none of the Scandinavian countries appears to have entirely succeeded in removing gender inequalities (Kamerman and Kahn, 1989), nor to have removed the higher risk of poverty which lone parents face, their strategy does appear to have successfully removed many of the obstacles to the employment of mothers in general (even if it was originally a response to employers' demands for women's labour). This high rate of employment has also been accompanied by a range of other policies which might be expected to improve lone parents' income prospects.

At the time the information was collected, Danish policies included universal child benefit, paid at the same rate for all children, plus an extra amount for lone parent families, a system of advance maintenance payments for children related to the absent parent's income but with a guaranteed minimum paid by the government, a similar payment for children of a widowed parent and those where paternity cannot be proved which is paid at the same level as the guaranteed minimum, relatively generous employment policies, such as parental leave and leave to look after sick children, as well as one of the highest levels of childcare services in the EC. (But see Villadsen, this volume, for a discussion.)

If the Danish example were to be followed in this country, current concerns would need to be turned on their head. Policies targeted at lone parent families are unlikely to do much for families in general but policies targeted at all families might do a great deal to help lone parent families.

Notes

1 The major source of up-to-date information about the number of lone parents is the General Household Survey which relates to Great Britain not the UK. The definition that it uses is slightly different in that dependent children are defined as all those under 16 and those aged 16–18 in full-time education.

2 The study on which this paper was based was published as a Commission document in 1989, *Lone Parent Families in the European Community* (V/545/89-EN). This, in turn, was based on reports from an expert in each of the twelve EC countries. These were not published independently, although copies may be available from the experts who are listed in the main report. Jane Millar and Jonathan Bradshaw were advisors to the report. Unless otherwise specified, information and statistics provided in this Paper are based on these country reports which were completed at the end of 1988.

References

Family Policy Studies Centre (1990) *One parent families*. Fact Sheet.

Lord Chancellor, Secretary of State for Scotland, Secretary of State for Social Security, Secretary of State for Northern Ireland and the Lord Advocate (1990) *Children Come First: The Government's proposals on the maintenance of children*. HMSO, Cm 1263.

Brown, J (1989) *Why don't they go to work? mothers on benefit*. Social Security Advisory Committee, Research Paper 2, HMSO.

European Commission (1982) *One Parent Families and Poverty in the EEC*. V/2541/2/82EN, Brussels.

Kamerman, S B and Kahn, A J (1989) *Single-parent, female-headed families in Western Europe: social change and response*, International Social Security Review 1/1989, International Social Security Association, Geneva.

Lefaucheur, N (1987) *Les 'familles monoparentales' existent-elles? 'Do lone parent families exist?'* Paper presented at the Seminaire Franco-Espanol, Madrid Centre National de Recherche Scientifique, Paris.

OPCS Monitor (October 1990) *General Household Survey, Preliminary Results for 1989*.

House of Commons Hansard (1990) *Written Answer 26 February 1990 col.59–60*. HMSO.

Moss, P (1990) *Childcare in the European Communities 1985–1990*. Women of Europe Supplements 31, 1990, Brussels.

Moss, P (1988) *Childcare and equality of opportunity*. European Commission, Brussels.

Millar, J (1989) *Poverty and the lone parent family: the challenge to social policy*. Avebury, Gower Publishing.

11 Reconstructing Scandinavian welfare

Søren Villadsen

1 The Scandinavian welfare state model

Introduction

Relations are often difficult between parents and a child. This is also the case with the decentralised welfare state model in Scandinavia. Born from a liberal father and a Social Democratic mother the child developed quite a complex nature. Social science in Scandinavia has been rather preoccupied with this so-called 'Scandinavian Model'. What will become of it?

Apart from normal national chauvinism this interest derives from a mixture of empirical research and more or less theoretical observations regarding the nature of welfare states in Scandinavia. The intensified interest in this welfare state model is of course strongly influenced by ongoing reconstruction policies in the various countries and by possible effects of European integration and harmonisation. With eight years of bourgeois coalition governments in the Danish case, reconstruction policies are perhaps most visible here, but many social and political processes are of a common nature between the Nordic countries. Sweden's and Norway's possible future entry into the EC will strengthen the joint nature of reconstruction policies in these countries – and perhaps the departure from some of the fundamental principles of the Scandinavian Model.

The purpose of this paper is to analyse the ongoing reorganisation process. What are the effects on social welfare provision and on local democracy? The reorganisation process may lead away from what has been supposed to be a consensual, welfare state regime and perhaps lead into a much more polarised and atomised society – with the consent of many of the important national actors in the very same system! How is such a development to be understood, and what kind of central variables and structures should be analysed in the presentation of the reconstruction process?

To understand changes and patterns of consensus or conflict the paper starts with a brief introduction to some of the central structures and aspects of the Scandinavian Welfare System (SWS). After that three areas are selected with the purpose of giving more specific information about changes (the welfare concept, labour market policies, and social security). The purpose here is to investigate whether there are fundamental changes of principles at play, such as changes in social citizenship. Special emphasis is laid on the Danish case because of the very active reconstruction policy and because of some rather extreme developments of the welfare state organisation in this country.

Changes in the institutions of democracy, decentralisation and participation are also vital parts of the reconstruction process and should be studied in the perspective of a global reconstruction of welfare state institutions. These democratic institutions were developed as important dimensions of the welfare state system and of social citizenship.

The Scandinavian Welfare System – some basic components

The Scandinavian welfare state has been one of constant develop-ment and change. It can hardly be said to have been fully developed before the recent process of reconstruction was started. The period of a developed welfare state structure only lasted a few decades (and in certain respects only one decade) before new policies pointing in other directions started. With bourgeois coalition governments and a much deeper industrial crisis in Denmark than in the other Scandinavian countries reconstruction here takes on a more fundamental character.

The Scandinavian Welfare System (SWS) is generally associated with the following features (Esping Andersen and Korpi, 1983–4; Rold Andersen, 1984; Amoroso, 1983–4):

1 General, manysided and encompassing public welfare service provision.
2 Universal and relatively high standards of social service provision, free of charge (for services considered essential) and paid by taxes (a major part of these being progressive income tax). Services are guaranteed by legal rights to citizens.
3 A large public sector involved in redistribution of incomes to the poorer parts of the population, ie a claimed principle of solidarity. Social policies are aiming at the integration of the totality of the population, not just at particular target groups.

Einhorn and Logue (1989), having studied Scandinavian welfare as participant observers, stress the following four disparate elements in the SWS:

1 '. . . a network of transfer payments from those currently employed to those who are not.'
2 '. . . the provision of certain social services based on need rather than on the ability to pay.'
3 '. . . the need to manage the economy . . . by minimising cyclical and structural unemployment . . .'
4 '. . . serious effort to adjust the market economy at the micro level of wage formation to curtail its tendency to generate unemployment.'
                            (Einhorn and Logue, 1989, p143–4)

Esping Andersen and Korpi describe the SWS by saying that it is a characteristic example of an 'institutional welfare state' seen as a contrast to the 'residual welfare state', where public intervention plays a much less important role, a lot more is supposed to be handled by the market and public intervention is not taken for granted in case of social problems occurring (Esping Andersen and Korpi, 1983–4, p9 ff.).

Jespersen (1990, p1), concentrating on the Swedish 'archetypal' example of the model, stresses three main features, '(1) The percentage of GDP disposed by the government, (2) the rather favourable trade off between unemployment and inflation, and (3) the high degree of wage/income equalization.'

Besides these features other aspects of the SWS have been debated and mentioned as integrated parts of this kind of welfare state. One of these features is the strong position of trade unions and the Social Democratic Party. Membership of trade unions is today nearly universal (between 80 and 90 per cent) and in this respect in strong contrast to all other EC countries. The enormous differences in trade union membership between selected countries can be seen from Table 11.1, which also includes rather recent figures that may only be estimations. In the Danish case figures from manual workers as well as those from salaried employees are given. There seems to be some internal disagreement about the actual level of membership, since data are collected in different ways.

It should be noted that, while affiliation to trade unions in Denmark has continued to increase, the opposite trend is visible in most other European countries. Trade union membership in Denmark is closely linked to unemployment insurance benefits that again are highly dependent on state support and state policies. This is one of the reasons why the strength of tri-partite institutions, particularly regarding labour market policy-making and implementation, has been emphasised.

Even neo-corporatist tri-partite arrangements have been mentioned as distinguishing features of the Scandinavian Model and the SWS (Amoroso, 1983–4). Since much of this has disappeared in the Danish case with the exit of Social Democratic minority or coalition governments from 1982 and these features exist elsewhere, they

Table 11.1 Trade union affiliation percentage for workers and salaried employees, 1980–5 and 1987, in various EC countries

	1980–85	1987*	
Denmark	80	80	
UK	60	48	
FRG		43	
Netherlands	40		
France	20	10	

Denmark	Manual workers	Salaried employees	All
1940	54	43	51
1950	61	52	58
1960	67	54	62
1970	74	53	64
1979	84	77	80
1987	91	87	88

*Quoted from le Monde. UK figure corrected by N. Manning.

Sources: The Danish Federation of Trade Unions, The Internal Market and the Social Dimension. Copenhagen, 1989. Levevilkår i Danmark. Statistisk oversigt 1988. København: Danmarks Statisk og Socialforskningsinstituttet. The percentages are members as a proportion of all workers and salaried employees.

may perhaps rather be understood in relation to a different kind of 'model'.[1]

All these principles are now either in a process of reconstruction or under debate. Some changes are rather fundamental, others only incremental and not changing the welfare system yet. But the point in this paper, which will be dealt with in more detail below, is that other elements are perhaps even more fundamental in the SWS than described in the points cited above.

The economic size of the public sector as a distinguishing feature of the SWS has recently been questioned. More detailed analyses show that 'real' differences in size between developed welfare states such as The Netherlands, West Germany and Denmark are perhaps in reality not very impressive (Forum for Industriel Udvikling, 1990; Rold Andersen, 1990). In these analyses the private provision of pensions and other welfare services in Holland and Germany and some other factors are taken into account when comparing volumes of the public sector in countries that are very difficult to compare. This may of course be quite right, but nevertheless the fact remains that these welfare policies are public and have a particular structure in the Scandinavian case.[2]

In the period of rapid economic growth in the 1960s the welfare state collective consumption in Sweden and particularly Denmark grew relatively very fast in comparison to other European countries (not to mention the U.S.A.). But growth particularly at the local level continued after the economic backlash in 1974 a backlash that was felt by far most dramatically in Denmark, whereas Norway (large production of North Sea oil under state control) and Sweden (industrial and economic policies) were much less influenced and had much lower unemployment rates.

As a crude analysis of these figures I have presented index-figures in Table 11.2, where any percentage for collective consumption for each country in 1960 equals 100. The countries are placed in two groups, the Scandinavian ones and other European countries. Inside these groups countries are ranked according to the size of their proportion of collective consumption in 1980.

In the Scandinavian case it can be noticed that Sweden and Denmark have had a much higher relative growth in collective consumption than the other countries. The growth in Norway started later and thus does not influence these figures too much. Norway is different from Denmark because of some important state owned industries. In this respect Denmark has a very liberal system. Also in Denmark's case spending on defence is relatively lower than in other countries, which makes the proportion of other types of collective consumption more similar to the Swedish case and the growth even more impressive. We shall look into the development in the 1980s in Section 3 of this chapter.

The questions of spending and size of collective consumption at aggregate levels are difficult to estimate precisely. Instead of concentrating on this aspect the present author has suggested that one should look at the structure of the public sector and the administrative culture and practices as some of the key elements in the SWS and certainly if any kind of particular model for the Scandinavian countries should be suggested (Villadsen, 1989 and forthcoming). The policy process, the practices and the structure of

Table 11.2 Collective consumption as a proportion of GNP, 1960–80 in selected countries. Transfer incomes excluded.

	1960	1980	1980-index
Sweden	15.8	28.9	183
Denmark	12.3	26.8	218
Norway	12.9	18.8	147
UK	16.6	21.5	129
Germany	13.4	20.1	150
Holland	12.8	18.0	141
France	13.0	15.2	117

Source: Rold Andersen, 1984, p26. (Based on OECD statistics)

the public sector and of public welfare provision certainly singles out this model as something different in relation to other kinds of market economies or even welfare states.

An enormously important role is played by local government (the 'commune') in the Scandinavian countries, which means that in all economic and social respects the enormous size of local government is a vital part of this particular administrative and political welfare system; but other and related structures are also of major interest in this connection. As a crude illustration one figure can be mentioned here. 71 per cent of all public employees in Denmark are employed in communes and counties (regional communes only responsible for certain specialised services). The equivalent figure in the UK is about 40 per cent and in the south of Europe the figure is close to 10 per cent. There are some important policy consequences of this ongoing and self-propelling decentralisation process. In Section 2 of this chapter the consequences of decentralisation of welfare services are discussed further.[3]

Public, private and mixed social service organisation at the local level: an example from day care for children

The public service organisation would on the surface seem to fit only partly with the principle of the SWS that welfare services are publicly provided. Though major reforms as mentioned above have made social services a government responsibility and particularly a local government task, a number of mixed or even private organisations still exist at the level of implementation. This is most frequent within health services (General Practitioners and a number of specialised medical services etc). But all this is under rather tight public control regarding prices, quality etc. Also in day care for children various mixed forms exist, and these are going to be briefly discussed as one example of mixed organisational principles within a unified social service system.

Reforms of the welfare system have generally been of a very thorough nature. The major complex of reforms in the 1970s included the following main elements:

1 Reorganisation and professionalisation of social services in principle in one organisation as a unified social service system integrating a whole range of different state, local government and private services at the local level as a public responsibility but still using mixed forms of organisation in many areas.

2 Decentralisation or perhaps rather 'communalisation', ie organisation and large scale development of welfare services within the reorganised local government system. But the

decentralised system was to be kept under public control from clients and from central state agencies.

3 Maintenance of some private and semi-public organising principles particularly in health services protecting the market for medical commodities, but also regarding some day care centres, homes, kindergartens etc.

Various kinds of mixed organisations at the local government level exist with looser or tighter control from state agencies. The case to be mentioned here is that of nurseries, kindergartens and day care centres for older children. Most children go to a kindergarten before starting in school at the age of six years (first year is a pre-school class). Since the proportion of women in the labour market is extremely high particularly in Sweden and Denmark (80 per cent and still growing, 90 per cent of women between 25–29 years, which is close to the proportion of males in work), most families or single parents use the various institutions for children. This is also caused by the fact that children start late in school and only stay there for a few hours during the first years – and never stay there late in the afternoon unless they participate in club activities or other voluntary activities. The proportion of children in kindergartens, nurseries, daycare centres or private day care is very high, but varies a lot between local authorities.

In Figure 11.1 day care for children in various types of institutions

Figure 11.1 Day care enrolment for children in all Danish local authorities 1983–91 (prognosis)

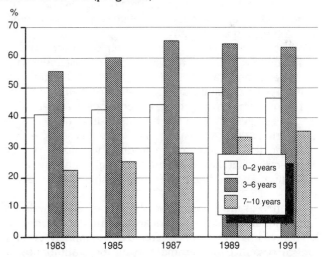

Source: Redegørelse om den offentlige sektor, Danish Ministry of Finance, 1989, p52.

is shown. 50 per cent of babies are in day care (nurseries or private homes subsidised and controlled by local authorities), 65 per cent of those between three and seven years are in kindergartens etc., but only 35 per cent of the youngest school children are in some sort of (officially recognised) day care. School children are increasingly cared for in school-day care in the afternoons and in the early mornings.

One of the interesting things about the organisation of this local government responsibility is that a lot of it is organised as mixed or even private enterprise – but under local government control. Many kindergartens are part of some kind of national organisations, for instance the Social Democratic influenced 'Free Kindergartens', various Christian kindergartens and many other types, organised as so-called self-governing institutions. This term is rather exaggerated, though, because of local government supervision, economic control etc. Nevertheless, parents' boards in these institutions have a few powers that do not exist in institutions that are under direct local government control. The tradition of more or less self-governing social or cultural institutions is reflecting a strong historical tradition of 'movements' and free education.

2   Decentralisation under control

The public sector is very different in the European countries. Even within states that more or less fall into the category 'institutional welfare states' political and administrative structures and practices vary a lot. One of the interesting features of the SWS is the reliance on a large local government administrative system and a democratic structure supporting this system.

Offe's discussion of strategies for rationalisation of social service administration has a lot of relevance also for Scandinavian and Danish social service administration (Offe, 1984). Offe's point is that welfare policies will be under constant pressure from opposite kinds of demands from workers and employers respectively. The only way out of this dilemma for the administration is to implement different strategies for rationalisation of the social services. Reforms like that tend to be implemented through top-down procedures. This is exactly what has happened through very encompassing administrative and political reforms of the social services in Denmark.

Two reforms in the Danish case should be mentioned. The first and fundamental one was the local government reforms around 1970. This reform meant much larger, amalgamated 'communes', a universal system of government in all local authorities, a pro-fessional, administrative organisation led by the mayor, the finance committee and the chief executive. Social service and social policies had their own board, which had its own administration within local government and was given a certain discretion. A number of tasks, which proved to be a continuous process, were transferred to or collected at local and in some cases regional government level. Eventually about 60 per cent on average of all local government spending took place within social services.

The welfare state gradually developed into a number of local welfare states, 275 to be exact, with the communes as the implementing level of nearly all welfare policies and increasingly also as policy makers. The Association of Local Governments became one of the very important bargaining organisations in this development period. Budgets and staff grew fast during the 1970s as a natural consequence of task reforms and the growth in traditional areas.

Decentralisation in Denmark can be seen as a sort of compromise between liberal principles of decentralisation drawing on for instance Tiebout (1956) and more centralised Social Democratic welfare state practices (Villadsen, 1989). The principle is based on a strong, functional division of tasks and responsibilities and a certain local autonomy presumably designed to take power away from the central state. Welfare provision through the 'commune' that is responsible for all sorts of social, educational, cultural and environmental problems has thus become a basic structure in a system of local welfare states.

Decentralisation first became an ideological principle for reforms and development of welfare state institutions. Then it became a strategic element in the reconstruction of public organisations, public control and public participation. In this respect decentralisation is changing from a tool for a global change of the SD-liberal compromise into a much more radical conception of decentralisation with much less emphasis on equality between different local authorities and the legal aspect of citizenship.

3 Reconstruction policies

The parents of the Danish welfare state are not fond of their child. Neither liberal or Social Democratic politicians are defending their own creation. But aspects of the model, particularly the decentralisation principle, are developed even further and praised by all parties. In this chapter some of the major and debated areas for reconstruction policies are analysed. The areas selected are key areas of welfare state policies and have all been subject to reorganisation and debate on principles. There have been important changes in the overall economic development despite some commentators' belief that most of the reconstruction process belongs to political rhetoric. It is true that a new style and a new spirit characterise for instance all important government reports. (But also recent Scandinavian SD-manifestos.) Instead of the traditional yearly publication about public budgets a new publication since 1988 discusses the status and future of the public sector.[4]

Cutbacks in the public sector have changed the development in welfare spending and the real wages of public employees in particular have been great losers in this process. As mentioned in the first section of this chapter, the size of the public sector in economic terms has been discussed and analysed recently. Some of these analyses are summed up in Table 11.3.

The interesting result of the corrections in the table that exclude interests of public debts (very important in the Danish case) and aid for the developing countries plus some other points caused by different tax principles, is that differences between these countries disappear at the gross level – not regarding the internal structure of public budgets and welfare benefits' distribution.

Another way of looking at this is the tax structure and the level of taxation. Here too variation between the European countries is considerable. Personal income taxes are relatively much higher in Denmark and the other Scandinavian countries than in the rest of Europe (29.3 per cent in Denmark, 12.7 per cent in the UK, 11.9 per cent in FRG, 7.6 per cent in France in 1986) (OECD, 1988) whereas labour market contributions show the opposite tendency. In Denmark the level is low, 1.8 per cent, France is in the lead with 21.5 per cent. VAT and other indirect taxes show differences, but not as impressive as in the other cases. The over-all result of this puts Denmark in the lead within the EC with a 59 per cent total tax proportion of the GFI, and the FRG in the other end among the countries discussed here with 41.6 per cent.

Table 11.3 The size of the public sector in Denmark, FRG and the Netherlands. GDP at factor prices.

Percentage of GDP	Denmark	FRG	Holland
(Without correction)			
Collective consump.	30.8	25.3	18.9
Income tranfer	33.1	22.4	40.7
Total	63.9	47.7	59.6
(With correction)			
Coll. consumption	28.8	24.9	20.5
Income transfer	22.2	23.8	29.9
Total	51.0	48.7	50.4

Source: Rold Andersen, 1990, p130.

This structure of public incomes is of course a reflection of the Scandinavian and particularly the Danish way of financing and organising welfare services – and because local authorities rely on income taxes for an increasing part of their activities.

Changes in the welfare concept

Arguments from the new right have particularly and with renewed strength questioned some of the basic principles of the welfare state. The collective principle for welfare provision was and is based on the idea that social problems are **social**, ie they should be treated as a problem for society. A public effort should be made to solve the problem or ease the pain for those hit by these problems. Full employment and the need to reorganise social services as described above strongly stimulated this effort. Maintenance of an ordinary life and reintegration into society and the labour market was the guiding line. Swedish labour market policies became an ideal.

In practice things have been different at least to a certain degree, but not altogether. Some of the ambitions regarding re-integration have not been fulfilled, particularly not in the Danish case, and other programmes for early retirements etc have been introduced to lessen the direct impacts of unemployment. Local governments have met increasing problems in their management of poverty, unemployment and socialisation because of a stagnating tax base, fewer resources caused by cut-backs in state block grants, spending limits and a number of other controls and interventions.

In recent years there has been practically no growth in the private sector in Denmark, a small growth in Norway and a reasonable growth in Sweden. This has put Denmark behind other countries in many economic and labour market areas and is reflected in negative attitudes in the population regarding the possibility of solving, for instance, poverty problems.

In the Eurobarometer, *The Perception of Poverty in Europe* (1990), the attitudes in England, Denmark and Ireland are much more negative than in the rest of Europe regarding possibilities for 'the pauper's chances to make it through'. Many years of high unemployment and political frustration have made their mark on political attitudes and resulted in a decreasing political activity. In Denmark the perceived visibility of poverty and the perceived importance of cuts in welfare benefits as a reason for poverty are felt. But in contrast to Southern European countries there is also a widespread belief that poverty is caused by the individual's laziness and unwillingness to do something for themselves.

This point of view is increasingly reflected in the political rhetoric stressing personal responsibility, strengthening the family, trying to support (non-existing?) social networks etc. Perhaps a more unpleasant aspect of this trend is an increase in racist attitudes, violence and discrimination against certain foreigners, restrictions towards political refugees etc.

Changes in the labour market concept

One of the major changes in most welfare states has been the rejection of Keynesian economic policy. This has particularly been the case in England (see for instance King, 1987 or Jessop *et al*, (1989). Full employment has been a less important objective and perhaps even only an object in the long run. The political rhetoric is not quite clear on this point which certainly is of a different nature in the Nordic countries. Since 1974 Denmark has had a relatively high unemployment rate, often at about 10 per cent[5], whereas Norway and particularly Sweden have had very low figures indeed and a very active labour market and industrial policy.

In Denmark the state has increasingly withdrawn from any general responsibility in relation to labour market problems, unemployment etc. Much of this has been changed into a local government responsibility aiming at particular target groups such as young unemployed, but because of the protection of the market and private enterprise the possibilities for effective management of these problems at the local level are rather limited. Other activities are simply left to organisations or to the market to solve. And in 1989 and 1990 unemployment has been growing slowly. The ambitious paragraph in the Danish constitution from 1953 about the right to work is not quoted very often in central government's announcements these days.

Changes in the social policy concept

The problem with the reform of social laws in the mid 1970s was the timing: they were created in a period inspired by economic optimism, high employment and Keynesian economic policies. The main strategy was to see and treat social cases as 'social events' that should be re-integrated into society and the labour market. The principles of the reform were in strong contrast to Beveridge and Bismarckian principles for social security which for a large part are based on the insurance principle, with a minor role for public intervention, and privately paid insurance for the employed (originally workers) as a basis for rights to welfare benefits (Rold Andersen, 1984, ch2).

The main principle for the social reforms in Denmark in the 1970s was to stress the role of public production (or control) and allocation of social services. The main producer and allocator was designed to be the newly reformed commune through a unified social service system integrating a wide range of state, private, semi-public and local government services in one system. Prevention of deeper crises for households and individuals was stressed as a major task for local government social services, besides services in relation to children, the elderly and other target groups.

Dramatically rising unemployment figures in Denmark soon created a rather different environment for these strategies. But though economic pressure on local government spending gradually grew, the basic decentral organisational structure remained the same or was even stressed further through new tasks such as employment policies, environmental protection and housing for elderly persons.

One important strengthening of the unified local government social service system was caused by the decentralisation of labour market policies. State withdrawal from employment policies and subsequently also from labour market education was an important signal. Employment services were more and more directed towards special target groups, particularly the young unemployed, and were treated as an aspect of the now completely decentralised social policy area.

Today local governments and particularly heads of social service committees complain that they cannot meet these responsibilities without any state support. For central government, 'exit' seems to be one of the options they want to see used much more in the future. User charges in highly sensitive social policy areas are not quite new, but the combination of decreasing real wages for many groups and increasing user charges imposed by central government may certainly increase many people's desires not to pay for services by choosing exit. A recent conflict may illuminate this problem. A bourgeois local authority wants to expel all children of unemployed parents from kindergartens. There are already rather high user charges in kindergartens for normal incomes, and legislation is based on the principle of a general pedagogical service for all parents who want to send their children to an institution. The local authority has won the first round of this conflict with local parents.

Decentralisation has increasingly replaced general and guaranteed welfare benefits. The policies towards this end include the gradual abolition of a number of complaint boards and possibilities in relation to local decisions. This is described as a logical consequence of decentralisation. As mentioned above, since some parts of welfare provision are based on a total estimation of the situation of the particular client, variations between local authorities will in all probability increase with less regulation from above (state control) and from below (complaint possibility to higher levels).

4   Democracy and participation: backwards or forwards?

According to a developed concept of social citizenship (Marshall, 1950) political rights and even institutions for participation are as important as legal rights and social rights. In the SWS the crucial aspect is that social and political institutions are closely interwoven in an institutional pattern of local democracy. Public participation has been a central aspect of the development of the decentralised welfare state. The connection to decentralisation has given participation a mixed character consisting of three elements.

One element is the democratic self-government existing in boards and committees in schools, day care and other institutions. They may in some cases serve as truly democratic self-governing bodies, but may also serve other purposes that are mentioned as the following two points. The second element is participation existing as a means for public control with local authorities partly taking the place of direct state control or existing parallel to other (state organised) control institutions. This is typically found for instance in regional and urban planning. The third is participation seen as an organisational structure in a mixed society. Functional explanations seeing these institutions as serving mainly purposes of political integration should be placed under this heading.

Reconstruction policies are mixed in their approach to participation. In ideal terms the market is preferred to democratic institutions within the welfare service. But the principle of radical decentralisation has in a few cases (such as schools) been connected to elected boards. The general policy, however, has been to reduce the number of boards, hearings and participation thereby reducing public control with public service. Industrial democracy is definitely not on the Danish government agenda – on the contrary: in the few cases where a kind of industrial democracy has existed within the public sector it is in the process of being removed or it is removed already.

But public service at the local government level is still closely connected to participation and local democracy, which is difficult for a state with, after all, limited powers to get rid of. One problem for reconstruction policies is therefore that public service provided by local government is very popular among users, according to a number of surveys. And users include nearly everyone.

5   The future

There are external pressures for change. The second referendum in Denmark regarding the EC in 1986 was about the single market and those in favour of integration in Europe got nearly 60 per cent of the votes. The first vote in 1972 had more or less the same result in Denmark, whereas Norway had a small majority against. Sweden, which until now did not want to become a member, mostly because of its neutrality, is probably joining forces with the new Norwegian government to become members quickly. So the Scandinavian countries have been in different positions though gathered in the Nordic Council with a single labour market, free trade and a passport union, numerous cultural agreements etc.

There are however important differences between the Nordic Council and the EC. The Nordic co-operation is based on consensual agreements between autonomous governments (though including some semi-autonomous regions or countries), not on a hierarchical government given the right to become a sovereign policy-maker.

With the major organisations in Denmark now supporting the process of integration and with changes in the attitudes in Sweden and Norway the future of public service structure in these countries is not easy to predict.

But internal pressures for change are also widespread. The crisis in the private sector in Denmark and in private-public relations is an important background for the continued political attacks on anything that is public. In a recent paper the necessity of developing institutional solutions to social problems if the Scandinavian Model is going to survive is pointed out. Since this is not happening at the moment, the model must be in crisis, caused among other things by the weakening of the SD-party (Amoroso & Andersen, 1990). But perhaps the crisis in the private economy and the self-propelling forces of decentralisation are just as important.

If the Scandinavian Model is a child of Social Democratic Parties and trade unions – with liberal forces as the other parent, one should not forget – then this is a sad case of neglect. Political attacks have been very aggressive, and defence seems rather reluctant, unsure and unconvincing. And some ideas borrowed from the new right philosophy are increasingly appearing in the SD vocabulary.

One of the more interesting documents from the SD party appeared after a 'leak' in a Swedish newspaper and subsequently in total in the Danish trade unions' journal (*Samak-rapporten*, 1989). Increasing user charges and marketisation are accepted in a lukewarm way and also some of the basic assumptions from the new right regarding the public sector are presented as a new strategy for the SD parties.

A very recent article by a former social democratic minister[6] is also very interesting. In this article the point of view is expressed that the Nordic Model developed over more than a century is nearly worn out and that a change in fundamental principles is necessary. 'The basic ideas in the Nordic Model would be able to continue, even if essential parts of the social security system were taken out of the public sector to be financed by the two labour market parties.' In other words a return to a much more continental and pre-SWS situation. To speak of a 'Nordic Model' in this connection seems a bit far fetched. But the lack of SD enthusiasm for the kid, the decentralised welfare state, is easy to see – but perhaps not so easy to understand.

Decentralisation under control is being reconstructed. Radical decentralisation, marketisation, user charges and acceptance of inequality even in public service are some of the results of the ongoing reconstruction processes, With the lack of love from both parents the decentralised welfare state is in a deep political and social crisis mainly initiated from the top. In the longer run fundamental changes of social citizenship and the political culture are inescapable.

Notes

1 Mishra (1984) puts Sweden and Austria in a category together because of the corporate pattern and the strength of trade unionism in these countries.
2 It should be noted that in the Swedish case huge and active labour market and pension funds of a semi-public nature have been developed over a number of years and have played a central part in industrial policies.
3 This question of decentralisation, the Left and central-local conflicts over welfare policies is further dealt with in Søren Villadsen, 'Local Socialism and the New Right' in Villadsen, 1990.
4 See particularly 'Redegørelse om den offentlige sektor, 1988', Finansministeriet that until now has been the most ideological of this kind of state publications.
5 On top of the unemployment figures come nearly three times as many persons on early retirements, on long term welfare benefits etc.
6 Erling Olsen, former minister of housing, in Information, 8.10.1990.

References

Amoroso, B (1983–4) 'Den skandinaviske models udviklingsperspektiv'. *Tidsskrift for politisk økonomi*, Vol 8, No 1.

Amoroso, B and Andersen, O W (1990) *Reconsidering the Scandinavian Model.* Paper presented at a conference by the European Association for Comparative Economic Studies.

Andersen, G Esping and Korpi, W (1983–4) 'Fra fattighjælp til velfærdsstat'. *Tidsskrift for politisk økonomi*, Vol 8, No 1.

Andersen, B Rold (1984) *Kan vi bevare velfærdsstaten?* Købanhavn, AKF.

Andersen, B Rold (1990) Den danske model i EFs indre marked. Finansieringen af de offentlige udgifter i Danmark i 1990erne. Lundbeckfondens prisopgave 1989. København, Jurist- og økonomforbundets forlag.

Einhorn, E S and Logue, J (1989) *Modern Welfare States, Politics and Policies in Social Democratic Scandinavia*. New York, Praeger.

Jespersen, J (1990) *What happened to the Scandinavian Model?* Paper presented at the AISSEC-conference, Verona, September.

Jessop, B *et al* (1989) *Thatcherism*. Polity Press.

King, D (1987) *The New Right*. London, Macmillan.

IO (The Danish Federation of Trade Unions) (1989) *The Internal Market and the Social Dimension*. Copenhagen.

Marshall, T H (1950) *Citizenship and Social Class*. (New ed. 1973.) Greenwood Press.

Ministry of Finance (1988–9) *Redegørelse om den offentlige sektor*. Købanhavn.

Mishra, R (1984) *The Welfare State in Crisis*. Wheatsheaf Books.

Offe, C (1984) *Contradictions of the Welfare State*. Hutchinson.

Rasmussen, E (ed) (1990) 'Den offentlige sektors rolle i 90'ernes samfund.' *Forum for industriel udvikling*.

SAMAK-rapporten (1989) *De nordiske arbejdebevægelser*.

Tiebout, C (1956) 'A pure theory of local expenditure'. *Journal of Political Economy* 64:416–424.

Villadsen, S (1990) 'Local Socialism and the New Right'. In Villadsen, S (ed) *Big City Politics, Problems and Strategies*. RUC, Forlaget Samfundsøkonomi og Planlægning.

Villadsen, S (forthcoming) *Reconstruction of Public Service and Local Democracy*.

12 Women in the labour market: policy in perspective

Angela Dale

Introduction

Since the 1950s there has been wide-ranging and continuing change in employment and labour market structures and in women's role within them. The purpose of this chapter is to consider some of these changes, and to assess their significance for women. An underlying theme of the chapter is a concern with equality of opportunity and achievement between men and women.

If women are to achieve greater equality of employment it is likely to be at the expense of the existing male workforce (Crompton and Sanderson, 1986) and will also challenge the existing division of labour within the home. Only if there is change in the occupational structure (for example a marked expansion in higher level jobs) or in the demographic structure, could greater occupational equality be achieved without a challenge to male positions. A discussion of women's position in the labour market must therefore incorporate a consideration of the employment relationship between men and women.

A historical context

To understand the current employment relationship between men and women it is essential to consider the factors that were influential in encouraging, and also controlling, women's labour market participation in earlier decades. The post-war years were a time of considerable labour shortage. During the fifties and early sixties this had been partly met by recruitment of immigrant labour from the Commonwealth. However, during the mid-sixties, when Britain was imposing restrictions on further immigration, the government identified the extent of the continuing shortage of labour.

A Fabian pamphlet of 1966 stated, 'One of the basic economic problems of our time is shortage of manpower ... The reason extra manpower is so urgently required is that the rate of economic growth of the economy depends on it. The more people who work the more goods and services we can produce' (Fabian Society, 1966). The National Plan had forecast a 'manpower gap' of 400,000 by 1970. At the same time, it was predicted that the 'dependent population' would reach nearly 60 per cent of the total by 1970 and that this would result in increased demands on the social services, and education. Third, marriage rates were rising, thereby reducing the supply of 'middle-aged spinsters' who, traditionally, had high rates of employment. (Eighty-two per cent of all single women aged 15–60 were in the labour force at the 1951 Census (Klein, 1959).) Between 1951 and 1961 the proportion of unmarried women aged 25–54 fell from 42 per cent to 32 per cent and it was predicted that, in coming years, this would decrease to 20 per cent. Married women had a substantially lower labour force participation rate – about 25 per cent of all married women in the early 1950s, although this had risen to 29 per cent by the 1961 Census. In 1961, 59 per cent of married women in paid work worked full-time – the great majority of them having no dependent children.

These three factors – the needs of an expanding economy, the increase in the 'dependent' population and the decline in numbers of single women, produced considerable concern. The solution identified was to tap the 'reserve army' of married women and to establish jobs which would fit in with what was seen to be women's primary responsibility – home and children. Because of the strength of this ideology (probably related to Bowlby's work on maternal deprivation during the post-war period and the publicity which ensued), there seems to have been little incentive to follow the example of France and provide day care and after-school facilities which would have enabled women to work full-time; rather, the emphasis was on part-time working for mothers of school-age children. There was already a precedent for part-time working; it had been introduced during the Second World War for married women with child-care commitments as a way of enabling them to combine much needed work for the war effort with care of home and family (Walby, 1986).

There seems to have been a consensus from a variety of sources (the Confederation of British Industry, the Fabian Society and the Institute of Personnel Management) that the only way for the economy to meet the demand for extra workers was by persuading more married women to work. However, all three sources identified a reluctance by employers to accept married women and, if accepted, a reluctance to offer them anything other than unskilled work with no promotion prospects. (It is important to acknowledge that married women have traditionally had high participation rates in some industries – eg the Lancashire textile industry. Nonetheless, Walby (1986) provides a graphic account of the mobilisation of male opposition to this during the nineteenth century.)

A 1960 survey of employers (Klein, 1961) carried out for the Institute of Personnel Management, found that, generally, part-time workers were unpopular amongst employers and were used mainly for semi- and unskilled work, particularly as cleaners and canteen workers, clerical staff, typists, telephonists and receptionists. Klein summed up the results of the survey:

> One is left with the general impression that in most firms the employment of married women is accepted as a necessary expedient to tide over a period of labour shortage. Few managements, other than those traditionally employing female labour in large numbers, have yet accepted the idea that married women workers have come to stay. Adjustments to fit them into the existing labour force are therefore mostly made *ad hoc* and are not part of a long term labour policy. It will presumably need a longer period of full employment and industrial expansion before employers can be persuaded to regard married women as a substantial and useful part of their normal personnel, for whom working conditions will have to be created which will enable them to pull their full weight. (Klein, 1961, p39)

The perspective adopted by Klein, and that of other commentators at this time, assumed that women's domestic role was central, and that employers should construct jobs that would allow them to combine 'their two roles: home and work' (Myrdal and Klein, 1956). The way to do this was by providing part-time work.

However, there was still a reluctance on the part of employers. This reluctance may have been partly economic – at that time, full social security payments were needed if women worked over eight hours a week – and partly ideological, based on conceptions of women as unreliable workers, taking off time from work for domestic reasons. A CBI Working Party was established to 'undertake an appraisal of the obstacles to the employment of women' (CBI, 1967:4). The Working Party summed up: 'in nearly every case where part-time employees are now accepted and welcome, they were first introduced reluctantly. Once the first step is taken, most employers find such employees well worth while.' (CBI, 1967, p29).

Until the Second World War, it had been common practice, particularly in non-manual jobs, to impose a marriage bar which automatically removed women from their job on marriage, thereby denying any prospect of a career to married women (Lewis, 1984;

Walby, 1986). The effect of the marriage bar, even after its removal, must have been to promote a climate of opinion, amongst both employers and women themselves, that higher level jobs were not appropriate for married women.

In a nationally representative survey carried out in 1957, Klein (1961) found that 47 per cent of married 'housewives' amongst the sample expressed a desire for a job outside the home. This provides some indication of the pool of married women who might be expected to take employment if it were available. Over eighty per cent of these wanted part-time work. Quotations from women interviewed provide some indication of the extent to which they felt constrained by their positions as housewives and mothers.

It appears that, on the demand side, employers were able to exercise their preconceptions and prejudices in establishing jobs which they saw as suitable for 'part-time' working, whilst, on the supply side, many women were keen to return to paid work in a part-time capacity. Therefore, despite the labour shortage of the fifties and sixties, married women were not offered part-time jobs that gave them either opportunities or levels of pay which were comparable with those available to single full-time workers. By ensuring that women's jobs were segregated from men's and paid at a lower level, there was little challenge to men's jobs or levels of pay. Walby (1986, p207) suggests that part-time work represented a form of compromise between patriarchal and capitalist interests. She argues that 'Women's labour was made available to capital, but on terms which did not threaten to disrupt the patriarchal *status quo* in the household, since the married women working part-time could still perform the full range of domestic tasks.' The scene was therefore set for an expansion of low-level, low-paying, part-time working for married women.

Increased levels of female labour market participation

The 1951 Census recorded women's labour market participation at about 42 per cent (Joshi, 1988) and women formed over one third of the British labour force. A high proportion of women left the labour market either at marriage or family formation, only returning to paid work after a number of years absence, if at all. It was these women who represented the pool of labour which the earlier-mentioned studies had identified.

Women's labour market participation has increased dramatically since the 1950s, reaching 70 per cent in 1987 (Table 12.1). Despite the initial reluctance of employers, discussed above, the post-war increase in female labour has been almost exclusively through women with dependent children returning to part-time jobs

Table 12.1 Economic activity rates, women under 60, Great Britain

Year	Full-time	Percentages Part-time	Economically active
1901	–	–	34
1931	–	–	38
1951	37	5	42
1961	35	15	50
1971	33	22	56
1973	34	23	60
1975	33	26	62
1979	34	26	64
1981	33	25	64
1983	31	25	62
1985	33	27	66
1986	35	28	69
1987	36	28	70

Sources: Figures for 1901, 1931, 1951, 1961 from Joshi (1988) based on the Census of Population. Figures for 1971-87 from the General Household Survey published reports; self-definitions of full and part-time are used. For years 1931 and 1973-87 the lower age limit is 16. For years 1951-1971 the lower age limit is 15.

Table 12.2 Economic activity rates of women aged 16–59

	1971	1975	Percentages 1979	1983	1985	1987
No dependent children						
Full-time	49	52	51	46	47	50
Part-time	18	17	18	18	21	22
Dependent children						
Full-time	15	16	16	14	17	18
Part-time	26	35	36	32	35	37
Dependent child less than 5 yrs						
Full-time	7	6	6	5	8	11
Part-time	18	22	22	18	22	24

Source: General Household Survey published tables (based on Joshi, 1988)

(Joshi, 1988) (Table 12.2). Only since 1985 have women's full-time employment rates risen to the levels recorded in the 1950s.

An examination of the occupational distribution of male and female full-timers and female part-timers (Table 12.3) shows clearly the way in which part-time jobs are concentrated at the bottom end of the occupational spectrum. As such, women's part-time work has an occupational distribution which is distinct from both that of women and men working full-time. While these date relate to 1981, they nonetheless still represent a fairly accurate picture of the occupational distribution of these three groups to-day. Although large numbers of part-time jobs were created by employers, they have been highly segregated, particularly by gender. There are a number of reasons for this. Much of

Table 12.3 The occupational distribution of men and women working full and part-time

	Column percentages		
	men	women FT	women PT
	(1)	(2)	(3)
Professional - barristers, solicitors, accountants, university teachers, doctors, dentists, pharmacists	6	1	0
Teachers – all except university	3	7	2
Nurses – SRN, SEN, auxilliaries, medical technicians paramedicals and social workers	1	8	8
Intermediate – civil servants (EO to Senior Principal) computer programmer, systems analyst, librarian, personnel officer, manager, journalist	19	8	2
Clerical – typists, secretaries, clerks, receptionists, non-retail cashiers, telephonists	7	39	19
Shop workers – sales assistants, reps, petrol pump attendants, check out operators, cashiers	4	7	16
Skilled manual – hairdressing, cook, baker, weaver, tailor, police officer (RG IIIM)	39	10	6
Semi-skilled factory – assemblers, packers, graders, sorters, inspectors, machine operators, storekeepers	9	11	6
Child-care and domestic – school meals supervisors, canteen assistants, waitresses, care attendants	1	5	20
Other semi-skilled – agricultural workers, shelf-fillers, bus conductors, postal workers	6	3	4
Unskilled manual – cleaners, kitchen hands	5	2	16
All working	100 (51112)	100 (20216)	100 (14352)

The occupational classification is that of the Women and Employment Survey.
Part-time work is based upon self-definition.
Data refers to employees only.

Source: Dale (1987); Labour Force Survey, 1981

the post-war growth in the economy was in the service sector
– particularly in education, health, financial services, and hotel,
catering and distribution. These were all areas where women
were already highly concentrated and thus generated an increased
demand for 'female' jobs (Oppenheimer, 1970; Hakim, 1979).
These jobs tend also to be locally available and therefore fit in with
the domestic constraints of women with young children. However,
they are also of low status, highly segregated by sex and with low
rates of pay.

The effect of part-time work is not simply restricted to earnings
ability but also affects employment protection rights and eligibility
for an occupational pension. Analysis of the 1984 Labour Force
Survey (LFS) showed that 46 per cent of women who were in
'permanent' part-time jobs did not fall within most employment
protection legislation, either because of the short hours they
worked or the length of time they had been with their employer
(Dale and Bamford, 1988); also, only 15 per cent of part-timers
were contributing to occupational pension schemes (Dale, 1991).
Additionally, of course, many part-time jobs are established on a
temporary or casual basis. Even those part-time jobs which are in
higher level occupations, eg teaching, have typically not been seen
as career posts and have not been open to promotion.

It is therefore apparent that, while the number of women in paid
work has increased greatly over recent decades, this has done little
to reduce gender-based inequalities within the labour market. To
the extent that part-time work has been constructed as low-level
and low-paid, the expansion of part-time working amongst women
must be a major explanatory factor in gender inequalities within the
labour market.

Continuity of labour force participation and downward occupational mobility

Research carried out during the late 1970s and 1980s has demonstrated that, on their first return to work following child-bearing,
many women take part-time jobs at a lower level than the job
they had held before childbirth. Work history data from the
Women and Employment Survey (Martin and Roberts, 1984; Dex
1987) clearly show how movement into part-time employment
following child-bearing is associated with downward occupational
mobility. Such jobs, of course, conform to employers' perceptions,
discussed earlier, of the kind of work suitable for married women
with children.

This downward mobility is also responsible for considerable
occupational inequality between men and women, as well as

representing a considerable skill wastage. While no comparable data are yet available for men, cross-sectional comparisons suggest that at the stage in the life course when women are most constrained by domestic and child-care responsibilities, men are consolidating and improving their occupational position, typically by gaining professional qualifications and by moving into managerial and supervisory positions (Dale, 1987). Thus, in aggregate, men and women show a widening in occupational status over the life-course with married men moving up into managerial positions while married women move down into part-time personal service sector jobs.

Work in both Britain (Joshi, 1988) and the USA (Corcoran *et al*, 1983) shows that a break from employment followed by part-time working leads to a fall in income that is not recovered in later life, even if full-time work is taken. This must clearly be one factor which explains why the observed pay differential between men and women is still so high.

Greater continuity of employment over the life-cycle may be expected to help women in retaining their occupations and thereby avoiding downward mobility associated with family formation. The Women and Employment Survey showed that successive cohorts of women are returning to paid work more quickly after child-bearing. Also, the proportion of women returning to work within six months of their first birth has increased from 9 per cent for women with a first birth between 1945–49 to 17 per cent for those with a first birth between 1975–79 (Martin and Roberts, 1984). Although this may suggest that women are increasingly taking advantage of the statutory provision for six months maternity leave, the Women and Employment Survey showed no clear evidence of an increase in the proportion of women returning to full-time work. Rather, there has been an increase in the return of women to part-time work. If the part-time jobs available remain concentrated in the low level occupations shown in Table 12.3, this will exacerbate rather than reduce the disparity between men and women's employment at this stage of the life-course.

While it is tempting to make the simplistic assumption that part-time work is inevitable for women who have dependent children, this idea is quickly dispelled by international comparisons of women's employment patterns. Figure 12.1 shows the extent of full- and part-time working among women at five-year age intervals in France and the UK. It is evident that part-time working is much more prevalent in the UK and that it is particularly associated with the years of family formation. French women are more likely to retain a full-time job during the stage of family formation.

However, discontinuity of employment over the life-course and part-time work is not the sole reason for the observed differences in

Figure 12.1 Women's employment patterns in France and the UK

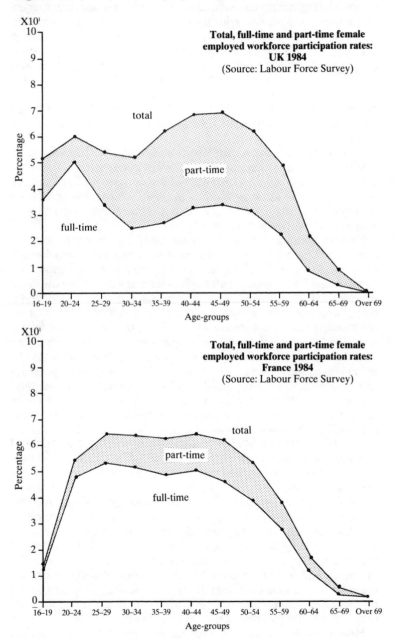

Source: Dale and Glover (1990)

men's and women's occupational status and earnings. As Beechey (1988) argues, it is important to look beyond the domestic sphere if one wishes to explain gender differences in employment patterns.

Legislation on equal pay and sex discrimination

Legislation introduced in the 1970s was, of course, aimed at providing greater equality of opportunity for women. The Sex Discrimination Act 1975 and the Equal Pay Act 1970, both of which came into effect in 1975, provided a mechanism whereby some of the grosser anomalies of gender discrimination in the labour market could be challenged. While the effectiveness of these Acts is often questioned, they have undoubtedly contributed to a climate of opinion in which it is less acceptable to deny jobs or opportunities to women.

Nonetheless, considerable male-female pay differentials are found not just in Britain but in most other western industrial countries (OECD, 1985). In Britain, data from the New Earnings Survey (DE, 1988) show that while women's full-time average earnings (exclusive of overtime) as a proportion of men's rose from 63.1 per cent in 1970 to 75.5 per cent in 1977, the 1977 figure represented a peak which has never subsequently been reached. In 1988, women's full-time earnings relative to men's were 75.1 per cent – still 0.4 per cent lower than the peak in 1977. This suggests that, while the Equal Pay Act had an effect on pay differentials immediately after it came into force, little has changed since 1977. It further implies that the 1983 Equal Pay (Amendment) Regulations, which allow a woman to claim equal pay with a man in the same employment provided her work is 'of equal value' to that of that man, has had little effect so far.

To formulate effective policies to promote greater equality for women, it is important to unravel the reasons for this. Is it explained by women occupying jobs that require lower levels of skill or education, or by women being paid at lower rates than men for jobs at similar skill levels? To pose this question raises the further, fundamental question of how skill is assessed and measured. A review of the Greater London Whitley Council job evaluation scheme, quoted by the Low Pay Review (1989), concluded that, when assessing skill level, choice of factors and the weight given to them was biased towards jobs traditionally held by men. Further, the scheme omitted factors that would recognise skills typical of women's jobs in local authorities.

Most research on male-female earnings differences is unable to make comparisons by skill level. However, the Social and

Economic Life Initiative (SCELI) collected data on three different measures of skill, relating to (1) human capital (2) discretion or choice and (3) job content. Research by Horrell, Rubery and Burchell (1989) drew comparisons between men working full-time and women working full-time and part-time. They found that 'from the specifically financial point of view, the most important issue for women, and in particular for part-timers is to achieve equal pay and equal benefits for jobs of equal skill and job content' (*op.cit.*: 34). This suggests that the 1983 'Equal Value' amendment may be helpful in obtaining higher wage rates for women. However, the authors go on to point out that, in practice, many of the industries and firms in which women work are highly constrained in their ability to pay higher wage levels and this, indeed, may be related to a policy of employing women.

The extent of occupational segregation by sex in Britain is considerable and strongly related to inequality of earnings. There is ample evidence that women in 'male' jobs have higher earnings than women working in 'female' jobs (Martin and Roberts, 1984). Part-time jobs, overwhelmingly filled by women, are much more highly segregated than full-time work and have considerably lower levels of pay. (In 1988 the average hourly earnings of women working part-time were £2.72 – less than 75 per cent of average earnings for women working full-time (Bryson, 1989)[1].) The 1975 Sex Discrimination Act may be expected to help women gain entry to occupations previously denied to them. However, problems of calculating an index which can provide a reliable measure of change in occupational segregation over time (Siltanen, 1990) mean that there is no firm consensus on whether segregation is increasing or decreasing. It is likely that there has been little consistent reduction in horizontal segregation between 1961–79.

However, changes are always most likely to be evident amongst those groups newly entering or re-entering the labour market. In particular, a comparison of successive cohorts is able to identify changes that may be expected to work their way through the occupational structure over time. The proportion of women entering higher education and the professions shows a steady increase over time which may lead to a change in the occupational distribution of women in the longer term. However, it cannot be assumed that this heralds a major change in patterns of occupational segregation generally. Work by Cynthia Cockburn (1987) suggests that sex stereotyping in YTS schemes is still very much in evidence and offers no prospect of short-term change – despite the fact that one of the explicit aims of YTS was to try to overcome it. Other research (Cross, 1987) has shown that YTS schemes are also reproducing existing forms of racial stereotyping within the labour market.

The greater representation of women in higher education

In the achievement of educational qualifications there is clear evidence that the percentage of women going into higher education is still rising. Thus women are moving towards equality with men in terms of entry to higher education. In 1965/56 women formed 28 per cent of all UK full-time university undergraduate entrants, whilst in 1986/7 they formed 42 per cent (DES, 1988). In 1987/8 they formed 49 per cent of all UK full-time polytechnic students (CSO, 1989).

In a number of professions which, in the past, had successfully excluded women, there is now near equality of entry between men and women. Crompton and Sanderson (1986) have recorded the rapidly increasing number of women entering medicine, dentistry, accountancy, banking and pharmacy. The Law Society's statistical report for 1989 reveals that women accounted for 46.6 per cent of solicitors qualifying in 1988/9, 51.9 per cent of candidates passing the solicitors' final exam in 1988 and 52.7 per cent of trainee solicitors registering between August 1988 and July 1989 (Guardian, 18.10.89). This expansion is not only related to the greater number of girls going into higher education and the removal of formal barriers to the entry of women, but also to the rapid growth of these professions, making it difficult to recruit sufficient men, especially in the south-east. The Women into Science and Engineering campaign must surely reflect the dearth of young men seeking to enter these professions, rather than the altruism of employers and professional bodies.

However, it remains to be seen whether the women now entering professions in equal numbers with men will manage to retain that equality at all levels of the career structure. At the moment women are extremely under-represented at the higher levels of most professions – for example, only about 13 per cent of hospital consultants are women (Allen, 1990).

Recent changes in the 1980s and 1990s, both in the occupational and industrial structure and in the demographic structure, are likely to influence the level of demand, not just in the professions but in all occupations and industries. This in turn will influence the extent to which government and employers are willing to promote women's entry to a wider range of occupations, and to retain women during the period of family formation.

It is important to point out that all the figures so far quoted are national statistics that do not enable the identification of any

distinctive patterns by ethnic minority group. No time series data
are available on employment participation by ethnic origin, and
numbers in non-white groups are generally too small to allow
separate analyses. However, the Department of Employment has
produced figures which combine three years' data from the Labour
Force Survey (with an annual sample size of about 200,000
individuals) which allow reliable employment estimates by ethnic
origin (CSO, 1989). These give some indication of the extent
to which national statistics submerge the distinctive employment
patterns of small ethnic groups.

The labour market experience of ethnic minorities

Estimates from the 1985–87 Labour Force Surveys show the extent
of variation amongst women from different ethnic origins; only
18 per cent of those from the Pakistani/Bangladeshi group were
economically active compared with 55 per cent of women from
the Indian ethnic group, 68 per cent in the 'white' group and 73
per cent in the West Indian/Guyanese group. It is only amongst
the 'white' group that part-time working is high – it is less than
30 per cent for the other groups. Rates of unemployment are
also considerably higher for the non-white women. It is therefore
important to recognise that most of the data discussed here are
dominated by the large white ethnic group and may not be an
accurate reflection of employment processes amongst minority
groups.

   During recent years there have been a number of major changes
that are likely to have an impact upon women's labour market
position in coming years. These changes, with the policy implications or opportunities that arise from them, are discussed below.

Labour market deregulation

Partly as a response to the economic recession of the early 1980s,
and partly in line with the Conservative government's preference
for market forces, there has been a general reduction in labour
market regulation. There has been a wide-spread adoption of the
concept and, to a lesser extent, the practice of 'flexibility' (Atkinson,
1984; Dale and Bamford, 1988; Pollert, 1988). There have been
an expansion and promotion of those forms of work which are
least subject to statutory regulation – part-time working, temporary
contracts and self-employment. Related to this is the move towards
privatisation and casualisation – for example, cleaning, catering and
waste disposal services in local authority and government must
now be tendered for by private contractors. The 1986 Wages

Act removed all workers under twenty-one years of age from the protection of the Wages Council and reduced the power of the Wages Councils for other workers. Self-employment has been heavily promoted by government, with the Enterprise Allowance Scheme providing a financial incentive to the unemployed who wish become self-employed.

There is considerable doubt over whether this opens up new opportunities for groups who might otherwise be excluded from the labour market, or whether it simply exploits the weak labour market position of these groups and thereby reinforces male-female employment differentials. Nonetheless, it is necessary to consider whether greater opportunities for 'flexible' working have made it easier for some women to earn an independent income. Westwood and Bhachu (1988) provide case study evidence of the way in which some women from ethnic minorities have been able to use opportunities for self-employment to achieve greater independence. However, the lack of regulation in the labour market also permits the exploitation of women, particularly from ethnic minorities (Mitter, 1986). As Phizacklea points out, it is important not to adopt a framework where 'dirty, arduous and poorly paid work is represented as a gift from the West to the women of the Third World' (Phizacklea, 1983:2).

Cause for concern over the impact of increasing levels of part-time working, particularly in the personal services, also comes from the Social Change and Economic Life Initiative. Generally, there has been an increase in skill levels amongst the workforce, although this has not been the case for those working in the lower levels of the personal service sector (Gallie, 1989). Thus the increase in these jobs has also brought with it deskilling relative to other sections of the work-force. This is particularly notable within part-time employment. Horrell, Rubery and Burchell (1989) also using SCELI data, argue that the growth of part-time work is likely to increase the polarisation within the labour market, with women part-timers having less skilled jobs, less pay and lower benefits than men while women in full-time jobs have similar benefits to men but nonetheless have lower rates of pay. This concern is supported by data from the New Earnings Survey (Bryson, 1989) which show a growth in the pay differential between women's full-time and part-time earnings since 1977, in both manual and non-manual jobs.

There is, then, evidence that one of the changes in the employment relationship between men and women over recent decades has been an increase in the proportion of women taking low-paid jobs with few prospects of promotion. The projected increase by the Department of Employment in women's participation levels in the age group 25–34, from 64 per cent in 1987 to 70 per cent in

1995, raises the question of whether this will be achieved by even higher levels of part-time working amongst women with dependent children. However, this rather gloomy prospect is tempered by predicted changes in both the demographic and the occupational structure during the 1990s.

The impact of change in the occupational structure and the demographic structure

During the 1990s employment growth is predicted to outstrip supply (Metcalf and Leighton, 1989). Employment forecasts carried out by the Institute for Employment Research (IER) (1988) predict an increase in total employment of about 1.2 millions between 1987 and 1995. At the same time, well documented changes in the demographic structure predict a fall of 1.3 millions in the labour force aged under 25, by the year 2000 (DE, 1989). Over the next ten years the proportion of the male work-force aged 16–24 will fall from 22 per cent to 17 per cent (Ermisch, 1990). Although the Department of Employment predicts that the civilian labour force will increase by about one million between mid-1988 and the year 2000, and 90 per cent of this increase will be amongst women, there will still remain a labour shortage. In the same way that the labour shortage of the post-war years caused employers to rethink their employment policies towards married women, the 1990s should witness a much greater recognition of the need to make better use of women's skills. Embryonic schemes to retain women during family formation and to encourage retraining by 'women returners' are already being put into operation in industries already facing shortages (eg banking). One of the interesting features of this predicted labour shortfall is that it is higher-level occupations which are predicted to expand the fastest. Forecasts by the Institute of Employment identify a 19 per cent increase in 'professional and related' occupations between 1987 and 1995; an increase of 10 per cent in management jobs and 8 per cent in craft and skilled manual work.

Recent changes in the structuring of occupational ladders may also be making it easier for women to advance vertically within higher level occupations. Lovering (1990) has argued that there is now a greater reliance upon objective measures of ability and success, which have replaced some of the traditional bases for promotion, such as length and continuity of service, which tend to militate against women's interests. There is also evidence that employers of professional workers are now less likely to demand frequent geographical mobility as part of the career process. This, again, is particularly helpful to women. What remains to be seen, however, is the extent to which these professional women will retain their occupational positions over the period of family formation or whether they will, like so many earlier generations, find themselves experiencing downward mobility at this stage.

A further question to be answered is whether this expansion of higher level occupations will simply widen the disparities between well qualified women and those women in part-time work, or whether there will be a 'trickle down' effect of benefit to all women.

Policy implications

The expansion of professional and managerial occupations provides an important opportunity for women to gain and retain higher level jobs. The staff shortages faced by employers should provide the incentive to introduce a great deal more flexibility and creativity into structuring jobs, for example by introducing part-time work into career grades. It also provides a considerable incentive for both Government and employers to provide child-care for working mothers. Whilst some progress has been made with the recent decision to allow companies to claim tax relief on work-place nurseries, child-care provision in Britain is still markedly lower than in most other European countries. As Metcalf and Leighton (1989) argue, the extent to which women with dependent children decide to work will be influenced by their net wage rate and also the cost of child-care. In a situation where women's wage rates are low and child-care costs are high, there may be little economic gain in taking a paid job. Higher wage rates and low-cost, good quality child-care would cause proportional increases in the labour market participation rates of women.

The predicted shortage in skilled manual and craft occupations (traditionally 'male' strongholds) may provide scope for reducing sex segregation. While pressures of adolescent conformity seem to be one of the factors that prevent young women from entering male dominated occupations (Cockburn, 1987), older women who are given the opportunity to retrain in non-traditional jobs may be able to serve as role models, thereby making it easier for younger women to take such jobs.

Conclusion

The current relationship between men's and women's employment needs to be understood not just in terms of the domestic division of labour, but also in the context of the barriers and control which, historically, have operated against women's but not men's employment. While it has always been the situation that many married women have held paid jobs, it is only in post-war years, with the removal of the marriage bar, that it has been possible for most women to hold a highly-paid or high-status job. Placed in this context, there has been a considerable advancement over the years. However, the very great rise in part-time working, and the almost total failure for higher-level jobs to be constructed on a part-time basis, give rise to considerable concern. A number of policy options are available for increasing equality between men and women in employment, and it is to be hoped that the shortfall of young people now entering the labour market will provide the impetus to ensure that the skills and abilities of both men and women are more fully used.

Notes

1 These figures come from the New Earnings Survey (NES). NES omits a large proportion of part-time employees, especially those on low earnings who do not qualify for National Insurance contributions; therefore the differential is likely to be even larger.

References

Allen, I (1990) 'Women Doctors.' In McRae, S (ed) *Keeping Women In.* PSI.

Althauser, R P and Kalleberg, A L (1981) 'Firms, occupations and the structure of the labour market.' In Berg, I (ed) *Sociological Perspectives on Labour Markets*, pp119–49. Academic Press.

Atkinson, J (1984) *Flexibility, Uncertainty and Manpower Management.* IMS Report No 89, Institute of Manpower Studies.

Beechey, V (1988) 'Rethinking the Definition of Work.' In Jenson, J *et al* (eds) *Feminization of the Labour Force.* Polity Press.

Becker, G (1985) 'Human Capital, Effort and the Sexual Division of Labor.' *Journal of Labor Economics*, Vol 3, No 1, Pt 2, ppS33–S58.

Blackburn, R and Mann, M (1979) *The Working Class in the Labour Market.* Macmillan.

Bryson, A (1989) 'Part-time Working.' *Low Pay Review*, No 37. Low Pay Unit.

Bulmer, M (ed) (1975) *Working Class Images of Society.* Routledge and Kegan Paul.

CBI (Confederation of British Industry) (1967) *Employing women: the employers' view.*

Cockburn, C (1987) *Two Track Training: Sex Inequalities and the YTS.* Macmillan.

Corcoran, M, Duncan, G and Ponza, M (1983) 'A Longitudinal Analysis of White Women's Wages'. *The Journal of Human Resources*, Vol XVIII, No 4, pp497–520.

CSO (Central Statistical Office) (1989) *Social Trends* 19. HMSO.

Crompton, R and Sanderson, K (1986) 'Credentials and Careers: some implications of the increase in professional qualifications among women.' *Sociology*, Vol 20, No 1, pp25–42.

Cross, M (1987) 'Black Youth and YTS: The Policy Issues.' In Cross, M and Smith, D (eds) *Black Youth Futures*. National Youth Bureau.

Dale, A (1986) 'Labor Market Structure in the United Kingdom.' *Work and Occupations*, Vol 15, pp558–90.

Dale, A (1987) 'Occupational inequality, gender and life-cycle.' *Work Employment and Society*, Vol 1, No 3, pp326–51.

Dale, A (1991) 'Stratification over the life-course: gender differences within the household.' In Payne, G and Abbott, P (eds) *The Social Mobility of Women*. Falmer.

Dale, A and Bamford, C (1988) *Flexibility and the Peripheral Workforce*. Occasional Papers in Sociology and Social Policy, No 11, Department of Sociology, University of Surrey.

Dale, A and Glover, J (1990) *An Analysis of Women's Employment Patterns in the UK, France and the USA: The Value of Survey Based Comparisons*. Department of Employment Research Paper, No 75.

Daniel, W W (1980) *Maternity Rights: The Experience of Women*. PSI.

DE (Department of Employment) (1988) 'Pay in Great Britain: Results of the 1988 New Earnings Survey.' *Employment Gazette*, November 1988, pp601–605.

DE (1989) 'Labour force outlook to 2000.' *Employment Gazette* April 1989, pp159–72.

DES Department of Education and Science) (1988) *Education Statistics for the UK, 1988*. HMSO.

Dex, S (1987) *Women's Occupational Mobility*. Macmillan.

EOC (Equal Opportunities Commission) (1986) *Women and Men in Britain: a Statistical Profile*.

Ermisch, J (1990) *Fewer babies, longer lives*. Joseph Rowntree.

Fabian Society (1966) *Womanpower*. Young Fabian Pamphlet No 11.

Gallie, D (1989) *Technological Change, Gender and Skill*. SCELI Working Paper No 4.

Goldthorpe, J, Lockwood, D, Bechhofer, F and Platt, J (1969) *The Affluent Worker in the Class Structure*. Cambridge University Press.

Hakim, C (1979) *Occupational Segregation*. Department of Employment Research Paper No 9.

Horrel, Rubery, J and Burchell, B (1989) *Gender and Skills*. SCELI Working Paper No 5.

Institute for Employment Research (1988) *Review of the Economy and Employment, Occupational Update 1988*. IER.

Joshi, H (1988) *Changing Roles of Women in the British Labour Market and the Family*. Birkbeck College.

Klein, V (1959) *Working Wives*. Institute of Personnel Management.

Klein, V (1961) *Employing Married Women*. Institute of Personnel Management.

Lewis, J (1984) *Women in England 1870–1950*. Wheatsheaf.

Lovering, J (1990) 'On Economic Restructuring, Spatial Change and Labour Market Segmentation in Britain in the 1980s.' In *Work,*

Employment and Society: A Decade of Change. British Sociological Association.

Martin, J and Roberts, C (1984) *Women and Employment: a lifetime perspective*. HMSO.

Metcalf, H and Leighton, P (1989) *The Under-Utilisation of Women in the Labour Market*. IMS Report No 172.

Mitter, S (1986) 'Industrial restructuring and manufacturing homework: immigrant women in the UK clothing industry.' *Capital and Class* No 27, pp37–80.

Myrdal, A and Klein, V (1956) *Women's Two Roles*. Routledge and Kegan Paul.

OECD (Organisation for Economic Co-operation and Development) (1985) *The Integration of Women into the Economy*.

Oppenheimer, V (1970) *The Female Labor Force in the United States: Demographic and Economic Factors Governing its Growth and Composition*. Greenwood Press.

Phizaclea, A (1983) *One Way Ticket*. Routledge and Kegan Paul.

Pollert, A (1988) 'The "Flexible Firm": Fixation or Fact.' *Work Employment and Society*, Vol 2, No 3, pp281–316.

Siltanen, J (1990) 'Social Change and the Measurement of Occupational Segregation by Sex: An Assessment of the Sex Ratio Index.' *Work, Employment and Society*, Vol 4, pp1–29.

Sutton, K (1989) 'Equal Pay: getting it right for women.' *Low Pay Review*, No 37.

Walby, S (1986) *Patriarchy at Work*. Polity Press.

Westwood, S and Bachu, P (eds) *Enterprising Women*. Routledge.

13 The right to work: justice in the distribution of employment*

Catherine Marsh

*An earlier version of this paper was presented to British Sociological Association Annual Conference at the University of Surrey, April 2–5 1990. The author is grateful to Nick Manning for his helpful comments on this earlier version. Some of the data reported in this paper was collected as part of the ESRC's Social Change and Economic Life Initiative, the fieldwork for which was conducted by PAS Ltd.

There is a significant gap in the literature on inequality and distributive justice. Much has been written about the distribution of income, yet little on the overall distribution of work. This is a serious omission, both because employment is the most important source of income to most households, and because it is an important source of value in its own right. Its distribution is a proper concern for those interested in social policy and social justice. The aim of this chapter is to open up this neglected area for discussion among policy researchers by challenging the traditional British divide between laissez-faire economic policy and more interventionist social policy. For various reasons, rights to income have proved insufficient to stop the tremendous gap in well-being between those with and without employment. The goal of the chapter is to promote reconsideration of a legally enforceable right to work.

Work or labour?

The lack of attention to the benefits of work stems, I believe, from an inappropriate model of the nature of work used by social scientists. Most languages, as Hannah Arendt points out (1957), distinguish between 'labour' and 'work' (*arbeiten* and *werken* in German, *travailler* and *ouvrer* in French, *laborare* and *facere* in Latin, *ponein* and *ergazesthai* in Greek). For Arendt, the distinction is vital to understanding what she calls the human condition. Labour is activity bound to the natural process of life itself, of keeping the body alive and capable of reproducing; it leaves no trace. Work, by contrast, is activity which produces an artificial world of things. Labour is universally regarded as painful and demeaning, whereas work is ennobling, civilising, worldly.

The social sciences have tended to concentrate on the labouring, unpleasant aspects of work. In the canons of neo-classical economics, work is defined in opposition to utility; it is leisure foregone in a trade off. Similarly, much sociology of work has rested upon the 'labour' model, with a focus on alienation, de-skilling and the degradation of labour. And what attention there has been in the philosophical literature on how jobs should be distributed, has been in a similar mould, with discussion centring on how to distribute and reward the least appealing jobs[1].

In agricultural societies, it might make sense to think of work as energy expended, as an outflow which has to be compensated by money or food sufficient to allow for the reproduction of the worker. However, in advanced industrialised societies such a simple input/output model of working is not so appropriate; the best efforts of classical economics fit less well. Most work in modern industrial societies is not 'labour' in the pejorative sense. The time has come for a re-orientation of perspective, with a more positive view of work as something with utility independent of the money earned for it.

The rewards of paid employment

Paid employment is the predominant mode of work in modern industrialised societies. Indeed, employment rates might be used as an indicator of economic development: the proportion of those of working age who are employed in the external economy (as opposed to self-employed or family workers) generally rises with economic growth. Sociological interest in domestic and other informal types of economic activity during the 1970s served a useful purpose in drawing attention to important but neglected contributions to overall social production. It took the mass unemployment in the early 1980s and some rather more careful empirical research to demonstrate that the informal sector did not really offer alternative access to valued goods and services to those not in formal employment: indeed, once unemployed, people often lost their very access to the means of informal sector work (Pahl 1984).

There are two reasons why it is still correct and desirable to focus attention on formal employment as a good whose distribution is a matter of policy concern.

Income

Formal employment accounts for the overwhelmingly largest element of the incomes of most households. First and foremost, therefore, deprivation from work is deprivation from income. If we fail to understand the dynamics and patterns behind the getting of work, we will never have a handle on the distribution of income (Piachaud 1987).

Some striking changes have taken place in the composition of the poor in Britain during the 1970s and 1980s. Households with unemployed heads have increased their representation strongly, and there has been a sharp decline in the extent to which households at the bottom of the income distribution had access to any earnings from employment. The gap between households with access to earnings and those without is very large; in 1988, for example, the median income in one-earner households was £197 per week, whereas households with no earners had a median income of £83 per week (CSO 1989: 70–71).

The state supports the incomes of the vast majority of those at the bottom of the income heap, and so bears some responsibility for the major income inequalities that exist. Some provocative recent research suggests that the modern welfare state has actually not done as good a job in closing the income gap between those in and out of work than did the forms of support available in Victorian times (Thomson 1984, but see also Hunt 1990). The failure to relate income support to previous pay means that the income gap between those on benefit and those in employment is probably greater than in many other European countries (OECD 1988; Marsh and Alvaro 1990).

However, the political task of trying to close the income gap between earners and those on benefit income is immense, particularly in a system of universal entitlement. The free-rider problem looms large in political discussions of welfare, despite the fact that there is a substantial minority who can be shown to work for wages which are pretty close to the income support they would be entitled to if claiming Supplementary Benefit[2].

Psychological rewards

Being in paid employment also brings many intrinsic, psychological rewards. Research on the effects of unemployment in the 1980s has been unanimous: the experience is miserable for virtually everybody – white collar or blue collar, men and women, young and old, black and white (Warr 1987). Even those on the Youth Training Scheme, a particularly poorly paid and low status form of employment, are at a great psychological advantage compared to their unemployed peers (Breakwell 1985).

There has, by contrast, been little research on the psychological effects of economic inactivity as opposed to unemployment, and little attempt to separate the effects of unemployment from the effects of low income. Since it is important for a general argument about the benefits of work, some new evidence about this is presented in Table 13.1.

The first row of Table 13.1 demonstrates once more that the mental health of the unemployed is depressed compared to the other groups. This is not just a spurious by-product of low income; when attention is restricted to people in households forming the bottom 8 per cent of incomes (second line of Table 13.1), the gap between the employed and unemployed remains. Furthermore, the combination of lack of employment and lack of money seems to have a deleterious effect on the psychological health of housewives.

To the best available psychological knowledge, the ill-health consequences flow from the objective deprivations that joblessness entails in people's daily routines and environment (Jahoda 1982; Warr 1987). While it is certainly true that the unemployed lack self-esteem (Eales 1986), this is more of a restatement of the psychological problem than a satisfactory explanation of why they feel so.

The distribution of paid employment in Britain

This century has seen a big increase in economic dependency, with striking increases in the retired population and a rise in the typical age of those entering employment. At the time of the 1981 census, only 43 per cent of the population was in employment (compared with 57 per cent at the 1911 census), and only one third was

Table 13.1 Psychological wellbeing by activity status

	Score on the General Health Questionnaire scale*		
	Employed	Unemployed	Housewives
All 20–60 year olds	0.8	1.2	0.9
20–60s in poor§ households	0.9	1.3	1.3

* – Scale formed from responses to questions about how often in the previous few weeks the respondent had: "been feeling reasonably happy, all things considered; been able to enjoy your normal day to day activities; been feeling unhappy and depressed; been losing confidence in yourself".
§ – Incomes less than one standard deviation below the mean of the logged income distribution.

Source: Social Change and Economic Life Initiative

in full-time work. This social change is rightly viewed both as a hallmark of national productivity and of the success of our systems of social insurance.

But there are also signs that not everyone welcomes this concentration of employment into the middle four decades of life. Most people would prefer to withdraw gradually from paid employment than be forced to retire at a fixed point (Parker 1982; Casey and Laczo 1989). There is a small but growing demand for all workers to have the right to periods of either part-time work or extended leave for family or educational reasons. Most young people on training schemes would prefer to be in work (Raffe 1988). While there would still be a set of important policy issues to address, the arguments about social justice would be very different if all that was happening was a redistribution of employment over individuals' lifetimes. But we may also discern several broad patterns of redistribution between individuals.

One significant part of the redistribution which has occurred has involved a transfer from men to women; the female participation rate has risen consistently whether in boom time or slump, with quite profound social consequences (see Dale this volume). To the extent that the rising female participation rate led to increased economic independence for women, it is to be welcomed. But we should note that almost all of the employment growth for women has been in part-time work. Moreover, the number of hours per week that part-timers worked dropped throughout the 1980s, while the number of hours of overtime worked by men increased (Marsh 1991). So in this respect the gendered distribution of work actually polarised. It is also important to note that changes in the distribution of work by gender has not, by and large, involved transfers between individuals in the same household; there has been a marked tendency for adult workers to cluster together in households, and adult non-workers to do likewise (Payne 1987).

And of course a major structural unemployment problem has persisted right through the 1980s. Estimates of the numbers affected vary depending on which definition of unemployment is used; we should probably add 50 per cent to the number of official unemployment claimants to represent the size of the discouraged labour force and the estimated register effect of those on government schemes (Marsh 1988). The problem is substantial even in the middle four decades of life; at a time in the middle of 1987 when claimant unemployment stood at 10 per cent overall, age-specific unemployment rates only fell to 7 per cent among those in their forties (*Employment Gazette* October 1990: S35).

There are worrying indications that the burden of unemployment falls recurrently on the same shoulders. Once an individual's employment history begins to be characterised by unemployment, it is very hard to escape (Gershuny and Marsh 1991). A group of long-term welfare recipients, alienated both socially and politically from other workers, appears to be growing in many advanced societies (Wilson 1985; Dahrendorf 1987; Alvaro and Marsh 1990). The idea that there exists an underclass beneath the labouring classes has a long history, and has often had undesirable moral undertones (Stedman Jones 1971; Mead 1985; Bulmer 1989). But several more sympathetic modern writers have suggested that unemployment has now become the axis of class division (Gorz 1982; van Parijs 1986–87). One final noteworthy aspect of the distribution of work is the growing correlation between unemployment and the level of qualifications (Table 13.2).

A quick reading of Table 13.2 might suggest that skills have become increasingly important for modern jobs. Yet studies of the skills of the unemployed and those demanded by employers with vacancies (Meadows *et al*, 1988; Smith 1988; Marsh 1990) fails to reveal any substantial degree of mismatch. A more plausible interpretation is that as the aggregate number of jobs available has fallen, employers have been able to be more selective.

Paid employment as a welfare good

In a nutshell, paid employment is highly desirable, yet there is a group of people clustered together at the bottom of the pile who cannot manage to find or at least retain it. But before turning to see whether the conceptual tools developed in the literature on distributive justice can profitably be applied to this problem, it is

Table 13.2 Unemployment rate among young (16–24) heads of households

	A-level or higher %	Some quals %	No quals %	τ_B
1973	2	2	4	.05
1974	3	4	7	.06
1975	5	6	13	.12
1976	1	3	15	.22
1977	1	4	16	.24
1979	2	3	22	.26
1980	5	8	13	.10
1981	6	13	35	.28
1982	10	14	40	.27

Source: General Household Survey (Dale and Bamford 1989)

necessary to think a little harder about how employment would fit into a theory of goods.

Discussion about appropriate principles of distribution have tended to take place with respect to goods which are scarce relative to desire for them, and where to give one person more would be to give another less. By discussing the distribution of work as if it were a good like others, the impression may be given that it too is inherently limited. In any labour market at any one time, this may be the case. But it is important to note there are no reasons **in principle** why the supply of jobs should be restricted. No economic theory exists which claims that full employment is in principle impossible (frictional unemployment due to job change aside) or that labour markets cannot ever clear; the debate is instead about the social and economic arrangements required to employ all those who seek work.

A distinctive feature of paid employment is that it cannot be bought: you get money for it, rather than give money to get it. (To be sure, at the beginning of the 1980s, stories appeared in the press of parents paying local firms to give their teenage children an apprenticeship, but this was only newsworthy because it offended the conventional sense attaching to the notion of work.) As a result, much of the theorising about justice and efficiency in the distribution of welfare just cannot be adapted to discussion of inequalities in the distribution of work; in particular, the crucial distinction between equality of resource use and equality of eventual utility cannot be applied productively[3]. Work is quite clearly a different sort of thing from traditional welfare goods.

Quite so, the neo-classical economist would say; work is the opposite of a good, it is what you trade **for** money to buy the things you want. This is unexceptionable as an empirical statement; after all, we have seen that it is overwhelmingly the most important source of income, and if you ask people the thing they most value in a job, pay looms very large. But as a definitional statement it is inadequate. If we took this line we could not explain why a significant minority work at such badly paid jobs, nor why the majority claim to enjoy their work so much that they would continue if they won the pools.

Indeed, there is a second way in which it would be wrong to view work as inherently scarce. One striking finding from various time use studies is that the more time people devote to any one activity, work included, the more time they also devote to almost any other, apart from watching TV (Robinson 1988). Subjective time is very different for different people[4], and there seems almost to be a feed-back element to human energy levels. Rather than view work as necessary hardship which people endure in order to earn the money to buy the things they really want, the psychological evidence reviewed above suggests that we view it as inherently valuable in its own right. But the case rests on the good representing a 'functioning', not a 'capability' (Sen 1985); the value inheres not in the **opportunity** to work, but in actually working. The utility that work brings is not incidental and substitutable, but central to wellbeing in modern societies. Whether, like Adam Smith, we focus on access to the means of decency, or, like Aristotle, on the opportunity to develop and exercise capacities to the full, indeed, almost whatever view of wellbeing and welfare one adopts, the conclusion is inescapable that, in modern societies, such wellbeing is extremely hard for unemployed people to obtain[5].

Rawls (1982) has established an influential hierarchy of timeless 'primary goods' which constitute the core concerns for distributive justice. It might be argued that place should be found in this hierarchy for paid employment. It would have to come after the negative liberties of thought and expression, freedom of movement and choice of occupation, after the powers and prerogatives of office, and after the all-purpose positive good of income. It might be deemed to rank with the final good in the hierarchy: the 'social bases of self-respect . . . – those aspects of basic institutions that are normally essential if citizens are to have a lively sense of their own worth as moral persons and to be able to realise their highest-order interests and advance their ends with self-confidence' (1982:166). But to ask one particular institution to supply a primary good would be contrary to the enterprise of trying to justify a set of goods which are independent of any particular set of social arrangements or goals. Whether we accept the notion of primary goods or not[6], it is hard to argue that paid employment should be one: asserting a right to work independent of a right to income in agrarian society where labour is indeed arduous, for example, would be a nonsense.

Moreover, as well as being an individual good with individual ethical implications, work is also a social good; making things and providing services are key social activities. It is not only economically irrational but also socially divisive to exclude people systematically from these basic activities; even if those affected were so alienated that they did not perceive their situation as deprivation, it would still be something for society to be concerned about.

Principles of distributive justice

We must recognise that there are many different distributional systems, appropriate to different kinds of goods, and that different criteria of just allocation pertain to each (Walzer 1983). There are three principles which one could use to provide an ethical justification for particular distributions of work: utilitarian, meritocratic and rights-based. These are not exhaustive of all the principles that might be proposed, such that if two could be dismissed one would be left by elimination[7]. They do, however, represent the most common ways of talking about social justice. Utility and desert will be treated relatively briefly, since the argument for them is not very strong. Much more sympathetic consideration will be given to the idea of a right to work.

Utility

If we make minimal assumptions about what people are, want and need – merely that they are rational and capable of making decisions – we may be content to argue on the basis of some broad-based notion of utility. The goal of promoting the sum of human happiness by whatever means is in fact an ethical goal but one which appears not to involve value judgements – to have the force of scientific calculable rationality behind it. Opponents of utilitarianism argue that merely maximising the sum of welfare outcomes has some particularly nasty ethical consequences, in rewarding those best capable of converting goods into utility. However, while utilitarianism does not intrinsically imply a commitment to equality, its defenders (eg Hare 1982) argue that, since people with little get so much more pleasure out of the same goods as those with a lot, 'approaches towards equality will tend to increase total utility' (1982: 27).

Utilitarian arguments, if applied to the distribution of work, might favour a more egalitarian distribution than the one we have. Indeed, one plausible hypothesis is that work is a good to which not only diminishing marginal returns apply but also diminishing total returns, at least as far as hours of work are concerned. So, on utilitarian grounds, we might be able to derive a powerful criticism of some aspects of the current distribution of work.

However, since utilitarianism makes such weak assumptions about what it is that humans need, it is bound to argue that money could substitute for work. Yet, if the argument proposed above is right, dole is not a substitute for work, and cross-domain compensation is not possible.

Desert

In popular discussions of justice in allocating work, the appropriate principle of distribution is held to be one of desert: people often express a greater sense of outrage when a skilled worker is made redundant than when an unqualified person fails to find a position, as if somehow the skilled worker did not **deserve** this.

The ethical language seems to be derived from perceptions of justice at the level of the individual appointment, when the employer is faced with the choice of several candidates: if he or she is to act fairly in the public eye, the job must go to the most deserving[8]. In the field of employment, desert becomes having the 'appropriate' qualifications, skills and experience. While some jobs require quite specific skills and qualifications, many others require more general qualifications or skills. The rules of the qualification game are bound by notions of equality of opportunity: they must be universal, widely diffused and generally accepted as legitimate filters for employers to use.

But such individualistic equality of opportunity in the competition for placement is perfectly compatible with large numbers failing even to get onto the bottom of the ladder. Desert is not a good way of thinking about equality of outcome in terms of the **aggregate** allocation of jobs. The only way to argue that the unqualified in society do not 'deserve' any job would be to have a very egalitarian view of the distribution of abilities, and to argue that lack of qualification represents the outcome of a conscious choice not to exercise those abilities.

It is true that some social groups have managed to use the rules of desert to seek social justice in employment. In many countries, if women, members of ethnic minorities or handicapped people can show that the rules of desert have been breached, they can seek legal redress for unfair treatment. The limited generalisation of the idea of desert to identifiable social groups for whom fair play is backed by law does not, however, generalise further to an allocative principle for work as a whole. Those at the bottom of the qualification heap would never be able to turn such legislation to their advantage.

The inappropriate principle of desert survives in much discussion about unemployment because there is much greater public commitment to equality of opportunity than to equality of outcome (Weale 1989). This is paralleled by social scientists, who have also shown themselves more concerned about procedural than substantive justice; Swift (1988) observes acutely that the reason for this is a paucity in the theory of social goods. This support for equality of opportunity is buttressed by the charitable popular view of qualifications, accepting their face validity as the institutionalisation of merit. But we saw above that qualifications may serve a different purpose when used as an aggregate allocative principle. In the extreme, they may function as a legitimating exercise, to cool out the failures of the educational and imposing individual responsibility for the condition (Bourdieu and Passeron 1977).

Rights

Rights provide a third way of thinking about justice in the distribution of work.

Two radically different traditions invoke a 'right to work'. The earlier is an individualistic, economic right, formulated in Hanoverian times in attempts to remove various restraints on trade sanctioned in the Elizabethan Statute of Artificers. This negative right prohibited any trades and localities from monopolizing particular occupations[9]. The right to work in this sense has plenty of modern reverberations in the rights of strike breakers to cross picket lines and so on. The other tradition is associated with the political left, a collective, positive right demanded of a state to provide employment. Such a right to work is enshrined in the constitutions of state socialist societies, but it is also mentioned in the constitution of market societies – the Spanish, Italian and Swedish, for example.

Surprisingly, it is only in the first sense that a right to work appears in Marshall's influential discussion of citizenship and real social entitlement. For Marshall (1949; 1964), it is a right in the negative sense, which ironically was claimed historically in a legislative package which involved the repeal of the Elizabethan poor laws and the rights to income support that they provided. He did not include it in his package of positive social rights which would empower people to fully exercise their citizenship, and it has rarely been proposed as a legally enforceable right in social democratic welfare states (with the partial exception of Sweden).

On a legal, constitutional interpretation of what a right is and how it is claimed, a right to work has only really ever existed in socialist societies. In such societies, no unemployment benefit is payable; defenders of the Soviet arrangements, for example, argue that 'Jobs are preferable to monetary benefits in all respects, as many Westerners are sadly learning today – preferable in terms of human dignity, feeling of self-worth and psychological well-being' (cited in George and Manning 1980: 57–58). It remains to be seen whether the current move towards marketisation of these societies will involve the destruction of the right. But there is no reason why a right to work should not form part of a social democratic state. Before we consider some of the details of how it might be effected in Britain, let us first deal with some powerful critics of the idea.

Arguments for and against a right to work

There are formidable obstacles to establishing a positive, enforceable right to work.

First, it attacks a cornerstone of British policy: the good in the social domain should be pursued by guaranteeing rights, whereas in the economic domain, the government should only act as handmaiden to the market[10]. From the start, the architects of the welfare state looked to economic policies controlling the level of demand in the economy rather than to individually enforceable rights to fulfil economic goals such as full employment. However, there was actually little hostility among the architects of the welfare state to the idea of government providing people with work directly if the marketplace could not[11]; they just did not think it would need to come to that. While the division between the economic and the social might have been acceptable under a government committed to use demand management to promote full employment, it has become less supportable as unemployment has become the main employment policy of the Conservative administration of the 1980s.

Second, there is antipathy to any introduction of legal processes into the economic arena. The antipathy comes both from those involved in fashioning our social policy institutions, who have not wished to involve the full process of the law in arbitration of rights (eg Titmuss 1971), and also from lawyers who have shied away from getting involved (Hepple 1981; Jaconelli 1980). Hepple, for example, upholds the distinction between economic and social policy, arguing that state is unlikely to be able to grant work as of right if its economic policies of full employment fail. Such a right to work would be inimical, he argues, to the edifice of British labour relations legislation, in which money has always been the compensating medium. But such arguments centre around the idea that such a right offends a tradition: they are not arguments in principle.

There are eloquent critics of the principle, even among close friends of equality and social justice. Elster (1988), for example, argues that the notion of a right to work is conceptually confused – not all good things in life are to be distributed as of right; there can no more be a right to work than there can be a right to love. The intrinsic benefit that work brings, he argues, is self-esteem, and to distribute work as welfare to people would therefore be self-defeating. There are several counter-arguments, however. Self esteem, as we saw, certainly comes with work, but is not the mechanism which produces psychological advantage. Even jobs on government training schemes – jobs held in low esteem both by incumbents and others – have important psychological benefits. Furthermore, while we may not know how to succeed in creating a loving environment, creating jobs is not so difficult – it was possible to turn an economy round from deep depression to full employment in six years in order to establish the warfare state in the 1930s when there was political consensus about the need to do this.

A final objection involves an economic version of Elster's self-defeating argument. There cannot be a right to work, economists argue, because the work that governments would be able to provide would never be economically viable: it would be cheaper to keep people on the dole. This is a variety of argument by definition: if there was a valuable job that needed doing, the marketplace would be doing it. But the argument that the market is already engaged in all the possible productive tasks is absurd if it is meant as an empirical claim. (There are also objections by economists to the inflationary effect of government job creation on wages; these are not arguments about **rights** as such, however.)

However, even if the chorus of objections to the idea is not as compelling as its volume suggests, it is important to rehearse the positive reasons for proposing such a right. The best argument is an extension of Marshall's important ideas, even if he would not have accepted the extension. Guaranteeing people by right the necessary means to play their full part as members of a civic community is fundamental; in modern societies, the right to work must be included. Our entire system of social insurance has employment at its heart, and people who make a claim on the state for support while they are unemployed are faced with a duty to seek work. The norm of reciprocity demands that they should in turn be guaranteed employment if the market fails them.

Policy considerations

If the right to work is to be more than a 'miserable pious wish'[12], it is important to flesh out the details a little, to show from whom it might be claimed, and what it might look like.

When it comes to job creators, there are three possibilities: governments, employers and workers themselves and their organisations (Hepple, 1981). The third possibility is not envisaged as extending positive social rights; the right to work claimed against other workers is negative right against restraint on trade and need not detain us.

Markets have not had a good record over the last 200 years in providing sufficient employment for all able-bodied adults. Even in the early decades of modern industrial capitalism, when free competition was relatively unfettered by laws and regulations by today's standards, labour markets did not clear and wages did not downward adjust until they reached a level at which work was offered. By contrast, the full-employment of the post-war years – the important formative period for much modern thinking about welfare – was the result of government policy, and seems in retrospect to have been quite exceptional. Employers are never going to be persuaded that they should expand to take on workers as their contribution to solving a problem of lack of demand for labour[13]. The rules of their game are about profit and loss, not social justice. Most industrialised countries have now accepted that it is unrealistic even to expect employers to be sufficiently long-sighted to invest many resources into education and training, let alone job-creation programmes.

The only other possible creator of employment is the state, either national or local. Townsend (1979: 926) places his hopes in local government without justifying why he does so, but most people believe that there is little that British local government on its own can do about job creation. Central government, which already heavily subsidises nine in ten of households at the bottom of the income distribution after all, is the most natural choice of an institution to distribute work to those whom the market fails.

Governments can affect employment in a wide number of ways. They can provide selective incentives to employers to take people on in specific job-creating industries or regions where help is felt to be needed; they can manipulate tax and national insurance policy to encourage job creation; they can legislate limits to hours of work; they can provide enabling welfare facilities such as childcare. Governments fully committed to providing employment for all would probably decide to try encouraging and support market mechanisms before stepping in to create jobs themselves. Indeed, if they knew that ultimately they had a statutory obligation to find jobs for all the marketplace casualties, they would have a very strong incentive to scrutinise the employment consequences of their other policies in advance.

But governments can also create jobs directly. To get an idea of what would be possible, there are plenty of models to turn to. Countries as diverse as Sweden and the United States have work schemes for the unemployed. But some of the most inspired examples of what a committed government with an activist executive can do come from the schemes which formed part of the New Deal in the US in the 1930s. The organisers were opposed to what they termed 'leaf-raking projects'. Many of the jobs involved white collar and skilled workers, who were paid the going rate. The bulk of the projects involved construction: building and renovating thousands of roads, schools, parks, hospitals, airports and playing fields. But projects also included surveying harbours, painting murals, building computers, compiling and analysing climatic data, teaching adult illiterates, establishing orchestras, and many other innovative and productive activities (see Badger 1989: 191–244). There are plenty of similar projects of this kind that could usefully be done in Britain today given a modicum of political will and imagination.

There are, however, two big stumbling blocks. The first is money. Real employment schemes are costly to establish; Roosevelt, for example, found himself repeatedly under political attack for the demand that the New Deal schemes placed on the exchequer. Government work schemes in the USA and Sweden cost a lot more per head than do the various training schemes in force in Britain (Digby, 1989). But the true social cost of unemployment is also very large, and is not revealed by the accounting schemes used in different branches of government each with their own narrow categories of cost and benefit. If the increased demands that unemployed people make on health and social services could be offset against the cost of schemes, they might not look so expensive.

The second problem is that most government work schemes of this kind have been compulsory: they have been the only way in which many unemployed people could claim benefit. Very different analyses from that proposed in this chapter, which suggest that the problems of unemployment are not so much due to the lack of jobs as to a vicious circle of inadequacy and dependency on the part of the poor (eg Mead 1985), have led policy makers in the Reaganite era in the US to compulsory work schemes as a solution. Compulsion was often the price paid for extracting the necessary funds from Conservative administrations for such schemes.

There is no doubt that compulsion would be fiercely resisted in Britain. One reason may be, as Digby (1989) suggests, that the British welfare system has never quite lost the associations of the Victorian poor laws, with its exploitative out-relief. Another is that the trade union movement in Britain has not in the past shown much enthusiasm for government regulation in any arena, being one of the fiercest supporters of the divide discussed above between free market economic policies and directive social policies, vociferously opposing the element of compulsion in the Restart scheme.

If we accept that compulsion would never be politically possible in Britain, one solution might be to propose a two-tier structure. The state could continue to provide a level of benefit which was enough to feed, clothe and house people at the very basic level of adequacy[14] which would be provided as a safety net to those who preferred to seek work on the open market to accepting the work the state provided. However, work would also be available on government job schemes, paying wages within one standard deviation of the national average. If the above arguments are correct, given the choice of dole and workfare, very few indeed would choose dole.

But under the right conditions, there is nothing inherently terrible about expecting work from people in return for money. The conditions would involve some important guarantees to ensure that the state would not be granted a commanding position over the individual that it could abuse. It would seem unreasonable (and geographically and ecologically inefficient) to insist that people should have to move house to find work. Genuine training would have to be given where it was necessary; indicators of the genuineness of the training would be the resources that were put into it, and the willingness of the trainees to stick the course if offered a job half way through. And sensitive rules would need to be developed for the participation of those with responsibility for young children. Under such conditions, if real work (as opposed to 'leaf-raking') were offered at reasonable rates of pay, much opposition could melt away.

Conclusion

Unemployment prompts consideration of some central issues concerning the distribution of resources in society. It is partly a distributional issue between firms, who can be thought of as taking part in 'competitive unemployment', seeking to enhance their profitability by reducing their own labour force as far as possible while transferring the social costs of maintaining surplus labour to the general exchequer (Blackburn 1987). It is also a distributional issue between workers: by and large the disadvantaged bottom end of the workforce sustains the brunt of the problem.

While most people concede it is wasteful to allow productive capacity, human or material, to lie idle, they will accept it so long as they believe that only markets can generate jobs, and that governments have no role in providing employment. By exploring the feasibility of a right to work, it is hoped that the assumptive basis of this approach may have been shaken. It would probably not even prove necessary to change the traditional terms of the equality debate too radically: a right to work could be presented as a fundamental part of equality of opportunity, especially for the young, giving them a chance to get on the ladder.

If we say that there is nothing governments can do purposely to create work when market opportunities fall short, we are near to saying we lack the ability to control the society in which we live and the institutions through which social life is organised. Yet comparisons across history and across countries suggests that governments can create work directly, given the political will. At a time when unemployment rates have turned up once more and no-one is forecasting an early downturn, it is vital that such a political will be found.

Notes

1   eg Hirsch (1977). Walzer (1983) has a chapter on what he calls 'hard work', and discusses appropriate distributive principles for the horrid jobs in society. His contribution is distinctive in that he also contrasts this with sought-after jobs that merit the name 'office'.

2   In 1979, in households where there was at least one earner, 3 per cent received less income that they would have been entitled to if they had been claiming social security payments, and 14 per cent of households received less than 140 per cent of their entitlement (calculations based on the dataset supplied with Dale *et al* 1984).

3   This applies with even more force to Le Grand's (1983) more complex distinctions between equality of public expenditure, equality of final income, equality of use, equality of cost and equality of outcome.

4   In a phone-in programme in January 1989 on BBC radio about the long hours of work done by junior doctors, one such doctor who phoned in said that one compensation for working upwards of 100 hours per week was the tremendously 'concentrated sense of living' that it gave one.

5   This is not to argue that most work actually allows people to develop their talents to the full: indeed, Blackburn and Mann (1979) argue that most manual jobs in one local labour market do not involve as many skills as are used in driving a car.

6   Walzer (1983) provides one critique of these ideas.

7   Need might be considered a distinct principle of distribution. However, the notion of need has been claimed for each of the three principles here: Dasgupta (1988) links needs with rights-based approaches, Le Grand (1984) links them with desert, and utilitarians claim that marginal utility provides its own criterion of need. The term is therefore insufficiently discriminating.

8   Walzer denies this; desert, he argues, looks backwards and rewards achievement, whereas appointment to offices can be justified on grounds of someone's potential. However, if an appointments' committee decided to select an underqualified and experienced man on the grounds that he had greater 'potential' than a better qualified woman, a tribunal would need evidence based on past achievements of some kind, on qualitative if not quantitative grounds, to justify this decision if the woman brought a case.

9   'All people are at liberty to live in Winchester, and how can they be restrained from using the lawful means of living there?' (Chief Justice Holt, 1705, cited in Marshall, 1949; 1964).

10   Britain, for example, has no general minimum wage legislation, and is also almost alone in European countries in having no general regulation of hours of work.

11   Beveridge, for example, believed in both the rights and duties of citizens to work, over and above rights to income: '(N)o man will be able to draw benefit for any day for which there is a suitable job available to him. On the other hand, if there is not a job, the Plan proposes that benefit should be paid in full, however long unemployment has lasted, though it proposes also that if unemployment has lasted for more than a limited time, provision

of an income should be accompanied by training and occupation. That is common sense and humanity.' Beveridge on Beveridge, cited in Piachaud 1987).

12 Karl Marx's description of the 'right to work' in the *Class Struggles in France* (1952:62).

13 They may be conjoined to employ a quota of 'green card', or handicapped workers, but even this is extremely difficult to enforce.

14 It is arguable that the current social security arrangements in Britain do not permit this now, especially on the housing front as it affects young people.

References

Alvaro, J-L and Marsh, C (1990) 'The unemployed as an underclass in Spain and the UK.' Paper presented to the XIIth World Congress of Sociology, Madrid, July.

Arendt, H (1957) *The Human Condition*. University of Chicago Press.

Badger, A J (1989) *The New Deal: The Depression Years, 1933–40*. Macmillan.

Blackburn, R M (1987) 'The economics of unemployment: a sociological interpretation.' University of Cambridge: Department of Applied Economics paper in Sociology.

Blackburn, R M and Mann, M (1979) *The Working Class in the Labour Market*. Macmillan.

Bourdieu, P and Passeron, J-C (1977) *Reproduction in Education, Society and Culture*. Sage.

Breakwell, G (1985) 'Young people in and out of work.' In Roberts, B, Finnegan, R and Gallie, D (eds) *New Directions in Economic Life*. Manchester University Press.

Bulmer, M (1989) 'The underclass, empowerment and public policy.' In Bulmer, M, Lewis, J and Piachaud, D (eds) *The Goals of Social Policy*. Unwin Hyman.

Casey, B and Laczo, F (1989) 'Early retired or long-term unemployed? The situation of non-working men aged 55–64 from 1979 to 1986'. *Work, Employment and Society* 3(4), 509–526.

Central Statistical Office (1989) *The Family Expenditure Survey 1988*. HMSO.

Dahrendorf, R (1987) 'Why we can't afford an underclass.' *New Statesman*, 12 June.

Dale, A and Bamford, C (1989) *General Household Survey Time Series 1973–1982 Codebook*. SN 2361, ESRC Data Archive, University of Essex.

Dale, A, Gilbert, G N, Rajan, L and Arber, S (1984) *Exploring British Society: Social Science Teaching using the General Household Survey*. Unit 3: Poverty and Income, University of Surrey; data available through the ESRC Data Archive at University of Essex.

Dasgupta, P (1989) 'Needs and rights.' Paper presented to the Cambridge Seminar on Inequality and Social Justice, January.

Digby, A (1989) *British Welfare Policy: Workhouse to Workfare*. Faber and Faber.

Eales, M (1986) 'Unemployment and Depression'. PhD thesis, Bedford and Royal Holloway New College.

Elster, J (1988) 'Is there (or should there be) a right to work?' In Gutmann, A (ed) *Democracy and the Welfare State*. Princeton University Press.

George, V and Manning, N (1980) *Socialism, Social Welfare and the Soviet Union*. Routledge & Kegan Paul.

Gershuny, J and Marsh, C (1991) 'Unemployment in work histories.' In Gallie, D, Marsh, C and Vogler, C (eds) *The Social Consequences of Unemployment*. Oxford University Press.

Gorz, A (1982) *A Farewell to the Working Class: an Essay on Post-Industrial Socialism*. Pluto Press.

Hare, R M (1982) 'Ethical theory and utilitarianism.' In Sen, A and Williams, B (eds) *Utilitarianism and Beyond*. Cambridge University Press.

Hepple, B (1981) 'A right to work?' *Industrial Law Journal*, 10: 65–83.

Hirsch, F (1977) *Social Limits to Growth*. Routledge & Kegan Paul.

Hunt, E H (1990) 'Paupers and pensioners: past and present.' *Ageing and Society*, 9: 407–30.

Jaconelli, J (1980) *Enacting a Bill of Rights: The Legal Problems*. Clarendon Press.

Jahoda, M (1982) *Employment and Unemployment: A Social-Psychological Analysis*. Cambridge University Press.

Le Grand, J (1983) *The Strategy of Equality*. Allen and Unwin.

Marsh, C (1988) 'Unemployment in Britain.' In Gallie, D (ed) *Employment in Britain*. Basil Blackwell, 344–375.

Marsh, C (1990) 'The Road to Recovery? One Week's Vacancies in Chesterfield.' *Work, Employment and Society*, March.

Marsh, C (1991) *Hours of Work of Women and Men in Britain*. Equal Opportunities Commission, HMSO.

Marsh, C and Alvaro, J–L (1990) 'A cross-cultural perspective on the social and psychological distress caused by unemployment: a comparison of Spain and the United Kingdom.' *European Sociological Review*, 6(3): 1–19, September.

Marshall, T H (1949; 1964) 'Citizenship and social class.' The Marshall Lectures, Cambridge 1949, reprinted in *Class, Citizenship and Social Development*. University of Chicago Press.

Marx, K (1952) *Class Struggles in France 1848 to 1950*. Progress Publishers.

Mead, L M (1985) *Beyond Entitlement*. The Free Press.

Pahl, R E (1984) *Divisions of Labour*. Basil Blackwell.

Parker, S (1982) *Work and Retirement*. Allen & Unwin.

Payne, J (1987) 'Does unemployment run in families? Some findings from the General Household Survey.' *Sociology*, 21: 199–214.

Piachaud, D (1987) 'The distribution of income and work.' *Oxford Review of Economic Policy* 3(3).

Raffe, D (1988) 'The status of vocational education and training 2: the case of YTS.' Paper presented to the ESRC/DE workshop on Research on Employment and Unemployment, London: Department of Employment, January.

Rawls, J (1982) 'Social unity and primary goods.' In Sen, A and Williams, B (eds) *Utilitarianism and Beyond*. Cambridge University Press.

Robinson, J P (1988) *How Americans Use Time*. Westview Press.

Sen, A (1985) *The Standard of Living*. In Hawthon, G P (ed). Cambridge University Press.

Stedman Jones, G (1971) *Outcast London*. Oxford University Press.

Swift, A (1988) 'Inequality of what?' Nuffield College mimeo.

Thomson, D (1984) 'The decline of social security: falling State support for the elderly since early Victorian times.' *Ageing and Society*, 4: 451–82.

Titmuss, R M (1971) "Welfare 'rights', law and discretion." *Political Quarterly*, 42(2): 113–132.

Townsend, P (1979) *Poverty in the United Kingdom*. Penguin.

van Parijs, P (1986–87) 'A revolution in class theory.' *Politics and Society*, 15(4): 453–82.

Walzer, M (1983) *Spheres of Justice: a Defence of Pluralism and Equality*. Basil Blackwell.

Warr, P (1987) *Work, Unemployment and Mental Health*. Clarendon Press.

Weale, A (1989) 'Equality, social solidarity and the welfare state.' University of East Anglia, Centre for Public Choice Studies, mimeo.

White, Michael (1987) *Working Hours: Assessing the Potential for Reduction*. Geneva: ILO.

Wilson, W (1985) *The Truly Disadvantaged*. Yale University Press.

14 The social division of welfare: a class struggle perspective

Kirk Mann

Introduction

In this chapter I want to examine how changes in the labour process influence access to the labour market and to occupational welfare. The first part of the chapter looks, albeit briefly, at some of the theoretical issues and the second considers these in respect of the development of occupational welfare in the light of a study carried out in Leeds. It will be argued that the concept of a 'Social Division of Welfare' (Titmuss, 1958; Sinfield, 1978) continues to provide the basis for a general theory of social divisions and welfare. However, and in contrast to Titmuss who first outlined the idea of a social division of welfare (henceforth SDW), it will be claimed that this has to be seen in the context of a capitalist labour market and how workers respond to and contest their location within it. Those contestants who are relatively successful can escape the stigmatising and debilitating effects of dependency on public welfare. An important aspect of this contest is the form and direction of class struggle. When competition for a 'better' position within the social division of labour takes the form of 'dual closure' (Parkin, 1979), social divisions will be reinforced. Moreover, the framework within which the contest takes place is set by changes in, and control of, the labour process (Therborn, 1983). The most recent manifestation of such changes has been referred to as 'post-Fordism'. Finally, I shall argue that the division between those who rely on public welfare, and the successful contestants who gain access to occupational welfare, is likely to be one of the prominent features of social divisions in the 1990s.[1]

The Social Division of Welfare

The essay on the SDW by Titmuss was written in the early 1950s as a retort to a number of critics on the right of the Tory Party. They had argued, and *The Times* and *The Economist* supported them, that the establishment of post-war welfare programmes had deleteriously affected Britain's economic position. Moreover, they claimed that the redistribution of resources from the middle classes to the working class, which they believed 'THE' welfare state facilitated, was unnecessary. In many respects critics like MaCleod and Powell were articulating a position we currently identify more closely with the Conservative Party in the 1980s and 1990s. Titmuss's response remains important for three reasons. First, it was a wonderful piece of polemic; second, it was descriptively the more accurate; and third it provides the possibility of a more theoretically informed approach to 'welfare' (Titmuss, 1958).

Titmuss argued that the critics were wrong to regard the welfare state as a unitary whole, which redistributed resources from the middle classes to the poor. It was more accurate to regard the welfare state as three related systems of welfare.[2] These three systems were fiscal welfare, social/public welfare and occupational welfare. Each element of the SDW met similar needs, according to Titmuss, but it was only public welfare on which critics focused. The welfare received by the middle classes such as tax subsidies (of which mortgage relief, currently estimated at costing the treasury £7,000,000,000, is most often cited), and occupational welfare (such as company pensions, which cost the Treasury £10,000,000,000 in 1990) tend to be neglected by critics (Inland Revenue, 1990). It is occupational welfare which will be focused upon here and it is the distinction between this and public welfare which is the most significant for any account of intra-class divisions.

Unfortunately Titmuss's work has not really been taken seriously by many outside Social Administration. Although the SDW thesis touches on many of the central concerns of the social sciences over the past thirty years – eg housing classes, working class affluence, inequality, and most recently consumption cleavages – the SDW, as a theory, has largely been neglected. For students of Social Policy the concept has generally been used descriptively or polemically (see Field, 1981; Goodin *et al*, 1987; Walker, 1984b). There are two main reasons for this neglect. First the distinction between Social Policy and Sociology as it developed in the late 1960s and early 1970s meant that theory and empirical policy research were moving toward a divorce. As with many divorces the initial period of separation provoked considerable hostility and mutual antagonism. Titmuss, as Professor of Social Administration at the LSE, and a vocal critic of student unrest, was seen as an empiricist. Second, Titmuss relied heavily upon a school of sociology – functionalism – which was not fashionable by the late 1960s. Moreover, as Rose (1981) has observed, Titmuss's grasp of sociological theory seems to have been somewhat tenuous. Nevertheless, there are a number of points he made which are worth reviewing.

The point which Titmuss makes most strongly is that welfare divisions are 'related to the division of labour in complex, individuated societies' (1958, p42). It has been the creation of dependency which has compelled the state to intervene but, he argued, the three systems of welfare meet similar needs by different organisational methods. He goes on: 'The dominating operative factor has been the increasing division of labour in society and, simultaneously, a great increase in labour specificity' (1958, p43). Durkheim's *The Division of Labour in Society* (1933) is cited by Titmuss and he clearly draws on the concept of the 'moral regulation of society' as the means to overcome the isolation promoted by the division of labour. The SDW arises, therefore, as a response to, and a function of, the dependencies created by the division of labour. Since dependence is socially generated it is unjust, in Titmuss' view, for the state to meet these needs more favourably for some than for others. He goes on to claim that the SDW further promotes self-interest, individuation, sectionalism and social conflict as the most powerful social alliances attempt to improve their position through one element of the SDW and the weaker groups are less able to do so. This can be seen most clearly in respect of occupational welfare where 'the drive to buy good industrial relations' (Titmuss, 1958, p53) has benefited those most able to exert pressure.

This brief synopsis of the most interesting aspects of Titmuss' thesis ought to highlight both its strengths and weaknesses. The strength lies in the link he makes between labour specificity, the social division of labour, the labour market and social divisions. To illustrate the weakness of the functionalist approach we need only examine the question of labour specificity since this is central to his argument.

Titmuss suggests that labour specificity occurs in complex individuated societies and that this is a function of industrialisation *per se* (1958, pp42–3). Certainly industrialisation generates specific forms of need but, it can be argued, these do not automatically result in an individuated society (Kumar, 1978). Nor does Titmuss locate 'increased labour specificity' within the framework of contests over working practices and the control of labour. Thus he misses the point about such changes and fails to acknowledge the impact of, for example, scientific management thinking, on labour specificity.

Frederick Taylor's ideas were not an inevitable consequence of industrialisation but were specifically designed to increase the profitability of companies (Braverman, 1974; Fox, 1985). Industrialism in Britain was certainly accompanied by the pursuit of profit but they are independent variables. Thus changes in the labour process are still largely, but not exclusively, driven by the desire to maximise profits. However, employers may be hindered in the pursuit of their goals by the demands and activities of organised labour. Occupational welfare, therefore, will be provided by employers either to pacify their employees or to legitimate proposed changes in the organisation of work.

Despite the flaws in Titmuss' analysis it is worth repeating that he was addressing social divisions, consumption patterns, welfare provisions and labour specificity in the 1950s. In doing so he provided the basis for further analysis and the opportunity for social policy to engage with some of the most interesting sociological concepts and questions. The first of these which needs to be addressed is social closure theory.

Social closure

When Parkin (1979) wrote his 'bourgeois critique' of Marxism he simultaneously insisted that Marxists had to relocate agency within their accounts (ie they had to address **how** the working class behaved) and that Weberian sociology could explain this behaviour by a theory of social closure. Murphy (1988) has expanded upon Parkin's account and points out that the theory of social closure has gained support during a period of sectionalism and economism on the part of the labour movement.

Parkin claims social closure takes three forms. Firstly, exclusionary social closure serves the interests of dominant groups and helps to maintain their privileges. This type of closure can be manifest through various forms of social action. The legal right to control particular resources (he refers to the ownership of the means of production), 'credentialism' and the education system are some of the ways in which the privileged exclude subordinates and maintain their position. This is the familiar Weberian concept of the monopolisation of life chances. It involves those at the top maintaining their privileges by excluding others. A second form is usurpatory closure, which occurs when a collectivity exert pressure against those who hold power, resources and privilege. Thus 'strikes, sit ins, marches, picketing . . .' (Parkin, 1979, p74) are cited as evidence of usurpatory closure. This is how those at the bottom respond to those at the top. Thus far Parkin's account of class formation is similar to a dichotomous Marxist model. Indeed, he acknowledges this himself when he suggests that the two forms of closure express 'the familiar distinction between bourgeoisie and proletariat' (1979, p46).

The most attractive and distinctive feature of Parkin's account, however, is the identification of 'dual closure'. It is this form of closure which promotes intra-class divisions and is significant for the revised theory of a SDW. Dual closure occurs when a subordinate group/class exerts usurpationary closure in order to challenge the dominant class and simultaneously excludes members of their own class. An example of this might be the trade union closed shop which makes it easier for workers to combine and challenge their employer but tends to exclude other members of the working class, most notably women and black workers. Thus Parkin asserts

> . . . exclusionary closure is an aspect of conflict and cleavage within social classes as well as between them. . . . This is also a way of saying that exploitation occurs within the subordinate class as well as against it, since the forms of collective action involved entail the use of power in such a way as to create a stratum of socially excluded inferiors (1979, p89).

There are problems with Parkin's account when it comes to identifying those who are excluded and why (Barbalet, 1982). From where does the power to exclude and define a stratum of socially excluded inferiors derive?

Unfortunately Parkin is somewhat confusing in this matter since he states quite boldly that it is the State which assigns excluded groups an inferior legal status (1979, p96). However, as the quote above illustrates, he has also claimed that dual closure itself serves to 'create a stratum of socially excluded inferiors'. Moreover there is ample historical evidence that particular groups are given an inferior legal status following their exclusion from what Miliband (1974) calls 'the defence mechanisms of the working class'. As I have argued elsewhere (Mann 1986), from the first the working class has made and re-made itself through the form and direction that struggle has taken. The exclusion of the Irish in the nineteenth century cannot be simply attributed to the State and certainly there is ample evidence of patriarchal values being used to exclude women from certain trades in feudal England (Middleton, 1985). Thus the working class has 'made' itself as a divided class. Nevertheless, and despite the confusion in Parkin's account of the basis of social power, the concept of dual closure remains useful and will be integrated into the theory set out below. The second aspect of a revised theory of the SDW is taken from the labour process debate.

Labour process, control and exclusion

The labour process is really quite a simple concept. It refers to the organisation of work and the constant attempts of employers to control what their employees actually do when they are working. If an employer can break down the tasks performed by their employees into the different elements it may be possible to achieve more rapid production at lower costs. For example; if the production of a car was carried out by one person it would take a very long time to make a car and the worker would have to have a variety of skills. The rate at which cars would be produced would have to be extremely flexible and the worker would have to have considerable discretion/control over the whole process. If, as has happened, the production of cars is broken down into each constituent element, with the use of assembly lines and times set for each and every detailed task, the rate of production can be controlled more easily by the employer. The multi-skilled worker can be replaced by a host of cheaper unskilled labour trained to perform very specific tasks. Divisions between workers are encouraged by the construction of pay and grading systems which, in turn, promote sectional and economistic demands. Moreover, the control that the worker previously had will have been considerably reduced if not entirely eradicated (Braverman, 1974). However, this ignores the fact that workers actively resist such changes and that with the demise of old skills new ones are created.

The crucial point to be drawn from the labour process debate for the argument here is that control of the labour process can empower some workers. Deskilling, the focus of much of the earlier literature on the labour process (Braverman, 1974), is only one feature of change in the labour process. Equally significant is the manner in which employees respond to change and attempt to assert some measure of control (Edwards, 1982). In the 1950s and 1960s control of the labour process by employees, even unskilled employees, was frequently addressed in terms of demarcation lines, so-called 'restrictive practices' and the closed shop. Cockburn's (1983) study of the print industry demonstrates how, despite the new technology, workers maintained their relatively privileged position. By using the apprenticeship scheme, and control over entry to the trade, the union was able to retain its knowledge of, and control over, the production process. The result was that, by and large, women and black workers were excluded from one of the most lucrative trades.

In the public sector control of the labour process may be less important than control over entry. Following the abolition of the Metropolitan counties in the early 1980s and in the move towards privatisation, unions at both national and local level insisted upon 'ring fencing' arrangements. These ensured, like many new technology agreements, that those currently employed would retain their jobs and that competition from outside the enterprise was minimal (Ascher, 1987; McCloughlin and Clark 1988). Consequently, the previous exclusion of black workers and women was maintained despite claims that the organisations were 'equal opportunity employers'. However, it is the historical legacy of exclusion, particularly the sexual division of labour and hostility to immigration, that has probably been most significant in enabling some sections of the working class to gain a relatively more privileged place within the social division of labour, and hence the SDW, than others (Mann, 1984, 1986).

It is in this context that dual closure seems most appropriate. In resisting the changes that employers want, employees themselves compete for a place in the labour market. Gaining and retaining a more privileged place in the labour market will, however, frequently depend on the ability of workers to organise over the control of the labour process (Therborn, 1983). This is a point which is emphasised by writers who claim that we have entered a post-Fordist era.

Post-Fordism and dual labour markets

Post-Fordism is in many respects simply the most recent development in the labour process debate but it takes a broader perspective. One of the more interesting aspects of the debate surrounding post-Fordism is the claim that social divisions will be firmer in the future. Central to these claims, although rarely expanded upon, is the part played by occupational welfare. There are of course different versions of the post-Fordist thesis but they tend to point to similar issues: an increasing demand from employers for 'flexible working', autonomous work groups, work group regulation and quality control by the workers themselves, the sub-contracting of services (eg catering, laundry, transport, cleaning, maintenance etc) and the creation of a skilled flexible core of full-time employees complemented by part-time and/or temporary workers. (See Aglietta, 1987; Atkinson, 1984; Atkinson and Gregory, 1986; Piore and Sabel, 1984; Bagguley, 1989).

As Bagguley (1989) has pointed out, there are some difficulties with the theories of post-Fordism. Too often the concern is with the impact of change on white male workers who might traditionally be regarded as 'skilled'. Similarly the focus tends to be on the private manufacturing sector, and the numerically larger public and service sectors are neglected. The specific part played by women workers, who are often crucial in the new technology industries performing routine and repetitive tasks – eg PC operators, micro-chip production, etc – and in the peripheral and service sector can be overlooked. This is not to deny that there are significant changes in the labour process but there are also some important continuities. Most notably the history of exclusion of specific groups from the 'core' has to be acknowledged (Mann, 1984). It is surely no accident that the services which are contracted out and/or rely on part-time and temporary staff are precisely those to which women and black workers are often confined. Moreover, there is nothing peripheral about the use of low-paid, insecure, unsocial, routine work with, as a rule, few forms of occupational welfare. The changes that have occurred have relied heavily upon such workers and the much vaunted 'flexibility' of the post-Fordist era comes at the cost of insecurity for those excluded from the 'core'.

A further problem with post-Fordism theory relates to its similarities with the older dual labour market thesis. As in dual labour market theory the coherence of the account depends on showing that there is a large measure of segregation between one sector of the labour market and another. In the dual labour market model the distinction is between the primary and secondary sectors, and in post-Fordism between core and periphery (Barron and Norris, 1976). This segregation may be demonstrated in some industries and some enterprises, but it is certainly not the case more generally. Consequently, whilst it is possible to identify certain forms of intra-class division – most notably in respect of gender and race – there is insufficient evidence of the type of segregation necessary to support a dualist model. If there is not a duality between core and periphery, or primary and secondary, then the account has to be much more heavily qualified (Blackburn and Mann, 1979).

Despite the flaws post-Fordism is significant for students of social policy because commentators highlight the impact of occupational welfare on social divisions. Like the dual labour market model, post-Fordism suggests that occupational welfare serves to distinguish the core from the periphery. Company pensions, share participation, profit sharing, relocation grants, assistance with removals, subsidised travel, company cars, membership of BUPA, subsidised opticians and dental services, free or subsidised purchases of products, free or cheap footwear and clothing, generous sick pay schemes, and a host of other 'fringes' serve to distinguish the 'core' from the periphery and the primary from the secondary sectors (Green *et al*, 1984). Titmuss's claim that an individuated society pursuing sectional interests, and the employer's desire to 'buy' good industrial relations, promote social divisions, appears to be borne out. However, this is to assume that:- a) there is segregation in the provision of occupational welfare and: b) employers are the active agents in the development of occupational welfare. Our research suggests that both of these assumptions are, at best, only partially true and that there are other factors which may be far more significant (Mann and Anstee, 1989).

Occupational welfare

There exists an assumption in the literature on 'occupational welfare' which is both surprising and unacceptable. Throughout the literature it is claimed that employers **offer** occupational welfare. This supports Titmuss's claims and, to a lesser degree, the idea that such benefits are the perks of being in the 'core' sector. Green *et al* (1984) even go so far as to claim that occupational welfare is best understood in the context of a dual labour market thesis. Leaving aside a number of criticisms which have been made of this thesis (see Blackburn and Mann, 1979; Walby, 1990) there is an obvious and immediate difficulty with this claim. The dual labour market theory itself relies very heavily on the unequal distribution of occupational welfare to demonstrate segregation in the labour market. Indeed, one of the key features of the primary sector, it is claimed, is that 'fringe benefits' are provided. So Green *et al* were stating that the way to explain fringe benefits is to use a theory which itself points to fringes to explain the labour market. This is at best circular and at worst a nonsense.

Green *et al* (1984) provide an excellent quantitative study using existing official data and, as a description of how unfairly distributed occupational welfare is, their work is second to none. (That was their aim after all.) However, as an explanation of how occupational welfare develops their account is not very helpful. Perhaps their most provocative claim is that trade unions are largely insignificant in promoting occupational welfare. Having been an AUEW (Amalgamated Union of Engineering Workers) convenor who had negotiated an improved sick pay and sick leave scheme, a long service bonus scheme, free boots and work clothes (from a catalogue which included some clothes deliberately designed for wearing outside work), a heavily subsidised canteen (choice of three menus, Continental, English and Asian), and an occupational pension scheme, I certainly felt as if I had been significant in getting management to provide occupational welfare. Management never approached me and said they were offering to improve the occupational welfare package. What is more, between 1976 and 1983 a host of information had been made available to trade unionists engaged in negotiating occupational welfare (eg

Ward, 1981; Lucas, 1977). Indeed, at the time I was reading claims that trade unionists were minor actors in the development of occupational welfare, first the EETPU (the electricians' union) and later the AEU announced their own package of benefits for their members, negotiated with the City of London (Bassett, 1986). Simultaneously other unions, most notably the General and Municipal along with the Transport and General, responded that in their view employers ought to provide these benefits. Only the public sector unions suggested that the state ought to provide all forms of welfare, and they soon went quiet when it was pointed out that occupational pensions in the public sector were generally much better than in the private sector. If, as Green *et al* suggested, trade unions were marginal to the development of occupational welfare packages, it seemed that the unions themselves were oblivious to this fact. Faced by widespread confusion over the part played by trade unions in promoting occupational welfare, and armed with a theoretical model which suggested that it had to be seen as an aspect of industrial relations conflicts, we decided to get our boots muddy and investigate how occupational welfare had developed. Interviews with trade union representatives, both full-time officials and shop floor representatives, and the managers or employers of 38 establishments in the Leeds area were conducted in late 1987. These establishments were broadly representative of industry in Leeds and covered seventeen different industrial groupings (see Mann and Anstee, 1989).

The study

The expectation that trade unions, works committees and employee associations had played a part in the introduction of occupational welfare was, not surprisingly, borne out (see Mann and Anstee 1989). Both trade unionists and employers agreed that occupational welfare was a constant theme in negotiations and that the trade unions had often initiated proposals for schemes. There were, however, some important variations, and trade union negotiators were by no means homogeneous in their attitudes. For example an interesting contrast was that between a games manufacturer, where employees were members of the printing and publishing workers' union SOGAT, and a major supermarket chain, where employees were represented by the General and Municipal (G&M). Both were effectively post entry closed shops, had a high percentage of women workers and surprisingly low labour turnover rates. When we discussed the benefits available to employees it became clear that, contrary to expectations, the shop workers were in a far better position. Apart from a host of benefits including sick pay, pensions, discounts on goods, Christmas bonuses, share participation and profit sharing, the supermarket also provided a 'well woman' clinic which visited the place of work on a regular basis in order to carry out cervical smear testing and breast screening. Both the company and the union did much to advertise this 'package of benefits', including using a glossy magazine to explain what was available. The company had even conducted a survey, carried out by a market research agency, into employee perceptions of the benefits available. In contrast the games manufacturer provided very few benefits, and of these the union had only negotiated over sick pay and pensions.

It seemed perverse that members of a print union were, in respect of occupational welfare, worse off than supermarket employees. Trade union folklore and the literature on industrial relations tends to portray workers in the printing industry as more aggressive in negotiations whilst shop workers are the poor relations. Our attempts at explaining this paradox remain tentative but there were a number of features which we felt were significant and illustrate the dangers of over-generalising. First, the structure of the two respective unions was very different. The G&M was far more in tune with shop floor opinion, and their annual negotiations with the company, and the manner in which the claims were arrived at, served to place occupational welfare nearer the top of the agenda. For example, each place of work and then each locality would draw up a list of items for the negotiators. These would then go to a regional conference and finally to the national conference before being presented to the employers.

In the case of the print union full-time officials were largely responsible both for drawing up the agendas and for negotiations, and it was clearly a more directive policy and practice. This had led in one instance to the union 'strongly advising' the membership not to join the share participation scheme. Only one employee took advantage of the scheme; she bought £5,000 of shares over five years. By 1987 those shares were worth £40,000 and as the official responsible for the initial advice told me – 'We had egg all over our faces, after that.' The relationship between the union officials and the shop floor, which in these examples meant men consulting with women shop floor workers, appeared to support the idea that the manner in which organised labour conducts industrial relations is extremely important. Thus, it is not the dual labour market or 'post-Fordism' that is significant but how those who sell their labour power pursue their interests.

However, these two brief examples also touch on a number of factors we had not considered. First, the attitude of the company was vitally important in the case of the supermarket. When the personnel director was interviewed he stated that they were prepared to provide 'fringe benefits' for a number of reasons.

1 It suited their labour market needs. They wanted to reduce labour turnover and fringes appeared to tie employees to the firm, particularly if the value of these was related to length of service. In the case of the games manufacturer this was unnecessary because wages, especially for women, were much higher than the 'going rate' elsewhere.

2 Although the costs of providing 'fringes' was ongoing they were also often relatively cheaper than wage costs. For example, an improvement in sick pay might be worth 1 per cent of an employee's total wage. However this cost might be less than 1 per cent to the company once the accountants had examined the pre-tax and post-tax liabilities of the firm. (This emphasises the point made in the introduction about the close fit between occupational and fiscal welfare.)

3 The supermarket felt it had to improve its image to consumers. It was thought that competitors, like Marks and Spencers and Sainsburys, were identified as 'good' employers and that consumers were influenced by such considerations. In a similar vein, and this was also common in both the bank and the building societies in our sample, the 'image' of the organisation **within** the organisation, (ie amongst employees) was also enhanced, it was felt, by providing occupational welfare. In this context it is significant that the games manufacturer was simply a provider of goods to retailers whereas the supermarket was more directly in touch with consumers.

These features of companies' labour market and marketing strategies highlight the fact that the conditions under which occupational welfare develops are not simply determined by the form and direction of class struggle. Trade union organisation, and thereby the form class struggle took in these cases, was seen to be **one** condition but not a sufficient condition of occupational welfare (Mann and Anstee, 1989, pp87–92). Both unions pursued 'pragmatic' objectives but they differed in the weight they placed on non-wage benefits. We felt that the difference was best explained by their negotiating structures and the differential ability of the membership to influence the agenda (Mann and Anstee, 1989, p101). For members of the print unions the negotiating agenda largely reflected the interests of the male employees for improved wages rather than occupational welfare. It bears repeating, however, that the unions' strategy was only one feature in a complex process. They had to identify and exploit opportunities provided by the employer's labour market and commercial strategy but were not able simply to dictate what they wanted.

In a number of the smaller firms we found that a combination of paternalism and employee pressure had played a part in the introduction of benefits. Where a small firm had no union the employers frequently claimed to be 'caring' for the workforce. However, benefits were, in the main, limited and of little material value. There is also a case for seeing paternalism as an industrial relations strategy. Fox (1985) has argued that it can be used to try and create a sense of 'belonging' and may be used quite cynically by employers to achieve their own goals.

Other factors which were significant were the history of the company and earlier practices, along with changes in government policy. Excellent historical studies by Hannah (1986) and Fitzgerald (1988) have emphasised the significance of occupational welfare in the past and its legacy for today. A good example of the 'custom and practice' case is the brewing industry where, among many more recent benefits, the provision of considerable quantities of free beer and cheap spirits dates back to at least the middle of the 19th century. Changes in government policy, notably in respect of pensions and sick pay, had been important in getting occupational welfare on to the agenda in firms where management had previously resisted introducing a scheme. As one full time union official stated:- 'Ironically the government has forced us to have a rethink and they have forced us to think about the sort of things we could get.' Likewise an official of the engineering workers' union stated that he had urged factory convenors to press for company pension schemes because:- 'the government pension scheme is so inferior we felt we had to concentrate on getting a good pension.' Here it appears that the union representative was prepared to acknowledge the failure of public welfare and the understandable desire to protect the interests of his members by ensuring they were able to get a better pension. Other respondents were also quite willing to agree that by improving their members' occupational welfare package they were simultaneously trying to escape the clutches of public welfare (see also Dunleavy, 1986).

Two further factors which were significant, and which relate to the earlier theoretical discussion, were 'harmonisation/flexibility' and labour market strategy. In both cases changes in the labour process had promoted occupational welfare. Harmonisation had meant that staff/manual distinctions were broken down and that the pension, sick pay and other benefits provided to clerical workers were extended to manual workers. However, this was often part of a package which involved new working practices, changes in technology and/or increased flexibility. Atkinson's 'core' workers, it seems, pursue occupational welfare as the *quid pro quo* for being 'multi-skilled'. Their importance as core workers enables them to get many benefits which, until as late as the early 1970s, were reserved for clerical workers and management. This poses the question of which 'benefits' that are reserved for managers today will be sought by the unions tomorrow. The EETPU is already pressing for company vehicles for maintenance staff!

Labour market strategies pursued by employers are more difficult to assess. For example, the bank in our study provided a package of benefits, including, amongst many others: mortgages, relocation grants, pensions, and loans, which, as the personnel manager put it, 'are second to none'. These were available, he said, because they needed to attract and retain labour. Likewise the building societies provided a host of benefits (of which a 4 per cent mortgage was the most attractive) worth in the region of £7,000 to an employee on £14,000. Both justified these benefits by stating that they served to attract labour. Both the building societies and the bank had lengthy waiting lists of prospective employees. On the one hand this would appear to support their claims but on the other it seems strange that they should continue to expand their package of benefits when they already attract considerably more staff than they can employ. Moreover, and in both cases, trade union and staff representatives claimed that they were the driving force behind the improved benefits. Without a more detailed longitudinal study of particular companies it is difficult to assess such claims. Nevertheless, it is significant that both the bank union and staff association representatives wanted to claim responsibility for improving occupational welfare. It would seem that the value of the benefits is appreciated and that everyone wants to get the credit for their introduction.

Where few benefits were provided there was a pattern of older industries or ones which continued with older methods of work. For example at a large steel stockholders the shop steward stated that the firm provided, 'Nowt, we get bugger all.' This shop steward went on: 'If it ain't in national agreements or law they gived us f**k all.' Once again the desire for occupational welfare, rather than public welfare, is what stands out.

In textiles and tailoring there was a difference between the small producers, who had virtually no benefits, and the very large producer and retailer (eg Burtons, Next). However, the large companies had not offered any new benefits, except credit facilities for retail outlet employees, nor improved their benefits since the 1930s. Indeed, according to the union the employers were withdrawing a number of established benefits, a process known in the U.S. as 'clawback'. The only notable exception to this was the provision of a company pension which had been developed in the last ten years.

All our respondents, managers, employers and trade unionists, acknowledged the pressure exerted by trade union and employee representatives for occupational welfare. This brief summary of our research suggests that one of the key features in the development of occupational welfare has been, and will continue to be, the tactics of the organised labour movement. Nevertheless, there were other factors and it is not being argued that trade unions are the sole actors. In some cases they will not play a part at all, but on a broader scale their activities will influence even the behaviour of anti-union employers. They will have to compete in the same labour market and may find they have to provide occupational welfare in order to attract labour.

Implications and conclusion

Our research does not allow us to derive hard and fast conclusions which can explain each and every development. Nevertheless, it was apparent that occupational welfare was a significant feature of industrial relations in contemporary Britain. Moreover, the wide variations in provision, and particularly the division between those in work with extensive packages and those who have to rely on public welfare, is noteworthy. With one or two important exceptions it is full-time male employees, in companies and industries which have introduced new working practices and technology, who have found it easier to improve their occupational welfare package. Other workers have used the organisation's desire for internal labour markets, or a 'good' image, or changes in government legislation as an opportunity to improve their benefits. Workers in part-time and temporary forms of employment, or in older industries using old working practices, are likely to get few occupational benefits. Only where organised labour exploits particular conditions will such workers gain access to the relatively more privileged benefits provided by occupational welfare. Thus women and black workers, who make up a disproportionate percentage of the low-paid, part-time and irregularly employed, are likely to be excluded from the benefits of occupational welfare. Likewise, the unemployed, single parents and older workers will invariably have to rely on public welfare. Once we look at housing, transport and other aspects of consumption these divisions appear even firmer (see Harrison, 1986; Murie and Forest, 1984; Walker, and Walker, 1987).

If large numbers of workers, particularly those in trade unions, are members of occupational pension schemes, share participation and profit sharing schemes, along with receiving a host of other benefits, whilst others are unable to gain entry to those firms which provide the benefits, or are forced to rely on public welfare, the potential for social divisions is obvious. Moreover, the political constituency for expanding public welfare will shrink whilst the social and economic cleavage widens.

Nevertheless, there is not sufficient evidence of segregation, yet, to support the rather woolly claims of those who point to an 'underclass' (Field, 1989;; Murray, 1990). There is a trend in which certain groups are consistently excluded and public welfare might more generally become residual services 'reserved for the poor' (Deacon and Bradshaw, 1984). There is no evidence that this has to be the case, as the women workers at the supermarket in our study would testify. The key factor, however, is likely to be how the organised labour movement addresses these questions. If it either decides to persist with economistic and sectional struggles, and/or fails to include the weakest sections of the working class in those struggles, social divisions will undoubtedly widen. Exclusion will be more significant and the political possibilities open to even the most radically socialist government more limited, since political support for public welfare will be confined to those who are forced to rely on it.

As far as the theoretical model outlined above is concerned, it appears that in general it holds true. I have suggested that occupational welfare is best understood from a class struggle perspective. Thus the SDW is 'made' in the course of conflicts and contests between classes and expressed in the realm of industrial relations. This is not to suggest that class struggle is the only factor; in some cases it may be insignificant. Nor is this a straightforwardly Marxist perspective, although it certainly draws on Marxist scholarship. The argument here departs from any narrow Marxist perspective in assigning the State a minimal role and in recognizing that class struggle can be expressed in sectional and economistic objectives. Thus the effect of class struggle may be to promote intra-class divisions based on access to occupational welfare and location in the SDW.

There are some important qualifications that need to be added and there will be a number of exceptions to be explained. In future it will be important to look at the question of social closure more closely to see how dual closure operates. It will also be necessary to try and weight some of the variables we identified to assess which are most significant in particular industries or areas. Once the necessary revisions are made of the SDW thesis it remains a particularly insightful approach to both divisions of labour and welfare.

Notes

1 I should add that these are tentative claims, designed to address the creation and maintenance of intra-class divisions. It will be necessary to qualify these claims and test them both in debate and empirically.
2 These three divisions do, however, need to be supplemented by a fourth in order to take account of the variety of largely unrewarded tasks performed by informal carers. I have in mind here child-care, looking after aged or infirm parents, preparing meals etc; and most of these services are carried out by women. They are so well established it seems inappropriate to call them 'informal' but the reader ought to be aware that this aspect of the SDW tends to be neglected.

References

The Economist, 5.6.1954.
The Guardian 14.2.1990.
Aglietta, M (1987) *A Theory of Capitalist Regulation: the U.S. Experience.* Verso.
Ascher, K (1987) *The Politics of Privatisation – Contracting out Public Services.* Macmillan.
Atkinson, J and Gregory, D (April 1986) 'A Flexible Future: Britain's Dual Labour Force.' *Marxism Today.* pp12–17.
Atkinson, J (August 1984) 'Manpower Strategies for Flexible Organisations.' *Personnel Management* 16:28–31.
Bagguley, P (February 1989) *The Post-Fordist Enigma: Theories of Labour Flexibility.* Lancaster Regionalism Group Working Paper 29.
Barbalet, J M (November 1982) 'Social Closure in Class Analyses: A Critique of Parkin.' In *Sociology*, Vol 16, No 4.
Barron, R D and Norris, G M (1976) 'Sexual divisions and the dual labour market.' In Barker, D L and Allen, S. *Sexual Divisions and Society*, Tavistock.
Bassett, P (1986) *Strike Free: New Industrial Relations in Britain.* Macmillan.
Batstone, E *et al* (1987) *New Technology and the Process of Labour Regulation.* Clarendon Press.
Blackburn, R and Mann, M (1979) *The Working Class and the Labour Market.* Macmillan.
Braverman, H (1974) *Labor and Monopoly Capital.* Monthly Review Press.
Coates, K and Topham, T (1986) *Trade Unions and Politics.* Basil Blackwell.
Cockburn, C (1983) *Brothers: Male Dominance and Technological Change.* Pluto Press.
Crompton, R and Jones, G (1984) *White Collar Proletariat: Deskilling and gender in clerical work.* Macmillan Press.
Curson, C (1986) *Flexible Patterns of Work.* Institute of Personnel Management.

Dunleavy, P (1986) 'Sectoral Cleavages and the Stabilization of State Expenditures.' *Environment Planning, Society and Space*, Vol 4, pp128–144.

Durkheim, E (1933) *The Division of Labour in Society*. Free Press.

Edmonds, J (September 1986) 'New Wave Unions.' *Marxism Today*, pp16–17.

Edwards, R (1979) *Contested Terrain: The Transformation of Work in the Twentieth Century*. Heinemann.

Field, F (1981) *Inequality in Britain*. Fontana.

Fitzgerald, R (1988) *British Labour Management and Industrial Welfare, 1864–1939*. Croom Helm.

Fox, Alan (1985) *Man Management* (second edition). Hutchinson.

Goodin, R E, Le Grand, J *et al*, (1987) *Not Only The Poor: The Middle Classes and the Welfare State*. Allen and Unwin.

Gordon, D, Edwards, R and Reich, M (1982) *Segmented work, divided workers: The historical transformation of labor in the United States*. Cambridge University Press.

Green, F, Hadjmatheou, G and Smail, R (1984) *Unequal fringes: Fringe Benefits in the United Kingdom*. Low Pay Unit, London.

Hannah, L (1986) *Inventing Retirement: the development of occupational pensions in Britain*. Cambridge University Press.

Harrison, M L (June 1986) 'Consumption and Urban Theory: An alternative approach based on the Social Division of Welfare.' *The International Journal of Urban and Regional Research*, Vol 10, No 2.

Hart, R A (1984) *The Economics of Non-Wage Labour Costs*. Allen & Unwin.

Inland Revenue (1990) *The government's expenditure plans 1990–91*. HMSO Cm 1021.

Kelly, J (1988) *Trade Unions and Socialist Politics*. Verso.

Kincaid, J (1984) 'Richard Titmuss.' In Barker, P (ed) *Founders of the Welfare State*. Heinemann.

Knights, D and Wilmott, H (eds) (1986) *Managing the Labour Process*. Gower.

Kumar, K (1978) *Prophesy and progress; The sociology of industrial and post-industrial societies*. Penguin.

Leadbetter, C (September 1987) 'Unions go to Market.' *Marxism Today*, pp22–7.

Le Grand, J and Robinson, R (1984) *Privatisation and the Welfare State*. Allen & Unwin.

Littler, C R (ed) (1985) *The Experience of Work*. Gower.

Lucas, H (1977) *Pensions and Industrial Relations*. Pergamon Press.

MacNicol, J (1987) 'In Pursuit of the Underclass.' *Journal of Social Policy* 16:3, pp293–318.

Mann, K (1984) 'Incorporation, Exclusion, Underclasses and the Unemployed.' In Harrison, M L (ed) *Corporatism and the Welfare State*. Gower.

Mann, K (1986) 'The Making of a Claiming Class – the neglect of agency in analyses of the Welfare State.' *Critical Social Policy*, issue 15, Spring.

Mann, K and Anstee, J (1989) *Growing Fringes: Hypothesis on the development of occupational welfare*. Armley Publications.

Massey, D (1984) *Spatial Divisions of Labour – Social Structures and the Geography of Production*. Macmillan.

McLoughlin, I and Clark, J (1988) *Technological Change at Work*. Open University Press.

Middleton, C (1985) 'Women's Labour and the Transition to Pre-industrial Capitalism.' In Charles, L and Duffin, L (eds) *Women and Work in Pre-Industrial England*. Croom Helm.

Miliband, R (1974) 'Politics and Poverty.' In Wedderburn, D (ed) *Poverty Inequality and Class Structure*. Cambridge University Press.

Murie, R and Forest, A (1983) 'Residualization and Council Housing: Aspects of the Changing Social Relations of Housing Tenure.' *Journal of Social Policy* 12:4, pp453–468.

Murphy, R (1988) *Social Closure – the theory of monopolization and exclusion*. Clarendon Press.

Parkin, F (1979) *Marxism and Class Theory: A Bourgeois Critique*. Tavistock.

Piore, M (1984) *The Second Industrial Divide: Possibilities for Prosperity*. Basic Books, New York.

Preteceille, E (1986) 'Collective Consumption, Urban Segregation and social class.' *Environment and Planning: Society and Space*, Vol 4, pp145–54.

Rose, H (1981) 'Rereading Titmuss: The Sexual Division of Welfare.' *Journal of Social Policy* 10:4, pp477–502.

Sinfield, A (April 1978) 'Analyses in the Social Division of Welfare.' *Journal of Social Policy*, Vol 7, pt 2.

Sinfield, A (1986) 'Poverty, Privilege and Welfare.' In Bean, P and Whyne, D (eds) *Barbara Wooton: Essays in Her Honour*.

Taylor-Gooby, P (1981) 'The Empiricist Tradition in Social Administration.' *Critical Social Policy*, Vol 1, No 2, pp6–21.

Therborn, P (1983) 'Why some Classes are More Successful Than Others.' *New Left Review*, 138, pp37–56.

Titmuss, R (1958) *Essays on the Welfare State*. Allen and Unwin.

Walby, S (1990) *Theorizing Patriarchy*. Basil Blackwell.

Walker, A (1984a) *Social Planning A Strategy For Socialist Welfare*. Basil Blackwell.

Walker, A (1984b) 'The Political Economy of Privatisation.' In Le Grand, J and Robinson, R *Privatisation and the Welfare State*. Allen and Unwin.

Walker, A and Walker, C (eds) (1987) *The Growing Divide: A Social Audit 1979–1987*. CPAG.

Ward, S (1981) *Pensions*. Pluto Press.

Wetherly, P (1988) 'Class Struggle and the Welfare State: some theoretical problems considered.' *Critical Social Policy*, issue 22.

Wilson, W J (1987) *The Truly Disadvantaged: The inner City, the Underclasses and Public Policy*. University of Chicago Press.

Windolf, P (1988) *Recruitment and Selection in the Labour Market*. Gower.

Wood, S (1982) *The Degradation of Work*. Hutchinson.

Wook, S and Windolf, P (1987) *Social Closure in the Labour Market*. Gower.